Digging
into
Popular Culture

Digging into Popular Culture

Theories and Methodologies in Archeology, Anthropology and Other Fields

edited by
Ray B. Browne
and
Pat Browne

Bowling Green State University Popular Press
Bowling Green, Ohio 43403

Contents

Introduction

Studies in popular culture have always ranged widely and penetrated deeply. No other discipline has so sought out the theories and methodologies used in other fields and brought so many of them to bear on a generalized study of the humanities and social sciences in an effort to explain the general status of human actions in society. Not satisfied with the outreach and inreach achieved so far, however, the popular culture student searches constantly for new insights and methods. The present collection of studies is yet a further effort to reach out and incorporate more materials from fields which have much to offer the student in popular culture.

Popular culture is the everyday, vernacular culture that comprises virtually all our lives. It is the way we live, the thoughts we think, the people around us and their activities; like the water the fish swims in, popular culture is the cultural air we breathe.

As such it has always been with us. Earliest mankind—because the communities were bound together by the sheer exigencies of existing—had only one culture, their everyday culture of existence. In 1381 John Ball looked upon the naked truth of the history of culture in his speech at Blackheath to the men in Wat Tyler's Rebellion when he quoted the anonymous couplet about privilege and elitism: "When Adam delved and Eve span / Who was than a gentleman?" But through the centuries as differences between individuals became real or seeming, the strong individuals exerted their power, and in order to bolster their superiority and privilege carefully and slowly separated ways of life and living into what they called superior and inferior—those separations established by some form of force, intimidation or declared and enforced superiority. In various societies this schism has been developed at various periods. As late as the sixteenth century in Western Europe society generally held together as one, though obvious breaks and separations were becoming clearly evident.

Through the ages this artificial separation of society has been maintained by some kind of force. Early on the evidences of superiority were best and most dramatically demonstrated by possession of objects of scarcity and value—artifacts which could be taken from and denied to the weak and could be declared superior by a trained or declared sensibility. Through the centuries artifacts have been nurtured in and

1

by a subtler aspect of culture which focused the power of intangibles on the separation of two—or more—classes, with artifacts, and many less concrete forms of material goods, and actions. As the difficulties of living close to nature in England and America became less severe after the eighteenth century the powerful and clever exploited every avenue and device to maintain and enhance their superiority.

For example, the so-called Age of Enlightenment in England was only relatively enlightened, and is a source of amusement and edification to us today. For instance, it was a given in England in the eighteenth century that one example of God's infinite wisdom was His endowing mankind with a nose conveniently situated so that eyeglasses could be worn on it. Of course such philosophy and natural science is not much different from a much later perception that God revealed His wisdom in creating air which will support airplanes in flight. Nor much more peculiar than a centuries-old proverb which reads that God created the Sahara Desert so that man would have a place of peace and quiet in which to rest his soul. Back in England, essayist Joseph Addison in a 1711 *Spectator Paper* (as Paul Shackel points out in his paper in this volume) asserted that city life had advanced far ahead of country life in his country. And French skeptic Voltaire, in 1733 (again as quoted by Shackel) opined that politeness—and the superiority of polite people over those who are not polite—is a "law of nature."

Such an attitude has long been held to be nonsense by the non-privileged and should have been unacceptable to intellectuals who ought to have been looking for truth and reality instead of intellectual justification for privilege. Perhaps Voltaire, in a wiser observation than proclaiming politeness a "law of nature," said: "Men use thought only to justify their wrongdoings, and speech only to conceal their thoughts." (Dialogue 14, Le Chapon et la Poularde, 1766). Unfortunately academics like to clone themselves in everything but garb and slogans. Thus they have been easily led into misunderstanding the glory of their proclaimed but not followed slogans: freedom of inquiry and attitude is the hallmark of the scholar. American education has too long followed the elitist attitudes of Western Europe, especially England, in thinking that the status quo should be maintained and simulated questioning and challenge to that status quo which threatened it the least was the most desirable and reassuring. Such an attitude was most comfortable for the Western European-American political and economic philosophy because it allows for, in Darwin's terminology, the superiority of the fittest, fastest and least accountable. But the attitude, especially intellectually and academically, is not appropriate for a democracy.

Regardless of the economic system which drives it, intellectual inquiry and activity, if it is to even approach its possible goals within reasonable time frames, must be quick to act independently, to recognize error and insufficiencies in direction and to adopt new and innovative ways to achieve goals. In the humanities—and literature especially— it is no good to replace one "ism" with another. It is fruitless to replace modernism, for example, with post-modernism, structuralism with deconstructuralism, Marxism with post-Marxism. Such theories and methodologies, when they are in vogue, are at best sharp-bladed axes which cut deep and cause spurts of blood but in the long run—as their transitoriness and replaceability indicate—do little to develop lasting observations and mature and enlightened insights. They are glitzy but faddish, doomed to live until undercut by another glitzy one. Far more than their authors would care to admit, these theories and methodologies represent the Madison Avenue approach masquerading as truths.

Enlightened and lasting observation is more likely to result from a bold realization of the need for new points of view about including new materials and new approaches rather than new ways to cut the same old deck of cards. Scholars are doomed to remain the drag edge of development of knowledge and understanding when they are content to remain naive, repetitive, unimaginative, tunnel visioned and reluctant to give up the old for an experimental new. One possible amelioration of such negativism is the realization that popular culture studies offer new materials and a new key to expanding understanding in both social sciences and humanities—and that popular culture studies should remain dynamic, open-minded and eager to adopt new materials and new means of study.

What is needed is more dramatic and genuine breaks with the conventional, both in theory and methodology and in subject matter. In a world like ours, driven by instant communication and by numerous fields containing their own languages and forms of literacy, it is daily demonstrated that studies of culture and society languish far behind those in the natural sciences. With scholars and students perceived as falling far behind urgent needs in the humanities, it is imperative that radical studies, if possible, need to be implemented as soon as possible. It seems that studies in popular culture provide a possible means of achieving some progress. Popular Culture, to oversimplify, consists of articulated artifacts.

That the attitudes and actions of a culture are contained in and revealed by that culture's artifacts seems self-evident. Just as a society's attitudes shape its artifacts, so too are those attitudes shaped by and driven by the artifacts, and revealed in them if one can read and understand the material objects. Art historian Alan Gowans has for forty years insisted that if one can fully "read" a work of art he/she can understand the culture in which it was created. So, too, and perhaps to an even greater extent, since it is fundamental to a culture's way of life, an artifact is a microcosm of a culture and reveals that culture when properly read and understood. A culture is the sum total of its artifacts, created and animated. The artifacts are the bone structure of a society and culture, which when articulated form the gestalt.

It should be realized that in culture studies all artifacts, all evidences of the life of a culture, demand study and understanding. Every manifestation of the life of a culture must have its due place in the fabric of that society. Some artifacts are obviously more important than others. But the serious interpreter of a culture must understand fully the total ramifications and implications of an artifact before consigning that artifact to its place in the culture, particularly if that artifact seems trivial and unimportant. In our own society, for example, we would need careful study before consigning the hula-hoop of the fifties, or the sneaker shoe in the nineties, to the back bin of triviality. Just as Andy Warhol is often quoted in his perhaps facetious remark that everybody deserves fifteen minutes of fame in our society, every artifact undoubtedly deserves a much more serious reading that it ordinarily gets in cultural interpretations of society.

Increasingly students in popular culture are recognizing the importance of artifacts in studies in such seemingly differing fields as cultural geography, literature, constitutional law, symbology, fetishism, iconology, tabooism, heroism, and in many others which at first blush might not seem deeply fruitful, such as anthropology, archaeology and particular approaches in sociology. But we need to look more closely into these fields for new subject matter, new ideas and new approaches.

Archaeology, for example, has through the years recognized the artifact—on one level or another—as fundamental. Before the 1950s, as Shuman points out in the lead essay in this collection, archaeologists were too often pith-helmeted grave robbers breathlessly going for the gold and clumsily destroying much of the priceless evidence of man's history as they tried to relocate Homer's Troy or the treasures of King Tut's tomb. After the 1950s, archaeologists realized that most priceless artifacts do not glitter, that all relics of the past, especially those of the popular culture, are of fundamental importance in the reading of past cultures. In fact, the importance of popular culture to the archaeologist and the archaeologist to the proper study of popular culture cannot be overstated. In truth, the opportunities of the archaeologist in bringing light to bear on the popular culture of the past is almost mind-boggling. It is almost as if archaeology is just turning the top soil on the first dig in the opportunities their researchers can provide to the study of popular culture.

Two examples spring to mind immediately. In Egypt the government is allowing excavation and study of less than five percent of the known graves of antiquity, holding back the others so that proper approaches to studying and preserving the relics can be clarified and solidified. Among those gravesites held back are some 3000 burial places of the common people of the times of the Pharoahs, graves which will eventually yield their own kinds of treasures to the properly trained and alert archaeologists, and through them to the student of popular culture.

Not far away, the mountains of the central Sahara Desert are now being recognized as having had a very rich past, rich in water and vegetation enough to support all the great animals of central Africa and a thriving civilization, and to have left rich deposits waiting for the mining of the archaeologists. Pictographs are being discovered in the area of the civilizations of Wadi and the so-called round-heads who existed 6000-10,000 years before Christ, and whose archaeological remains will reveal a whole new and dramatically significant civilization which has hitherto been unknown. Archaeologists already know that despite the drama of the find of the terra-cotta figures in Xi-an, China, the digs that will eventually reveal the artifacts of the common, everyday lives of the people who molded the figures and supported the life-style of the workers will be far more revealing than the terra-cotta figures themselves.

Another area of archaeology pregnant with possibilities of unfolding the life of the past is, of course, marine archaeology. The floor of the seas is a veritable treasure-chest, not only in gold and silver but also in artifacts of past cultures. The thousands of ships that litter the floor of the Mediterranean, the hundreds that lie intact on the bottom of the Caribbean, in the Atlantic along the coast of the U.S. are all loaded with treasures of the popular culture of the past. Merchant ships, military ships, pleasure ships, the barges of the powerful, the boats of the weak— all are laden with archaeological treasures and new evidence for the student of popular culture.

So too are the possible treasures of new directions in cultural anthropology studies. Anthropologists have long since departed from preoccupation with exotic tribes of distant and primitive civilizations. They realize that studying our own present-day peoples is far more important, more urgent. So urban and domestic anthropology serves as outreaches in the study of popular culture, just as popular culture is an indispensable tool in the study of urban, cultural anthropology. Each is vital to the other, both symbiotic, both in fact extensions of the other.

Likewise with the several other areas represented in this volume which might not ordinarily come to mind immediately when popular culture people are thinking about the various areas and methodologies which need to be covered in their study.

The various areas and approaches to those areas represented in this volume demonstrate how widely and deeply the net of popular culture studies should be cast if the field is to approach achieving its mission. Everyone in popular culture studies appreciates the value of Peter Burke's excellent study *Popular Culture in Early Modern Europe* (1978), mentioned above. But popular culture studies should go more deeply into roots and antecedents, as was done in Fred E.H. Schroeder's excellent *5000 Years of Popular Culture* (1980). Many could use as a kind of model David Hackett Fischer's monumental study *Albion's Seed* (1989), in which he describes four British folkways in the U.S. and their cultural course and impact. People interested in the use of popular culture in the development of literacy might want to use as a reference Jeffrey Brooks' *When Russia Learned to Read* (1985), in which he demonstrates the indispensability of popular literature in the development of literacy in an illiterate population. For sheer exhaustiveness of its subject, one will also want to consult David S. Reynolds' *Beneath the American Renaissance: The Subversive Imagination in the Age of Emerson and Melville* (1989), and to note how a scholar can read virtually every publication that is pertinent and available and still draw dangerously erroneous conclusions. The list of books concerned with outreach and peripheral subjects goes on and on. No introduction can or should cover them all.

Meanwhile the present volume begs to teach by example how popular culture is being used and should be used in areas outside the conventional ones of popular culture, and how popular culture studies can benefit from these examples. The essays demonstrate the value of popular culture materials in most fields of study—which is educational and comforting— and the possibility of value of these materials and techniques in popular culture studies. Each study is a cameo of open windows.

M.K. Shuman's paper, for example, outlines the general approaches of the archaeologist and tells us what we are inclined to suspect: that without a knowledge of the context of an artifact—where it was found, conclusive proof of its use, and what it meant in a social and human situation—one might well draw false conclusions. In other words, every artifact is an inlay in a background of popular culture.

Barbara J. Little, in her essay "Popular Culture, Material Culture: Some Archaeological Thoughts" demonstrates that foodways "can supplement, confirm and correct documentary information" because they add the hard undeniable artifact to supposition, theory and memory. In other words, a foodway in the hand is worth many in the memory.

Paul A. Shackel, in his study entitled "Consumerism and the Structuring of Social Relations: An Historical Archaeological Perspective," emphasizes the power of goods; "Goods provide a communicative medium of symbolic significance...and provide a medium for social domination as an expression of power and ideology."

In his essay "Visual Aesthetics for Five Senses and Four Dimensions: An Ethnographic Approach to Aesthetic Objects," John Forrest presents a tantalizing and elusive approach to how complicated an evaluation of esthetics of an object may be. His analysis calls for the very greatest sensitivity on the part of the scholar.

Malcolm Shuman, in his second essay in this volume, "Maya Popular Culture," turns to an in-depth demonstration of how in certain aspects of popular culture contemporary Mayan culture can be traced back to pre-Classic times. This is a fascinating use of comparative-historical popular culture to show a continuum in a society.

In the next essay, "Towards a Methodology of Disasters: The Case of the Princess Sophia," Coates and Morrison raise a point in scholars' search for what we ought to be interested in and want to know, and suggests an even more interesting one of whether the general public is wiser in its interests in popular culture than some tradition-bound scholars are. The point should cause us to pause and reflect.

Some popular culture scholars may be surprised at the full implications of Elizabeth Lawrence's essay, "His Very Silence Speaks," which shows how research in museums and among animals can cast light on the preoccupation museums and zoos have held for Western Europeans since the seventeenth century. The essay suggests much more work that needs to be done on the subjects.

Ade Peace's essay, "The City and the Circus Engagement: Symbol and Drama in the Adelaide Grand Prix," reveals the ramifications on a community of such an outdoor event as the Grand Prix. Much work needs to be done on the subject of outdoor entertainments, as he reveals and implies.

In his essay, "Truth and Goodness, Mirrors and Masks: A Sociology of Beauty and the Face," Anthony Synnott turns to an age-old subject and demonstrates how though the subject of nearly everybody's interest, the subject still needs much in-depth study in order to be understood.

In "The Landscape of Modernity: Rationality and the Detective," James Smead takes a subject that is popular today and gives us a new cultural and literary geography that draws a new three or four dimensional map that scholars might well use as a guide.

Finally, in his paper, "Media Based Therapy: The Healing Power of Popular Culture," Joe Moran probes into the subject of how popular culture can be used in therapy of our many emotional problems.

These then are eleven essays which probe into new, and familiar, subjects in innovative ways. Though beginning at various points and from several points of the compass, they all come together to suggest fuller, deeper, and more innovative ways to study subjects in popular culture.

Digging into popular culture requires the understanding that there are important treasures in all the various areas of research, that there are digs everywhere, that in order to comprehend the subject one must really dig into the many levels of culture and that to approach a satisfactory exploration of the subject, a student, as all of society said in the 1960s, must really "dig" the subject. With these understandings, the inquisitive seeker in popular culture is ready to search for new materials in all fields, and to bring to light much valuable information on which to base valuable and promising conclusions.

The net result may perhaps not be Bertrand Russell's "good society [which] is a means to a good life for those who compose it," but it can be at least a culture whose problems and potential solutions are less abused and misunderstood than they are at present.

Ray B. Browne
Pat Browne

Artifacts and Archaeology

Malcolm K. Shuman

In this paper Malcolm Shuman outlines the general approaches of the archaeologist and tells us what we are inclined to suspect: that without a knowledge of the context, the setting, surrounding an artifact—where it was found, conclusive proof of its use, and what it meant in a social and human situation—one might draw false conclusions. The main thrust of Shuman's argument is that care must be exercised to chart the total human content of an artifact, devoid of myth and hypothesis which say more about the archaeologist than the artifact. It is best, as Shuman says, if all theories are verified by fieldwork. Students working in popular culture should be prepared to enter the dig of their inquiry and find out how theories stand up among the people and how they need to be modified, rather than being bent and twisted to fit theory. As Shuman says, archaeology "is a profoundly human (and humanizing) endeavor that cannot be divorced from the matrix of human life." All culture is the skein of human life. Popular culture is especially close to a voice of democratic life.

Nearly fifty years ago, the American cultural anthropologist Clyde Kluckhohn ventured the opinion that most archaeologists working in Middle America were "but slightly reformed antiquarians" (Kluckhohn 1940:42). He went on to castigate them for a preoccupation with minutae at the expense of "a general attempt to understand human behavior." And while his criticism was justified, it might well have been expanded to include archaeologists working in other parts of the world. Indeed, considering the origins of archaeology, a preoccupation with artifacts rather than the people who made them has been a hallmark of the field since the days of Winkelmann. It is, after all, artifacts that are the observable and behavior patterns that are the product of inference.

For pioneers such as Schliemann, the behavior patterns were to be found in myth; the artifacts were but proofs of what was already assumed to be fact. For others, however, such as the French customs official Boucher de Perthes the process was reversed. Confronted with oddly shaped pebbles washing out of the Somme terraces, Boucher refused to accept the mythical explanation that these objects were left over weapons from the war between

9

the good and rebellious angels. Noticing that these artifacts seemed associated with the bones of animals unlike any modern species, Boucher declared them to be evidence of human life in a period more remote than anyone had to that date imagined. Today, of course, we know that Boucher's handaxes were products of the Paleolithic or Old Stone Age, a time roughly coeval with the Ice Age.

Perhaps the first attempt, however, to systematize the archaeological categorization of artifacts was that of Thomsen, who in 1836 was curator of what is now the National Museum of Copenhagen. Grouping his collection into items of stone and metal, he declared them to represent three separate, sequential stages—the Stone, Bronze, and Iron Ages. While his conceptualization was a museological device, designed to make order of his collection, and was extensively modified by scholars such as Montelius, the Three Age System, as it is called, has been with us, in one form or another, ever since.

By the end of the first quarter of the present century, these and other developments had provided archaeology with a firm foundation for future work. It was well-recognized that man's antiquity far exceeded what might be inferred from a reading of Scripture; it was accepted that myths, such as that of Homer's Troy, might contain at least a kernel of truth (although later archaeologists would argue endlessly about which level contained the Troy of the Iliad; see Wood 1985); and it was accepted that cultures had changed, though anthropologists would fight internecine battles to resolve the issues of how such change related to evolutionary process. Perhaps most important of all, sheer interest in distant places had caused the latter part of the nineteenth and the first part of the twentieth centuries to be a period of great archaeological discovery and exploration. The Maya (never really lost) were "rediscovered" by a new breed of archaeologists with formal training in their field; British and French scholars, such as Rawlinson, Wooley and Leyard exposed to daylight the ancient civilizations of Mesopotamia and Syria; the Wetherell brothers of New Mexico discovered the famous cliff dwellings of Mesa Verde.

Yet probably no event so kindled the imagination of the public as the discovery in 1922 of the Tomb of King Tut, by Howard Carter (Carter 1923-33). For generations thereafter the public image of the archaeologist was to be that of a pith-helmeted figure, revolver at his belt, native bearer trembling behind him with a torch. The image has been reinforced by innumerable cartoons; by such horror film classics as The Mummy, with Boris Karloff, and the Mummy's Ghost, with Lon Chaney, Jr.; by popular novels, such as those of Elizabeth Peters; and, most recently, by the Indiana Jones movies featuring Harrison Ford. It is hardly surprising, therefore, that the public image of archaeology, is that of the "tombs-and-temples" approach castigated by Kluckhohn half a century ago.

That this public image is incorrect goes without saying. Kluckhohn's was but one of several admonitions on the part of theory-conscious anthropologists and archaeologists in the 1930s and 1940s. Notable was the work of Kluckhohn's student, Walter Taylor, who, in *A Study of Archaeology* (1948), advanced the idea that the object of archaeology was the same as that of cultural anthropology; namely, the delineation of the "statics and dynamics of culture." It was important to Taylor that non-material aspects of culture be inferable by the material artifacts. Artifacts, he suggested, were not valuable solely as means of deriving cultural chronologies, but, rather, as objects that told something about the lifeways of extinct groups. This distinction has been crucial in American archaeology ever since. Or, as Willey and Phillips put it in their seminal 1958 study, "American archaeology is anthropology or it is nothing."[1]

As a consequence of the above, in today's archaeology the artifact is valued primarily because of what it tells about the people who made it. Put another way, archaeology has moved from a strict concern with the artifact as aesthetic object (antiquarianism), through the stage of artifact as temporal marker (strict cultural history), to the phase of artifact as cultural mirror. In this process, numerous techniques have been devised for the analysis of artifacts, as well as several schemes for the classification of artifact function.

Perhaps the most rudimentary of archaeological analytic procedures is that of typology, which, generally speaking, may be seen as the classification of artifacts into groups based on techniques of manufacture, morphology, appearance, and composition. Thus, Thomsen applied typology in its most basic form by classifying artifacts as stone, bronze, and iron. The Swedish scholar, Montelius, for example, related artifacts found in the same tomb, proposing that, thereafter, isolated but similar artifacts be dated to the same time period. Thereafter, archaeologists have focused on variations within each of these general categories, adding other materials as well, as the subject of typological investigations. In the United States, where bronze and iron were generally unknown prehistorically, the analysis of ceramics has assumed a position of preeminence in the study of pre-Columbian (and even historic European) peoples.

And while the value of lithic and ceramic analyses cannot be overemphasized, most archaeologists recognize that the data gained from such studies alone are extremely limited in what they tell us about cultural history, and even more limited in terms of what they say about culture process. A prime example is the contrast between certain finely-made projectile points and so-called pebble tools.

Since 1924, it has come to be recognized that Folsom points (Figure 1) represent the height of the flint-knapper's art. These thin, finely fashioned dart points, with a flute on each side for a wooden haft, and a delicately pressure-flaked edge, have been securely dated to between 9,000 and 8,000 B.C., in the American West (Forbis 1975). They were utilized by some of the first inhabitants of the New World to kill now-extinct forms of bison. Their dating has been secured through a meticulous analysis of the strata or earth layers in which they occur. From what we know of ethnographically described hunter-gatherer peoples, we infer that the Folsom people lived at the end of the Great Ice Age and roamed the Great Plains and desert Southwest in small bands of perhaps 20 individuals. From a burial at Midland, Texas, we feel that we probably even have part of the skeleton of one of these folks—as it turns out, a woman.

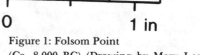

Figure 1: Folsom Point (Ca. 8,000 BC) (Drawing by Mary Lee Eggart)

Let us now consider the situation with regard to pebble tools. Pebble tools, it may be remembered, were found by Louis and Mary Leakey in Olduvai Gorge, Kenya, in presumed association with fossil hominids. Ergo, pebble tools are markers of a time in human prehistory before human beings learned the fine arts of the flint-knapper's craft. Now, pebble tools are by no means restricted to Africa. In point of fact, they have been reported in several locations throughout the United States. In one case, in Houston County, Alabama, a "complex" of such tools was described in the mid-1960s and the eminent French prehistorian, the late Francois Bordes, was invited to examine the find.[2] Not surprisingly, Bordes who had made his reputation describing the French Lower and Middle Paleolithic, declared that the tools were genuine and, presumably, old, although he entered the sensible caveat that since they occurred on the surface, their antiquity was unable to be proven (Bordes, personal communication). It would probably not be unfair to say that Bordes wanted to believe in the antiquity of these tools, although he was far too good a scholar to disregard the fact that there was no stratigraphic context with which to associate them. Later opinion, however, has tended to debunk the antiquity of the "Lively Complex" and similar complexes for a far more obvious reason: simply because something is well-made or poorly-made does not indicate its age. People who use bows and arrows (or rifles, for that matter) may also use pebbles for some tasks (Indeed, it has been pointed out that pebble tools function well for such work as the processing of seaweed!). Conversely, the beautiful Folsom points have never been equaled by subsequent peoples, as can be readily seen by comparison with a projectile point of about A.D. 1200 (Figure 2).[3]

And, whereas the Folsom point has been dated to within a fairly narrow time range, the point shown in Figure 3 spans a period of about 1,500 years. Clearly, within a millennium, social, political and linguistic patterns may all change, so that finding such an artifact by itself gives us only the most general information about the people who made it.

All of which points up the fact that a single artifact, devoid of context, tells us little about the manufacturer, and it is precisely this emphasis on context that separates the archaeologist from the collector. And yet even context can deceive. Consider the case of the Anasazi projectile points:

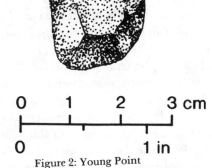

Figure 2: Young Point
(AD 1200-1500) (Drawing by Mary Lee Eggart)

These items, manufactured about 1,000 years ago by the ancestors of today's Pueblo Indians of the Southwest, have been collected for generations by Navajo medicine men, who place them in their sacred medicine bundles. Naive archaeologists, unaware of this fact, might easily assume, from the association of an Anasazi point with a Navajo burial, that the projectile point was produced by the Navajo. It is much the same as assuming from the excavation of a twentieth century museum that people of our era made Etruscan vases. On the other hand, the fact that an artifact is found, for example, at a lower level in the earth than might be expected (i.e., underlying other, typologically earlier artifacts) does not necessarily indicate greater antiquity for the lower object. The action of rodents (bioturbation) has been known to shove artifacts to lower levels. The digging of pits from a higher level will also deposit items at a depth greater than items in the surrounding, undisturbed earth. Consequently, archaeologists rely heavily on the observations of skilled geologists for their interpretations.

From the above, it should be obvious that archaeologists hesitate to draw conclusions without multiple analyses of artifacts, utilizing a number of techniques, of which typology is but one. One of the more interesting such supplementary techniques has to do with the analysis of wear patterns and techniques of manufacture. An entire subfield, experimental archaeology, has developed to reproduce the implements of prehistoric man, basing itself on the logical assumption that unless one knows how an artifact is manufactured, and what problems are associated with its production, much information about the tool's producer(s) is lost. It is one thing to discourse glibly about the use of stone tools for the skinning of game, and quite another entirely to cut up an antelope using lithic implements of one's own manufacture. On the other hand, archaeologists could expound endlessly about the cultural significance of scratch marks on bits of bone but when it was shown experimentally that such marks could be made by an animal—say a deer—grinding such a bone fragment into the sand of a creek by merely walking over it, the issue became moot. In short, experimental archaeology, by replicating both human and natural actions, gives the archaeologist insight into the technological aspects of a past age.

0   30
cm

Figure 3: Ledbetter Stemmed Point (1,500-1,000 BC) (Drawing by Don Hunter)

Third, some mention should be made of the location or distribution of artifacts. As has been implied above, the geological context of cultural materials is vitally important. But even beyond this the differential distribution of artifacts provides valuable information. In the early days of archaeology, work was too often limited to the exploration of elite tombs and residences (hence Kluckhohn's criticism). The picture of ancient life was thus one of pharoahs, kings and high priests. By the 1950s, however, fueled by Gordon Willey's work in Peru (Willey 1953), there came to be a recognition that there was far more to an archaeological site than the artifacts of high-status individuals. Willey placed an emphasis on settlement patterns, or the distribution of dwelling areas within an archaeological site. Following Willey, practitioners of the "New Archaeology," epitomized by Louis Binford and his students (Binford and Binford 1968), made a virtual fetish of settlement studies. In part, this was the result of the egalitarian currents of the 1960s, which deprecated elites. But the trend was also a much-needed corrective to past practices. Today, the archaeologist is generally interested in the relationship of intrasite areas to one another, and to such elementary (but often previously ignored) matters as population density. Thus, scholars have been able to postulate population sizes for the Mayan center of Tikal, previously thought to be a "vacant center" without substantial inhabitation (Figure 4). For the great center of Teotihuacan, in central Mexico, it has been possible to distinguish an area for merchants, one for priests, etc. (Figure 5, Teotihuacan). Related to this, but on a reduced scale, is the delineation of activity areas within sites corresponding to groups at the band or tribal level. The archaeologist dealing with a site in the Southeastern United States, for instance, will want to distinguish the village area (usually indicated by extensive ceramic deposits in a thick, blackish soil matrix) from the lithic workshop areas (indicated by extensive numbers of flint flakes and other stone debris). The presence of a mound will be further indication of a sacred or political precinct (mounds were sometimes used for burial, sometimes as platforms for temples, charnel houses, or the homes of chiefs). In this connection, some of the early work of the "New Archaeologists" blazed new ground. In one of the more imaginative studies, Longacre (1968) classified design elements on pottery and related the sherd types to where they were found within a Southwestern Pueblo. From this analysis, he was to argue for "post-marital residence in the vicinity of the wife's female relatives, with ceramic decoration learned and passed down within the residence unit (p. 99)."

And finally, the archaeologist learns from the very material utilized in the production of artifacts. In prior eras, it was all too easy for archaeologists to view exotic items as evidence of invasion by strangers; today, it is far more likely to see such objects as signs of trade. Certain types of stone found at the great Poverty Point prehistoric ceremonial complex in northeastern Louisiana derive from the Appalachian mountains and thus show the existence of a thriving trade network a thousand years before Christ. And while it is accepted that the Yucatan Peninsula of Mexico was invaded at some point by Toltecs from central Mexico, today Nahua potters from Puebla drive up the Gulf Coast with their wares, using pickup trucks, and sell them in the Maya villages for good (or inflated) Mexican currency (Figure 6, Modern Nahua bowl bought in Yucatan). Clearly, it is dangerous to infer too much on the basis of exotic artifacts in unlikely places. A far better case for invasion can be made on the basis of design elements associated with standing structures (e.g. feathered serpents, skull racks, murals).

Cross-cutting these concerns with artifact form, location, and substance are concerns with the function which an artifact served. Very early on, it came to be realized that some artifacts served a material purpose

Figure 4: Skyline View of Maya Site of Tikal, Guatemala

Figure 5: Site of Teotihuacan, Mexico, Showing Temple of the Sun

and others served symbolic ends. From this developed the often-employed distinction between utilitarian and non-utilitarian artifacts. Utilitarian artifacts include the projectile points actually used for hunting and warfare; pottery used for the preparation of daily meals; and (yes) even hunting rifles and military sidearms. Non-utilitarian items would include special artifacts designed for burial purposes; artifacts used in religious ceremonies; and presentation-grade guns that are never meant to be fired. Thus, the rather ornate tripod bowl from Costa Rica shown in Figure 7 is certainly a burial offering, while the sherds of undecorated ware shown in Figure 8 are probably from someone's cooking pot. This distinction between the useful and the symbolic, as obvious as it may seem, is hardly devoid of pitfalls. Figure 9 shows a fragment of undecorated pottery from the southeastern United States. It is referred to as Coles Creek Plain and was, presumably, a utility ware. Figure 10, on the other hand, shows a pot fragment with parallel incised lines. It is referred to as Coles Creek Incised. Both date from about the same period: roughly A.D. 900. Is the first to be classified as utilitarian and the second as non-utilitarian, because of the designs? The answer is clearly no, because it was a characteristic of the Coles Creek people to make incisions only on the two or three inches of their vessels immediately below the rims. Hence, both sherds might come from the same vessel. Presumably, such dilemmas can be solved by adequate samples of potsherds, provided one has a site that is sufficiently rich. Also, the presence of a burial might settle the issue, if the highly acidic soil has not destroyed all that remains of the bones.

Of far greater concern is the mental set of archaeologists who have, over the years, tended to relegate to the non-utilitarian category anything whose use is not readily apparent. This tendency has become so marked that it is a standing joke that anything unexplained must serve a ceremonial purpose. Thus, for example, the earthen wall around the Marksville mound site in central Louisiana (Figure 11) is identified in official signs as a "ceremonial wall," though not a shred of evidence exists to support that interpretation. More spectacular, perhaps, was the earlier interpretation of Maya stelae. These limestone monuments, erected during the period from about A.D. 300 to 900, bear the likenesses of Maya lords and warriors, along with glyphic texts (Figure 12). The calendrical content of the glyphs was soon decoded; the prose content of the glyphs is still only partially deciphered. Because the glyphs all bore dates in the Maya calendar, a novel explanation of the stelae themselves was developed: The stelae merely reflected the Maya preoccupation with time and the human figures were gods and goddesses. In this view, the Maya were conservators of a cult of time, based on a calendar that allowed them to reckon forward and backward for millions of years. The purpose of the calendar was largely astrological and was the tool used by the priesthood to control the masses.

Figure 6: Modern Nahua Bowl

Figure 7: Anccient Costa Rican Tripod Bowl

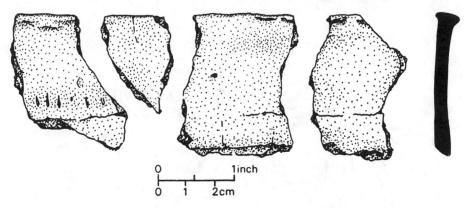

Figure 8: Sherds from Aboriginal Cooking Vessel, Avoyelles Parish, Louisiana
(Drawing by Mary Lee Eggart)

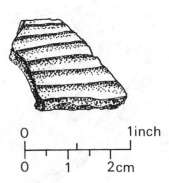

Figure 10: Fragment of Decorated
Aboriginal Pottery, US Southeast
(Drawing by Mary Lee Eggart)

Figure 9: Fragment of Plain Aboriginal
Pottery, US Southeast (Drawing by Don
Hunter)

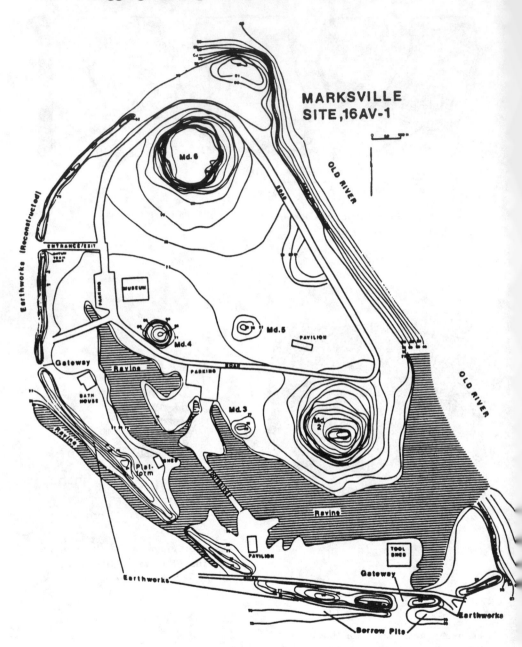

Figure 11: Map of Marksville Indian Site, Avoyelles Parish, Louisiana (Map by Dennis Jones)

Figure 12: Maya Indian Stela from copan, Honduras

A far more common-sense solution might have suggested itself had not archaeologists been caught up in the uniqueness of the Maya civilization, which they thought to be *sui generis*. It was not until the 1960s that the late Tatiana Prouskouriakoff noticed that the dates on closely grouped series of stelae fell within periods that could be comprehended by a single human lifetime, or, more precisely, a single reign. This observation, along with progress in glyphic decipherment, led to the now accepted view that the stelae, far from carrying the images of mythical beings, are monuments to rulers who actually lived, and who commissioned the monoliths to celebrate their accomplishments. Hardly a unique practice in the annals of politics!

The "New Archaeology" of the 1960s, recognizing the deficiencies of a method that tended to characterize anything unknown as part of some esoteric magico-religious system, sought a way out of this morass by an insistence on the formalization of archaeological arguments: henceforth, it would be anathema to advance a *post hoc* explanation that placed the unknown into such catch-all categories. Rather, archaeology should proceed from previously defined hypotheses, and many of these hypotheses could be drawn from ethnographic analogy and experimental archaeology.

It sounded good. Unfortunately, the New Archaeologists tended to excel at thought-work rather than fieldwork, and when hypotheses were not borne out, then new hypotheses had to be offered. These new hypotheses often seemed dismayingly similar to the old *post hoc* interpretations. Nevertheless, it was an admirable attempt to make all practitioners play fair and it created a new awareness of the basic rationality of human adaptive strategies. Maybe the artifact that seemed so outré to the American archaeologist, who grew up in an urban context, was merely a commonsense tool that served a basic need for a prehistoric person living in a different kind of world.

From the foregoing, it can be imagined that the process of obtaining archaeological knowledge from archaeological data is hardly a smooth one. Battles between the New Archaeologists and the traditionalists were acrimonious and sometimes seemed closer to gang warfare than scholarly dialogue. Even today, with the vanguard of the New Archaeologists approaching retirement, there is no such thing as a smooth, unimpeded accretion of archaeological knowledge. If each artifact represents a potential for knowledge, it also represents a potential for conflict, as interpretation wars with interpretation, and theorist decries fieldworker. The popular view of the archaeologist crying "Eureka" as he makes the epochal discovery is rooted in the myth of King Tut and has little to do with the everyday world of the archaeologist. Most archaeological knowledge is the result of a gradual picture developed from an analysis of several seasons of fieldwork.[4] The picture is further complicated by those archaeologists who excavate but never publish. It is a sad fact that, while they decry amateurs who wreck sites in order to recover artifacts, some archaeologists (and supposedly quite reputable ones, at that) have gone through the process of excavation, with its attendant destructiveness, and then have failed to write a report. The artifacts, soil samples, and their notes languish for years in dusty labs while the excavators go on to other projects, promising themselves that they will return to the original project when they get a chance. Sometimes, twenty years later, they steel themselves to the task and *do* publish. By that time, of course, the data are literally quite cold: The methodology has been superseded by new approaches and new interpretations have been developed that, had this information been available, might have been modified. Still, they publish, and it is better than nothing. Just as often, however, is the case of the archaeologist who dies or retires, leaving the notes and bags of artifacts to a future doctoral student on the prowl for a dissertation. It suffices to say that no write up at second-hand can approach the accuracy of a publication by the person who actually carried out the work.

The above is not to imply that archaeology is a useless undertaking; rather, that it is a profoundly human (and humanizing) endeavor that cannot be divorced from the matrix of human life. Like anthropology itself, it is an exercise in the paradoxical practice of self-study. Despite the slings and arrows of outrageous personality differences, or the slashes of warring methodologies, knowledge has been, and will continue to be, derived from a study of what past peoples left by the wayside, just as knowledge of our own lives is being preserved for future generations by the study of contemporary garbage deposits (Rathje). Yet there is something a bit disquieting in the notion that archaeology is only about knowledge. It is a bit as if saying that the only purpose in living is to work. The archaeologists of old, those maligned antiquarians portrayed in books and film, existed for the thrill of discovery and endured incredible hardships for the possibility of crying "Eureka" in the middle of a desert where no one would hear. They have been supplanted by a more earnest breed, with computers and radiocarbon laboratories, who look askance at the possibility that anything worth doing can possibly be fun.

If any one of these grim practitioners were asked, however, it would be almost certain that he or she first became interested in archaeology not because of a fascination with quadratic equations, or statistics, but because of the thrill of picking up arrow heads in a ploughed field, or seeing a filmstrip of crumbling ruins in a Central American jungle. And perhaps this is the triumph of archaeology as a humanistic endeavor—that it feeds on the romantic in each of us, and that far beneath the surface of even the most serious scholar there is still the child, imagining himself grown and in pith helmet, entering the tomb of King Tut and crying "Eureka."

Notes

[1]This situation is peculiar to the United States, where archaeology forms a field of study within departments of anthropology, and archaeologists receive degrees in anthropology, with specializations in archaeology rather than in archaeology itself. The situation is different in France, for instance, where somewhat less attention is given to the cultural matrix of artifacts and entire schemes are erected on complex statistical analysis of artifact types. As one French archaeologist remarked to the author when queried about what inferences might be drawn about lifeways, "I am an archaeologist, not an anthropologist.".

[2]Francois Bordes, personal conversation with the author, 1970.

[3]The rather natural assumption that "crude equals old" is also contradicted by an example from historical archaeology: As the industrial revolution progressed, the originally well-made cream wares of the late 18th century gave way to mass-manufactured ceramics in the 19th century. Was there a period of cultural collapse, as archaeologist might infer from this degeneration of technique? Hardly; rather, what we see, is a period of cultural transformation spurred by technological advances.

⁴An exception to this time is contract archaeology, where the constraints of time make it necessary to survey, excavate, and produce a report, often within a matter of weeks or, at most, months.

Works Cited

Binford, Sally R. and Lewis R. (Eds.) *New Perspectives in Archaeology*. Chicago: Aldine, 1968.

Carter, Howard. *The Tomb of Tut-Ankh-Amen*. 3 Vols. London: Cassell, 1923-1933.

Forbis, Richard G. *The Paleoamericans. In North America* (Ed. by Shirley Gorenstein et al), pp. 17-35. New York: St. Martin's, 1975.

Kluckhohn, Clyde. *The Conceptual Structure in Middle American Studies: Essays on Middle American Anthropology and Archaeology. In The Maya and Their Neighbors*. (Ed. by Clarence L. Hay et al), New York: Dover Publications, 1977 (orig. 1940). pp. 41-51.

Longacre, William A. *Some Aspects of Prehistoric Society*. In *New Perspectives in Archaeology* (Ed. by Sally R. Binford and Lewis R. Binford), Chicago: Aldine, 1968. pp. 89-102.

Taylor, Walter W., Jr. *A Study of Archaeology. American Anthropological Association Memoir* No. 69. Menasha, 1948.

Willey, Gordon R. *Prehistoric Settlement Patterns in the Viru Valley, Peru. Bureau of American Ethnology Bulletin* 155. Washington, D.C., 1953.

Willey, Gordon R. and Philip. *Method and Theory in American Archaeology*. Chicago: University of Chicago Press, 1958.

Wood, Michael. *In Search of the Trojan War*. New York: Facts on File, 1985.

Popular Culture, Material Culture:
Some Archaeological Thoughts

Barbara J. Little

Foodways, Little says, "can supplement, confirm and correct documentary information" because they add the hard undeniable artifacts to supposition, theory and memory. Foodways all demonstrate how wideranging a particular subject can be, including how human physiology responds to changing food, and how eating customs developed "esthetics" and correct ways of handling food. Archaeology gives a historical perspective that modifies temporal evaluations and smoothes out the vagaries of esthetics. Food can also be used to demonstrate the dynamics of hegemony. Little correctly points out that in her discipline, and we in ours, "Any discipline interested in things and in daily life needs observations, a vocabulary and a theory for talking about the active roles of both concrete and ephemeral representations and images of the mundane."

Archaeologists study garbage. Archaeologists study the past, the pyramids, the exotic. Archaeologists search for treasure. Every semester I ask my students newly enrolled in introductory classes, "What do archaeologists do?" The responses vary little: garbage, treasure, tedium, adventure, romance, science. Odder than the seemingly contradictory perceptions of archaeology is their basis in truth. We do study garbage; we do search for treasure, but the treasure has changed. Once archaeology focused its energy on the objet d'art, on aesthetically interesting pieces for public display. "Things, I see wonderful things," sums up Howard Carter's finally gratified search for the tomb of Tutankhamun. Public— and professional—imagination is fired by the possibility of recovering the past, thought to be forever lost. Things provide tangible proof of that recovery, provide some visible parts of lives long extinguished. "Artifact Lust" is what we anthropological archaeologists call the antiquarian passions that see an object as token or art devoid of original context. It is context, the full association of something, that allows interpretation and any sort of real understanding of the past.

This essay is about some of the ways that one type of anthropological archaeology studies the material remains of popular culture. The point to be made is that material culture is a basic aspect of our lives that creates and reinforces as well as reflects non-material culture. Much of modern anthropological archaeology focuses on its analyses on "lifeways" that are illuminated by the remains of everyday activities. Historical archaeology studies not only underground remains: the bits of bone and glass; but also the aboveground: buildings, gravestones, and archives of written and printed documents. Archaeologists should be interested in documents, i.e. in print culture and in other media for a reason other than their direct information. That reason is the portrayal of archaeology in such media. Before I discuss the way historical archaeologists look at popular culture, a few words are in order about the way popular culture has looked at archaeology.

Archaeology in Popular Culture

Archaeology has played a role *in* American popular culture since the late eighteenth century. European explorers and later settlers were struck by the impressive earthen mounds and earthworks that dotted the eastern half of the North American continent. Although many of these constructions are now destroyed, some survive as monuments and attractions for visitors. The sites of Cahokia near East St. Louis, Illinois and the Newark earthworks in Newark, Ohio are just two of the handful of surviving sites that come immediately to mind (see Wilson 1980).

The myth of the moundbuilders, which attributed these engineering feats to a "lost race" rather than to Native Americans, can be traced back at least to 1785 and grew in popularity through the nineteenth century (Willey and Sabloff 1980:20ff). It is no mere coincidence that such attributions, denying Native American creativity and organization, flourished while battles raged across the continent over possession of the land. It is also not an accident that the myth was put to rest by government-sponsored professional archaeology in the 1890s, just about the time that white settlers had succeeded in confining Native Americans to reservations (Shackel, personal communication).

Whether or not one can identify particular political or economic purposes behind a popular interest in antiquity and its remains, some myths of archaeology remain in popular culture. The most obvious current example is the portrayal of archaeology in the series of Indiana Jones films. (At the time of this writing the third had not yet been released.) There is portrayed the romance, adventure, and treasure—treasure recovered for a noble purpose, "for the museum." Such artifact lust, however, is not what most modern, professional archaeology is about. Popular perceptions that archaeology is concerned with objects, rather than with the more informative and time-consuming contexts, are damaging. Archaeology as treasure hunting encourages amateur searching and acquisition and results in the destruction of irreplaceable archaeological resources.

While it is not the point of this essay to bemoan the effects of popular culture, it is worth noting that an analysis will not necessarily turn into a celebration. There are, depending on one's perspective, both positive and negative aspects of any subset of popular culture. I personally think that *Raiders of the Lost Ark* is brilliantly entertaining and I am simultaneously fascinated, appalled, and thrilled by the mythology it enacts, not the mythology of the Ark, but that of archaeology.

Other representations of archaeology in popular film and literature are equally as fascinating. Almost inevitably archaeology is associated with a good mystery or a supernatural thriller. There is much more literature using archaeology or archaeologists as a theme than one might expect and my list of a dozen or so novels is certainly incomplete. *The Exorcist* and *The Omen* both use some archaeological discoveries. Another more recent work that immediately comes to mind is Tony Hillerman's detective novel *A Thief of Time*.

Archaeology's goal of recovering what was lost or of discovering the unknown in the past invites other themes of the unknown, both of human motive and of supernatural intent. The power of such imagery enhances as well as distorts the "realities" of archaeology. Those realities include the garbage aside from the treasure, the tedium aside from the adventure, and patient scientific analysis aside from romance and immediate gratification. The subject of the mythology of archaeology deserves more reflection, but I will leave it and turn to the less flamboyant (but no less fascinating) side of archaeology and popular culture.

Archaeology of Past Popular Culture

Archaeology has broadened its horizons. Once defined as the study of the prehistoric past, it is now better defined as a study of material culture through time. Material culture may be broadly defined as that part of the physical environment created or affected by cultural concepts. It includes such things as food, plates, houses, gardens, and the arrangements of villages, farms, and cities. In addition to excavation and analysis of prehistoric remains, modern archaeology includes such specialties as "living" archaeology or ethnoarchaeology, which is the study of material culture in currently functioning social and cultural systems.

Historical archaeology is part of the overall broadening of and maturation of the larger field. Kathleen Deagan offers a definition of historical archaeology upon which she thinks most would agree: "the study of human behavior through material remains, for which written history in some way affects its interpretation" (1982:153). That is, practitioners use the materials and methods of both history and archaeology. Goals vary; historical archaeologists have argued about the proper orientation of their field. Deagan also has pointed out that the field has been unfocused and erratic because of simultaneous attention to historical, anthropological, archaeological, and ideological questions (1982:171).

There are influential suggestions for focusing historical archaeology in order to make it more productive. Historical archaeology in this country has been largely concerned with European occupation and Robert Schuyler (1970) has identified capitalism and capitalist development and growth as the proper subject of our sub-discipline. Likewise Mark Leone (1977) has strongly encouraged the study of the organization and emergence of the production, distribution and exchange relationships of contemporary society. Handsman (quoted in Orser 1988) identifies our subject matter as "power, commodities and capital, class struggle and resistance, hegemony and masking." Charles Orser (1988) agrees, stating that once we recognize our subject as capitalism, historical archaeologists will be free to accomplish interdisciplinary research. Capitalism here refers to the whole developing culture of capitalism. It is not confined to industrial capitalism but rather develops from the 15th century on with mercantile capitalism, global exploration, colonization, and the development of a world economic system (Braudel 1979, Wallerstein 1974, 1980).

With the consumer revolution of the mid 18th century (e.g. Breen 1986) and the revolution in the English ceramics industry started by Josiah Wedgwood in the 1760s, mass production and consumption becomes increasingly apparent in everyday life and in the archaeological remains of that life. As a discipline that studies capitalism and focuses on material culture, historical archaeology is particularly well suited to address questions about things that are mass produced and mass consumed, but is not confined to these. The mundane accoutrements of everyday life can be studied not only for their place in vernacular, localized developments, but also for their role on a global scale. Industrialism, colonialism and social relations have effects on production and consumption which are tempered and channeled by local ethnic, economic, religious, political, and historical concerns.

Historical archaeology is an appropriately optimistic discipline. With a variety of rich data bases from both ground and archives it should be possible to examine both consumption and production. We should be able to reveal what persons of a variety of backgrounds were buying and selling, whether the commodities were material goods, appropriate behaviors, or useful ideologies. As optimistic as we are we must also be cautious. For as much as we learn about the meanings of goods and the uses of material culture—and there is a lot to learn—we must remember that objects as much as words are meaningful only in their proper social and cultural context as well as in their archaeological context.

It is beyond the scope of this paper to argue much about fine distinctions among popular culture, vernacular culture, and mass produced culture or those between all of these and high style culture. For my purposes that material culture associated with everyday life provides sufficient boundaries for research.

Historical archaeology, like all anthropological archaeology, asks particular kinds of questions of everyday life. Reconstructing "lifeways" is the archaeological analog to ethnographic description in cultural anthropology. One wants to describe how people live: the who, what, when, where, and why of food, crafts, industries, businesses, living arrangements, social relationships, political ideology, and cosmology.

Some of the most influential work in historical archaeology is that of James Deetz (1977, 1983). *In Small Things Forgotten* related changes in everyday material culture to broad cultural changes in worldview and cognition. Changes in architectural facades and floorplans, ceramics, foodways, trash disposal, gravestones, and other less archaeologically visible objects such as furniture are described in relation to changing emphasis on Anglo-American culture from medieval-style communality to Renaissance-inspired individuality. There is a great volume of work inspired by Deetz' ideas in the last decade (e.g. McKee 1987; Palkovich 1988). Deetz' observations about changes in the styles and uses of material culture become much more useful, I believe, when one thinks about the creative, teaching, socializing roles of artifacts and the built environment.

Before discussing such roles of material culture however, I want to provide some specific examples of the way historical archaeologists look at everyday life by considering questions of sustenance. I pick this topic because it is one of the most mundane aspects of daily life and it is a topic for which archaeological interpretation is relatively straightforward. It also provides an example of material culture which can be superficially dismissed as trivial and simple, but which actually holds complex and important meanings. As Douglas and Isherwood write (1979:73), "Even the choice of kitchen utensils is anchored to deep preconceptions about man and nature."

Historical Archaeology of Foodways

What do people eat and how do they eat it? The answers to such simple questions become complex, involving not just types of plants and animals and methods of cooking and serving, but also all the expected anthropological concerns with economic, social, political and religious constructs. There are many different sorts of questions to ask from many theoretical perspectives: How does the way people make a living change as the nature of settlement changes from frontier to native land? How does health and nutrition compare between urban and rural areas, between blacks and whites, between the new world and the old? How do foodways persist or change in response to overall change in social relationships and integration or segmentation? How does food become part of ethnic or gender identity?

Archaeological information can supplement, confirm and correct documentary information. There is often not much specific documentary information on day to day details. Of course, some sorts of written and printed material are helpful for suggesting what people were eating. Cookbooks, diaries, personal account books, probate inventories and other sources can reveal much about attitudes, ideals, preferred foods, and particular items. Archaeological excavation yields skeletal remains of domestic and wild fauna as well as often less well preserved remains of flora in the form of seeds, phytoliths husks, pollen or other plant parts. Examples from just a few archaeological studies will illustrate some kinds of questions that have been addressed.

Comparisons between archaeological and documentary data at the Mott farm near Portsmouth, Rhode Island revealed specific economic uses of animals. Joanne Bowen (1975) compared domestic animals listed in a 1736 probate inventory (the record of things owned at a person's death) with skeletal remains recovered from an archaeological deposit dating to the same time. She was able to distinguish uses of animals for family consumption, as draft animals and as items of export. Her study is successful at understanding the Mott family's integration into the sheep-exporting economy of Rhode Island in the 18th century. Although not large scale producers, the Motts were able to supplement their income as farmers by raising sheep for export as well as for home use of wool and meat.

Bowen concentrated her analysis on domestic animals, but wild food remains are equally informative. Proportions of wild to domestic food have provided some interesting information on slave sites in Georgia. Plantation slave diet was made nutritious and sufficient through the slaves' own efforts at collecting wild food rather than through provisioning by plantation owners, as some historical interpretation would lead us to believe (Singleton 1988).

Further interesting observations about sustenance are provided by the work of John Otto (1984) at Cannon's Point Plantation. Ceramics for serving food and the butchering patterns of animal bones were compared for sites of different socioeconomic and legal status: owner, overseer, and slave. Both slaves and the overseer owned relatively high proportions of serving bowls in comparison with the owner. Slaves owned proportionately more bowls than the overseer. In comparison with slaves, both owner and the overseer owned more flatware, i.e. platters and plates.

The owner owned proportionately more flatware (and more in absolute numbers) than the overseer or the slaves. Such data point to questions of dietary differences which are borne out by the butchering marks on food remains. Slaves were eating many more meals of stew and soups, made with meat chopped with a cleaver into chunks. Such meals require fewer cooking vessels and less care in tending than the roasts indicated by sawn animal parts and service on plates. The owner's family ate more expensive cuts of meat which took more careful preparation (by a servant or slave). Overseer cuisine had attributes in common with those of both slave and owner. Such differences in foodways point to both economic and cultural differences.

Ceramics are certainly involved in foodways and their change or persistence through time, and they also take us directly to issues of cost, wealth, status, and display. A useful technique for comparing costs of ceramics is Miller's index for ceramic scaling. George Miller (1980) has used potters' price-fixing lists, commodity price lists, and other documentary information to create a standard measure of costs with which to compare any particular collections of ceramics for the late 18th through the mid 19th century. Relative cost coupled with information on occupation, access to markets, rural or urban lifestyle, etc. can provide basic data with which to form further questions of relative wealth, display of wealth or the appearance of wealth, relationships among classes or other groups, and adherence to rules of etiquette and ownership of "proper" dining equipment.

Meanings and Uses of Material Culture

Etiquette and ownership of "correct" items bring us to issues of what goods are used for. In many ways goods are for competition which may be absolutely explicit or largely implicit and subconscious. In constructing understandings of how items of material culture act in structuring as well as reflecting values, ideas, and cultural "common sense," archaeologists have found useful the works of social theorists such as Louis Altusser (e.g. Leone 1988; McGuire 1988), Antony Giddens (e.g. Leone 1986; Shanks and Tilley 1987), Pierre Bourdieu (e.g. Miller 1987), Michel Foucault (e.g. Shackel 1989), Mary Douglas (e.g. Little 1988), and Antonio Gramsci (e.g. Little 1987), among others.

My own understanding of the uses of goods owes much to the work of Mary Douglas, especially her book with Baron Isherwood, *The World of Goods* (1979). Douglas emphasizes humans' metaphorical understanding of goods as markers of cultural categories. Goods make and maintain social relationships through the information system. Individuals who know the code of the information system endow goods with agreed upon values as category markers. Goods act to elicit and stabilize consensus about cultural categories and about what is valuable. In this way the universe is made intelligible and controllable.

In affirming that the consumption of goods is ultimately about power relationships, Douglas states that those in control of information seek a monopoly and try to prevent others from gaining that knowledge. Those without information control either withdraw and consolidate around remaining social possibilities or try to infiltrate the class of information controllers, presumably through emulation (Douglas and Isherwood 1979).

Those in the controlling group are in a position to impose particular meanings on goods, therefore create or reinforce cultural categories, thereby create consensus on values, and thereby extend hegemony into the world of goods.

Hegemony is a word used frequently, often without consideration of some of its implications. The Italian Marxist Antonio Gramsci developed the ideas of hegemony from Lenin's writings and the need to explain consent as well as conflict. Hegemony is a societal relation of domination by means of consent rather than by force. It is political and ideological persuasion used by a dominant class to convince the dominated classes that the status quo is just and proper. The power of the concept of hegemony resides in the addition of culture to a Marxist point of view, which traditionally relegates culture to the realm of the affected. In this way it is a valuable reconciliation of the materialist and idealist viewpoints. It is a powerful concept because it recognizes both abstract and concrete bases of social organization and culture. Hegemony also helps to explain social stability in the midst of conflict and allows the possibility of social change emerging from seeming stability.

The mechanisms through which hegemony operates logically consist of whatever is available as a means of communication for persuasion. There may well be competing messages and one should expect differential acceptance of messages. Not everybody "buys" the party line, whether figuratively as in political or religious dogma, or literally in the forms and styles of material goods. Those who do not buy the prevailing cultural "common sense" are of great interest, as they present the challenges, both to their own societies and to the historical anthropologist who seeks to make sense of the diversity within societies.

Often emulation is invoked as an explanation, yet it is not straightforward. Those who do not emulate upper class values and fashion are in a peculiar position in a capitalist economy. Douglas describes their action as withdrawal and yet pursuance of alternatives may well be as much celebration or affirmation as reluctant resignation. Hegemony is operating efficiently if adherents to such alternatives do not overtly challenge the dominant system's values. Of particular interest to historical archaeologists is the relationship between dominating and resisting cultures and their strategies.

Emulation can be read in different ways. Is it a way of challenging the cultural/social system or merely one's own place in that system? Emulation can be an effective strategy for challenging a particular social hierarchy, especially when rigid stratification begins to break down. In his book *Material Culture and Mass Consumption,* Daniel Miller notes that the "demand for goods may flourish in the context of ambiguity in social hierarchy" (1987:136). People lower in the hierarchy aspire to higher status through the purchase and display of material goods identified with higher status. Such action in turn stimulates the upper classes to maintain a differential between themselves and those perceived as lower class. Knowledge and understanding of quickly changing fashions works to exclude or include. Fashion uses the dynamic force of the object as a way of stabilizing the social system (Miller 1987:126).

Conclusion

I have provided some examples of ways that historical archaeologists have looked at the most mundane remains of everyday life and have made some broad observations on the kinds of concepts I find important. As with any discipline, specific data and the questions asked of it vary with theoretical orientation. Historical archaeology runs the gamut from functional environmental determinism to Levi-Straus style structuralism to symbolic anthropology to Marxist interpretations of ideology. The challenge, of course, is to blend theoretical perspectives to create a useful hybrid which will help interpret our fragmentary data. A "post-processual" archaeology (e.g. Hodder 1986) is one that accepts myriad approaches for looking at data and accepts insights gained from different perspectives, but rejects dichotomies, such as materialist vs. idealist, which tend to overly focus and unduly limit interpretation.

Historical archaeologists study material culture: garbage, standing architecture, tax records, probate inventories. Different information, clues, and questions are available in objects and documents. They are both material culture. Both are products of culture created from different perspectives, with different purposes, from different activities. Either sort of source raises questions of the other. Miller (1987:105) notes that Pierre Bourdieu "constantly affirms the effectiveness of order embodied in details such as dress, body movement and manners, and argues that it is a function of the mundane artifact almost always to be regarded as an example of mere 'trivia' unworthy of systematic academic study."

One general goal of historical archaeology, or of any discipline that takes the material world of culture seriously, is to achieve a better understanding of the uses and meanings of goods. How are they active?

How do they get empowered? How do they lose influence? Are there neutral goods or have all goods "lost their innocence?" (cf. Wobst 1977)

The observation that goods are neither innocent nor trivial is equally important for the study of popular culture and modern material culture and for archaeology. Any discipline interested in things and in daily life needs observations, a vocabulary, and a theory for talking about the active roles of both concrete and ephemeral representations and images of the mundane.

Works Cited

Braudel, Fernand. *Civilization and Capitalism, 15th-18th Century.* 3 Volumes. New York: Harper & Row, 1979.

Breen, Timothy. *The Meaning of Things: The Consumer Culture of Eighteenth-Century America and the Coming Revolution.* Paper presented at Winterthur Museum Conference: "Accumulation and Display: The Development of American Consumerism 1880-1920." November 7-8, 1986.

Bowen, Joanne. "Probate Inventories: An Evaluation from the Perspective of Zooarchaeology and Agricultural History at Mott Farm." *Historical Archaeology* 9:11-25, 1975.

Deagan, Kathleen. "Avenues of Inquiry in Historical Archaeology." In M.B. Schiffer, editor, *Advances in Archaeological Method and Theory*, Volume 5. pp. 151-173. New York: Academic Press, 1982.

Deetz, James. "Scientific Humanism and Humanistic Science: A Plea for Paradigmatic Pluralism in Historical Archaeology." *Geoscience and Man* 23:27-34, 1983.

―――― *In Small Things Forgotten.* New York: Doubleday, 1977.

Douglas, Mary and Baron Isherwood. *The World of Goods.* New York: Basic Books, 1979.

Hodder, Ian. *Reading the Past.* Cambridge: Cambridge University Press, 1986.

Leone, Mark P. "The Georgian Order as the Order of Merchant Capitalism in Annapolis, Maryland," in Mark P. Leone and Parker B. Potter, Jr., Editors. *The Recovery of Meaning, Historical Archaeology in the Eastern United States.* pp. 235-262, Washington, DC: Smithsonian, 1988.

―――― "Symbolic, Structural and Critical Archaeology," in D.J. Meltzer, D.D. Fowler, and J.A. Sabloff, Eds. *American Archaeology Past and Future*, pp. 415-438, Institution Press, 1986.

―――― "Foreward," in S. South, Editor. *Research Strategies in Historical Archaeology.* pp. xvii-xxi. New York: Academic Press, 1977.

Little, Barbara J. "Craft and Culture Change in the 18th-century Chesapeake," in Mark P. Leone and Parker B. Potter, Jr., Eds. *The Recovery of Meaning, Historical Archaeology in the Eastern United States.* pp. 263-292, 1988.

―――― *Ideology and Media: Historical Archaeology of Printing in Eighteenth-Century Annapolis, Maryland.* Ph.D. dissertation, State University of New York at Buffalo, 1987.

McKee, Larry. "Delineating Ethnicity from the Garbage of the Early Virginians: The Faunal Remains from the Kingsmill Plantation Slave Quarters," *American Archeology* 6:1:31-39, 1987.

McGuire, Randall H. "Dialogues with the Dead: Ideology and the Cemetery," in Mark
     P. Leone and Parker B. Potter, Jr., Eds. *The Recovery of Meaning, Historical
     Archaeology in the Eastern United States*, pp. 435-480, 1988.

Miller, Daniel. *Material Culture and Mass Consumption*. Oxford: Basil Blackwell, 1987.

Miller, George. "Classification and economic scaling of 19th Century Ceramics," *Historical
     Archaeology* 14:1-40, 1980.

Orser, Charles. "Toward a Theory of Power for Historical Archaeology: Plantations and
     Space," in Mark P. Leone and Parker B. Potter, Jr., Eds. *The Recovery of Meaning,
     Historical Archaeology in the Eastern United States*. pp. 313-344, 1988.

Otto, John. *Cannon's Point Plantation 1794-1860, Living Conditions and Status Patterns
     in the Old South*. New York: Academic Press, 1984.

Palkovich, Ann M. "Asymmetry and Recursive Meanings in the 18th Century: The Morris
     Pound House," in Mark P. Leone and Parker B. Potter, Jr., Eds. *The Recovery
     of Meaning, Historical Archaeology in the Eastern United States*. pp. 292-206, 1988.

Schuyler, Robert L. "Historical and Historic Sites Archaeology as Anthropology: Basic
     Definitions and Relationships," *Historical Archaeology*, 4:83-89, 1970.

Shackel, Paul A. Personal Communication, Spring 1988.

––––– *The Archaeology of Power and Domination: The Use of a Modern Discipline in
     Structuring 18th-century Society*. Paper presented at the annual meetings of the
     Society of Historical Archaeology; Baltimore, Maryland, 1989.

Shanks, Michael and Christopher Tilley. *Re-constructing Archaeology, Theory and Practice*.
     Cambridge: Cambridge University Press, 1987.

Singleton, Theresa A. "An Archaeological Framework for Slavery and Emancipation, 1740-
     1880," in Mark P. Leone and Parker B. Potter, Jr., Eds. *The Recovery of Meaning,
     Historical Archaeology in the Eastern United States*. pp. 345-370, 1988.

Wallerstein, Immanuel. *The Modern World-System II, Mercantilism and the Consolidation
     of the European World-Economy, 1600-1750*. New York: Academic Press, 1980.

––––– *The Modern World-System I, Capitalist Agriculture and the Origins of the European
     World-Economy in the Sixteenth Century*. New York: Academic Press, 1974.

Willey, Gordon R. and Jeremy A. Sabloff. *A History of American Archaeology* (Second
     Edition). San Francisco: W.H. Freeman and Company, 1980.

Wilson, Josleen. *The Passionate Amateur's Guide to Archaeology in the United States*.
     New York: Collier Books, 1980.

Wobst, H.M. "Stylistic Behavior and Information Exchange," in C.E. Cleland, Editor,
     For the Director: Research Essays in Honor of James B. Griffin. Ann Arbor, MI:
     Museum of Anthropology, University of Michigan. Publication #61, 1977.

Consumerism and the Structuring of Social Relations: An Historical Archaeological Perspective

Paul A. Shackel

Shackel emphasizes the power of goods, quoting Shanks and Tilley: "Goods provide a communicative medium of symbolic significance...and provide a medium for social domination as an expression of power and ideology." Undoubtedly he is correct. Perhaps the student of popular culture should be more attentive to goods and material objects instead of relying largely on electronic communication which may be more immediate and glitzy but not more long-lasting. Goods establish norms and culture flaws and must be understood. An ancillary of goods is probate records, which Shackel points out provide "a rich source of data for studying changing material culture patterns in early America." Students of Shakespeare will compare this with the great importance placed on the poet's will as he left his meager holdings to his heirs. Shackel demonstrates how convincing the study of goods can be. Having traced the development of goods in Annapolis, MD,—but it could have been any Colonial place—he concludes: "As mass produced goods became more available to the lower wealth groups, the artifacts increasingly reinforced standardized behavior of everyday life, thus creating the foundations of our modern day society." Many questions are raised here.

In this paper I demonstrate how particular goods operate in a specific social and physical setting and to explain the historical content of meaning, i.e. to perform what Ian Hodder calls a "Contextual Archaeology" (Hodder 1986:1). Of particular interest to this study is the use of popular cultural material, or mass produced goods, to create and reinforce a social hierarchy in society. I demonstrate how these goods eventually became the everyday material culture of the middle and lower classes and how they reinforced a new modern behavior, the basis of our western industrial society. I use Daniel Miller's (1987) argument for an emulation model which focuses on Enlightenment England and incorporate it into my analysis of material culture in colonial Annapolis, Maryland.

Miller explains that the symbolic use of material goods in a society increasingly oriented to consumption were used by interest groups to reinforce their position in social hierarchy. Building upon Neil McKendrick's work, Miller explains that when a well established hierarchy is present, new patterns of consumerism are extremely difficult, if not impossible. As the *ancien regime* lost power in Enlightenment England, there was a radical transformation of the amount and type of goods used in society. Goods which may have had little or no symbolic meaning during times of unquestioned hierarchy were now more active in creating meaning and reinforcing social asymmetry, since the old order was increasingly being questioned and threatened. As the consumer revolution accelerated mass manufacturing made goods cheaper and more available to different wealth groups. With these mass manufacturing of goods and the emulation of the higher groups by those lower, there was an increased ambiguity in the social hierarchy. Since the hierarchy was being threatened by emulation, there was a desire to reestablish differences. Therefore the wealthy began to acquire new goods, new behaviors, new social actions, and began to control access to knowledge about these goods to maintain social distance from the lower groups. The wealthy increasingly used new codes of behavior to segment themselves from other classes, until eventually the middle and lower classes emulated these new behaviors associated with mass produced goods. This new behavior was modern discipline, the foundation of our industrial society.

In the specific context of colonial Annapolis, Maryland, the explicit use of material culture in creating and reinforcing a social hierarchy and disciplined behavior appears suddenly during the 1710s and 1720s, plays a marginal role during the 1740s and 1750s, and reappears in the 1760s and 1770s. By the late 18th and early 19th century a significant proportion of all wealth groups are participating in the consumption of these goods. Associated with this change in material culture is a new order of behavior creating and reinforcing the segmentation of groups, and establishing the concepts of behavioral and material standardization and individuality. This new behavior, which Michel Foucault (1979) calls a modern discipline, is a behavior based on the measure of time to make human action more predictable, replicable, and measureable. This behavior first becomes noticeable among the wealthiest in Annapolis during a time of social and economic fluctuation. Stratification based on this modern discipline legitimized increasingly distinct group boundaries. The new discipline was thought of as a phenomenon of nature, therefore inevitable and unarguable.

The creation of a modern discipline is not a sudden result of the Industrial Revolution. It is one of a number of processes which began sometime in the late medieval period. The roots of a modern discipline may be attributed to the medieval monastic communities and their established rhythm in daily activities, their imposition of particular activities and their regulation and reinforcement of cycles of repetition (Foucault 1979: 149; Shackel 1987). Foucault writes that, "[f]or centuries, the religious orders had been masters of discipline: they were the specialists of time, the great technicians of rhythm and regular activities" (Foucault 1979:150). Through the late medieval period, time, motion, and human action became more replicable and in turn became more standardized, structured and disciplined. Time became increasingly segmented as it began to be divided into quarter hours, minutes and eventually seconds. With the development and wide acceptance of time discipline (Thompson 1967) also came an increased discipline of everyday life. Time discipline and other disciplines were attributed to nature and were so given a certain inevitability and power (Leone 1988).

Foucault (1979) notes that a disciplined behavior makes specific uses of time and of body movements. "[N]othing is to remain idle...everything must be called upon to form the support of the act required" (Foucault 1979:152). By applying to specific, mundane actions, discipline constitutes a type of infra-law levied, through rules for individuals, onto societies and groups. Repetitive behavior eventually becomes mechanical, yet fluid and natural, and allows for an increased "efficiency" (Foucault 1979: 170, 176, 222). Such rules and behavior became accepted and internalized. The success of this modern discipline relies on the supporting use of material culture which creates and reinforces disciplined behavior through appropriate use of everyday things.

Since everyday things have meanings that are part of a code or structure, exact meanings, which depend on relationships within the code, are not arbitrary but are historically created (Hodder 1986:1). "Goods provide a communicative medium of symbolic significance...and provide a medium for social domination as an expression of power and ideology" (Shanks and Tilley 1987: 131). Because goods are endowed with meaning and have an ideological and symbolic component, they are actively manipulated in social circumstances to structure relations in social strategies (Hodder 1982: 12, 85). It is the meaning and context of goods and their interactive quality which helps us understand how goods were used in the development of a modern discipline. Goods communicate through a whole set of clues which elicit appropriate behaviors in specific situations and contexts relaying the message of the behavior expected. They create and maintain social boundaries. Goods are a powerful medium which can be used to legitimate social order and which imply a common understanding or common codes of communication within and between groups. It is through this social interactive process that their meaning is created, used, reinforced and reproduced, making a set of operations for ordering the social world.

Competition to acquire these goods will produce boundaries that exclude outsiders. Those within a group will attempt to synchronize their consumption patterns with peers. In a developing complex or urban society, consumption goods are diversified and the upper wealth groups have a finely tuned perception of the meaning of goods in different social circumstances (Douglas and Isherwood 1979:118, 144, 180).

The Historical Context of the Naturalization of a Modern Discipline

Modern discipline distanced the upper wealth group from others while the elite were creating their own identity (Elias 1983: 103). This discipline, especially in the form of complex manners, appeared foreign and to some extent nonexistent in early medieval times. It increasingly became part of the perceived natural order of the elite in western civilization. An analysis of early etiquette books indicates that medieval etiquette was far from having strict disciplinary rules to guide people's eating behavior. These books, which were often written for the wealthy and literate, indicate that a typical table setting often consisted of a knife, trencher, and maybe a goblet. Solids were often taken by hand, liquids drunk from a ladle or communal glass. Two or three people would share the same trencher (Elias 1978). Rules were simple and usually consisted of prohibitions, such as those against spitting across the table or putting food that was already in one's mouth back onto the communal dish. By the end of the medieval tradition, rules for eating became more predictable, measurable, and replicable and were being internalized and part of what was made to appear as natural behavior. With this trend came an increasingly rigid discipline and complexity of behavior as well as an increase in the kinds of material culture which aided in the creation and reinforcement of this behavior.

By the 18th century the communal use of utensils was frowned upon by the gentry and detailed instructions were given for the specific use of these items. "Every movement of the hand...the way in which one holds and moves knife, spoon, or fork...[became] standardized" (Elias 1978: 101-108) as the elite were gradually accepting and socially manipulating the ideas of etiquette into a modern discipline.

By the 18th century, etiquette was increasingly seen as being part of the natural order and became part of the social strategy of power and domination. This phenomenon can especially be seen in the literature of 18th-century Europe. For instance, in 1711, Joseph Addison (1907 [1711]: 135-6) of England stated that the "polite world" of the city was far more advanced in the category of manners when compared to the country people. This modern discipline, he explained, was far closer to the first state of nature. And it was Voltaire, in 1733, who wrote in the dedication of his *Zaire* to an English merchant that "politeness is not in the least an arbitrary manner...but it was a law of nature" (as quoted in Elias 1978: 103). It was not until the middle of the 18th century, the eve of the Industrial Revolution, when there was a tremendous increase in the literature regarding rules of modern behavior, in the form of etiquette books, for the middle and lower classes (Shackel 1987). Encompassing these groups is truly a sign, I believe, of an ideology at work, creating and reinforcing a modern discipline among a new working class, the members of which formed the backbone of modern industrial life.

The Local Context of the Development of a Modern Discipline

Even though a modern discipline developed in Western Europe from the late medieval era and was well established among England's elite by the mid 16th century, this new discipline was not incorporated into colonial Annapolitan behavior until about the 1720s. Up until about 1715, Annapolis, the capital of the Maryland province, is considered by most historians to be nothing more than a medieval-like village with about 40 to 50 dwellings and a population of about 200 to 300 people (Papenfuse 1975: 5-34). A poem written in 1708 describes the town as having framed buildings where only a few houses were built well enough to keep out rain. Ebinezer Cook wrote (in Steiner 1900:24-30):

> Up to Annapolis I went
> A city situated on a plain
> Where scarce a house will keep out rain
> The buildings framed with Cyprus rare,
> Resemble much our Southwork Fair,...

Annapolis did not grow as a tobacco center, but rather functioned as a small political and social center.

During the 1720s there were several major social and economic fluctuations which threatened the established hierarchy of society. These events encouraged the elite to adopt the new form of behavior, modern discipline, and a new type of material culture, in order to re-establish the social order.

First, there were several long-term depressions in the Chesapeake during the 1700s. The most severe one occurred between 1722 and 1735 and resulted in tobacco riots in northern Virginia and southern Maryland. Tobacco warehouses were burned by the less wealthy planters who felt cheated as their tobacco was being overlooked by inspectors in favor of their wealthier neighbors' tobacco (McCusker and Menard 1986; Kulikoff 1986).

There are also signs of inflation in the Chesapeake during the 1720s and 1730s. Two components of a commodities price index, imported labor and manufactured goods, rose substantially during this time (Carr and Walsh 1977:15).

There are also several long term processes specific to Annapolis which correlate with the introduction of a modern discipline. First, the population of the city grew at a relatively slow pace for the first two decades of the 18th century. In the 1720s, however, the town population grew at a rate of about 65%. This growth was twice as fast as any other decade of the colonial era (Walsh 1983). Second, there was a dramatic redistribution of wealth in the city during the 1720s. During that time the wealthiest people in the city increased their share of wealth from 21% (held by 8% of the population) between 1700-09 to 85% (held by 20% of the population) in 1768-77. The poorest wealth group had its holdings diminished from 8% (held by 46% of the population) in 1700-09 to 2% (held by 30% of the population in 1768-77) (Russo 1983; Shackel 1987).

Another era of social, economic, and political stress in the colonies occurred prior to and including the beginning of the American Revolution. During this era the elites' privileged place in the social hierarchy was increasingly being challenged by dissenting religious groups (Isaac 1974, 1982). In order to reaffirm their place in society, the elite began to express their hegemonic control through overt expressions of material culture as well as through a new commitment to a modern discipline. It is during the 1760s, the golden age of Annapolis, that gentry members began to construct for the first time large five-part symmetrically designed Georgian style mansions. It was a way for the elite to explicitly demonstrate their power by expressing their knowledge of the laws of nature through expression of symmetry and segmentation.

All of these phenomena may have produced a competitive society which created distinct social groups in Annapolis through overt material expressions and a new order of behavior associated with a new material culture during the 1720s and the 1760s.

Historical data were analyzed to determine when etiquette books were introduced into colonial Annapolis, and who was using these guides. From an analysis of probate data the earliest behavioral guide books appear in Annapolis about 1720. This appearance was in the estate inventory of one of the wealthiest people in the city of Annapolis (Inventories 1720 4:197-207). These texts were found in other libraries, but exclusively among the elite throughout most of the 18th century (i.e. Inventories 1727 12:71-91; 1767 84:53).

By the late 1740s there were advertisements in the colonial newspaper, the *Maryland Gazette,* for the sale of libraries as well as a list of stolen books from the Free School. Both of these lists contained behavioral guide books (*Maryland Gazette* 1769, September 7; 1769, September 28).

This new discipline was seen as natural and embedded in nature, legitimizing strong group boundaries. An excerpt from a traveler's guide written by Dr. Alexander Hamilton of Annapolis in the 1740s provides an example. Dr. Hamilton was a prominent citizen, a member of the elite, and founder and president of the Tuesday Club, the most prestigious social club in Annapolis. In his travels through the rural area surrounding Annapolis he came upon a family of poor farmers who asked him to join them for dinner. He wrote in his diary:

They desired me to eat, but I told them I had no stomach. They had no cloth upon the table, and the mess was in a dirty, deep wooden dish which they evacuated with their hands, cramming down skins and all. They used neither knife, spoon, plate or napkin...(Bridenbaugh 1948: 8).

The farmers' dining habits were very similar to what might be found among the poor, and reflect many of the aspects of a medieval tradition. Hamilton's refusal to eat dinner is a fine example of the elite's naturalization of a modern discipline. Not only was the table not "properly" set, but the lack of utensils, such as the fork, which was introduced into American elite society only 50 years earlier, was considered rather repulsive.

Later in the Maryland Gazette, in 1746, an article was written describing how the idea of a new and modern discipline are natural processes that need to be cultivated. It stated:

A true taste is internally founded on nature. A man who models his taste a right with relations to natural Objects...will in reality become a great man. By the first taste, he understands how to lay his Garden, Model his House...and appoint his table (*Maryland Gazette* 1746 no. 70).

The evidence for behavioral guide books as early as the 1720s and the descriptions of this new regimented behavior found in Annapolis during the 1740s demonstrates two things. First, the social environment of goods is retrievable and can be associated with the development of a new modern discipline, in this case, formal segmented dining. Second, the meaning of these goods demonstrates that the penetration of a new discipline was in place among the elite by at least the 1720s in Annapolis. This new order of behavior was publicized in the *Maryland Gazette* as being natural and embedded in nature. The elite were the people participating in this modern discipline. They were using a naturalizing ideology to legitimize their place in society, as they distinguished themselves as being a distinct and cohesive class through a new type of behavior and the goods associated with it. As the consumer revolution increased with intensity from the early 18th century, it became more difficult for the elite to use a naturalizing ideology to claim their domination in society through a modern discipline. As goods became cheaper, the distribution of mass produced goods became widespread through all wealth groups, and so did the behavior associated with it.

The spread of goods and the rules for their use throughout social groups threatened the privileged hierarchy. To trace the use of new everyday items and everyday discipline I turn to probate data.

Probate Data Analysis

Some of these ideas of the naturalization of a modern discipline can be seen in an analysis of data from 18th-century Annapolis. In the early part of this century Annapolis appears to have had many characteristics of a medieval village, with urban lots, kitchen gardens and a variety of domestic animals. It was a town which strived for self sufficiency and had very little interaction with the rural community (Walsh 1983; Shackel and Little 1987). Probate records provide a rich source of data for studying changing material culture patterns in early America. If used with other historical data they provide a medium for a symbolic interpretation for the patterns of goods found. Probate inventories were done by two or three appraisers, familiar with the occupation of the deceased, who were appointed by a judge of a commission of probate. Their duty was to create a list of the goods and their current market values that were found in the estate (Main 1975).

Since material culture plays an active role in the creation and reinforcement of a modern discipline, an analysis of probate inventory data in a particular historic context may provide clues to the structuring and reinforcement of the social hierarchy. Especially during times of economic, social, and political stress, these goods in an historic context provide clues as to some of the responses used by the elite to explicitly segment themselves from lower groups.

One group of items which demonstrate the new order of behavior were those goods which are related to formal and segmented dining. Sets of plates were coded for in this analysis with the assumption that if sets of these formal and segmenting dining items were in the estate inventory, there was a high likelihood that people were practicing the ideas of disciplined behavior, with one person using one plate. These items were used at the table to segment the dinner into many parts, and to separate the diners from each other, rejecting the communal, medieval tradition of sharing a trencher. The elite of Annapolis, who had etiquette books in their libraries, were probably adhering to the rules therein, thus participating in replicable, predictable, and measurable behavior, a modern discipline.

When the data were analyzed for the first two decades of the 18th century for Annapolis, there was a noticeable similarity between the upper and lower wealth groups in terms of the types of material culture that they possessed. The only difference between the two groups was that the wealthiest people owned more. But during the 1720s there was a dramatic change in this pattern. Not only were the amount of goods owned by the wealth groups considerably different, but also the types of goods that the upper wealth group began to acquire were different. This change appears to be associated with the social and economic fluctuations in the city. As mentioned above these include a dramatic demographic increase, a tobacco depression, and a wealth redistribution.

Analysis of the probate data, suggests that sets of plates were rather rare among all wealth groups in early Annapolis, and social group boundaries appear not to be distinct, in terms of material culture (Table 1). These items were introduced into Annapolis society during the 1710s-1720s. At this point in time, the majority of ownership of these goods belonged to the wealthiest, while the lower wealth groups had a smaller proportion of these disciplining items.

Table 1   Urban - Presence of Sets of Plates.

Years

Wealth in Pounds	1688-1709			1710-1732			1733-1754			1755-1777			1778-1799			1800-1820		
	C	N	%	C	N	%	C	N	%	C	N	%	C	N	%	C	N	%
000- 49	9	1	11	24	3	13	33	2	06	33	1	03	5	1	20	1	1	100
50-225	3	0	00	27	3	11	18	2	11	30	5	17	12	5	42	4	2	50
226-490	4	1	25	12	2	17	11	1	09	9	2	22	9	6	67	3	1	33
491+		1	0	00	9	2	22	15	3	20	17	7	41	18	13	72	10	7	70

C = Total Number of Cases
N = Presence of Item
% = Percentage of cases

The proportion of sets of plates did not increase dramatically during the 1733-1754 time period. But, just before the American Revolution, the elite's position in society was challenged by dissenting religious groups composed of the middle and lower classes. In order to reaffirm their hegemonic control, wealthy Annapolitans significantly increased their participation in modern discipline by increasing their consumption in disciplining items, i.e. sets of plates, as well as other goods. During the late 18th century and continuing into the 19th century this disciplining behavior increasingly penetrated to the lower wealth groups.

Discussion

By the early 18th century no longer were group differences established by the quantity of material goods, but rather it was the types of artifacts and the new order of behavior, or etiquette, associated with it, that created group boundaries. There were wealthy landowners in Maryland before, but the establishment of a distinct and formidable elite that remained cohesive, yet individualized through a new discipline, was being established in Annapolis, Maryland in the 1720s. This new behavior, or etiquette became increasingly significant when the elite's place in the social hierarchy was again being threatened in the 1760s and 1770s. As the distance between the social groups was narrowing, the elite created a common front with the lower classes to defie the authority of the Crown in the name of liberty (Isaac 1982: 265-266; Leone 1984). Material culture, such as the tea ceremony, which was once exclusively used by the wealthy, was rejected among all groups. This uniform rejection symbolically united colonists of varying classes for the resistance against Britain (Breene 1986). In this socially competitive society the upper wealth group accepted this new discipline as a means of maintaining a social cohesion, creating boundaries from the lower groups, possibly establishing itself as a self-recognized class. By the beginning of the Industrial Revolution, the end of the 18th century, there was an increased number of behavioral guide books for teaching a modern discipline to the middle class. Along with the penetration of this new order of behavior, probably through emulation, was the spread of a new, mass produced material culture to the middle and lower wealth groups. As mass produced goods became more available to the lower wealth groups, the artifacts increasingly reinforced standardized behavior of everyday life, thus creating the foundations of our modern day society.

Works Cited

Addison, Joseph. *The Spectator* 1-4. London: J.M. Dent, 1907 [1711].

Breene, Timothy H. "The Meaning of Things: Consumer Culture of Eighteenth-Century America and the Coming Revolution," Paper presented at the Conference of Accumulation and Display. The Winterthur Museum and the University of Delaware, November 7-8, 1986.

Bridenbaugh, Carl. *Gentleman's Progress: The Itinerarium of Dr. Alexander Hamilton: 1744.* Westport, Connecticut: Greenwood Press Publishers, 1973 [1948].

Carr, Lois and Lorena Walsh. "Inventories and the Analysis of Wealth and Consumption Patterns in St. Mary's County, Maryland, 1658-1777." The Newberry Papers in Family and Community History, paper 77-46. Chicago: The Newberry Library, 1977.

Cook, Ebenezer. "The Sot-Weed Factor, or, A Voyage to Maryland." In *Early Maryland Poetry.* Edited by Bernard C. Steiner. Fund Publication No. 36, Baltimore: Maryland Historical Society, 1900 [1708].

Douglas, Mary and Baron Isherwood. *The World of Goods.* New York: Basic Books, Publishers, 1979.

Elias, Norbert. *The History of Manners: The Civilizing Process, Volume I.* Translated by Edmund Jephcott. New York: Pantheon Books, 1978.

_____ *The Court Society.* New York: Random House, 1983.

Foucault, Michel. *Discipline and Punish.* New York: Vintage Books, 1979.

Hodder, Ian. *Symbols in Action: Ethnoarchaeological Studies of Material Culture.* Cambridge: Cambridge University Press, 1982.

_____ "The Contextual Analysis of Symbolic Meanings." In *The Archaeology of Contextual Meaning,* Ian Hodder, editor. Cambridge: Cambridge University Press, 1986.

Inventories 4: 197-207. On file at the Maryland Hall of Records, Annapolis, Maryland, 1720.

Inventories 12: 71-91. On file at the Maryland Hall of Records, Annapolis, Maryland, 1727.

Inventories 84: 53. On file at the Maryland Hall of Records, Annapolis, Maryland, 1767.

Isaac, Rhys. "Evangelical Revolt; The Nature of the Baptist Challenge to the Traditional Order in Virginia, 1765 to 1775." *William and Mary Quarterly,* 3rd series XXXI: 345-348, 1974.

_____ *The Transformation of Virginia: 1740-1790.* Chapel Hill: The University of North Carolina Press, 1982.

Kulikoff, Allan. *Tobacco and Slaves: The Development of Southern Culture in the Chesapeake, 1680-1800.* Chapel Hill: The University of North Carolina Press, 1986.

Leone, Mark P. "The Georgian Order as the Order of Mercantile Capitalism in Annapolis, Maryland." In *The Recovery of Meaning: Historical Archaeology in the Eastern United States.* Edited by Mark P. Leone and Parker B. Potter. Washington, D.C.: Smithsonian Institution Press, 1988.

_____ "Interpreting Ideology in Historical Archaeology: Using the Rules of Perspective in the William Paca Garden in Annapolis, Maryland." In *Ideology, Power, and Prehistory.* Edited by Daniel Miller and Christopher Tilley. Cambridge: Cambridge University Press, 1984.

Main, Gloria. "Probate Records as a Source for Early American History." *William and Mary Quarterly* 32, 1975.

Maryland Gazette, September 28. On file at the State Law Library, Court of Appeals Building, Annapolis, Maryland, 1769.

Maryland Gazette, September 7. On file at the State Law Library, Court of Appeals Building, Annapolis, Maryland, 1769.

Maryland Gazette, August 26. On file at the State Law Library, Court of Appeals Building, Annapolis, Maryland, 1746.

McCusker, John J. and Russell R. Menard. *The Economy of British America: 1607-1789.* Chapel Hill: The University of North Carolina Press, 1985.

Miller, Daniel. *Material Culture and Mass Consumption.* Oxford: Basil Blackwell Press, 1987.

Papenfuse, Edward. *In Pursuit of Profit: The Annapolis Merchant in the Era of the American Revolution, 1763-1805.* Baltimore: Johns Hopkins University Press, 1975.

Russo, Jean. "Economy of Anne Arundel County." In *Annapolis and Anne Arundel County, Maryland: A Study of Urban Development in a Tobacco Economy: 1649-1776.* Lorena S. Walsh, editor. N.E.H. Grant Number RS 20199-81-1955. On file at Historic Annapolis, Inc., Annapolis, Maryland, 1983.

Shackel, Paul A. *A Historical Archaeology of Personal Discipline.* Ann Arbor: University Microfilms, 1987.

Shackel, Paul A. and Barbara J. Little. "Cows, Printers and Capitalists and the Growth of Annapolis." Paper presented at the Council for Northeastern Historical Archaeology Meetings, St. Mary's City, Maryland, October, 1987.

Shanks, Michael and Christopher Tilley. *Re-constructing Archaeology: Theory and Practice.* New York: Cambridge University Press, 1987.

Thompson, E.P. "Time, Work-Discipline, and Industrial Capitalism," *Past and Present* 38: 56-97, 1967.

Walsh, Lorena. "Annapolis as a Center of Production." In *Annapolis and Anne Arundel County, Maryland, A Study of Urban Development in a Tobacco Economy, 1649-1776.* Lorena Walsh, editor. N.E.H. Grant Number RS 20199-81-1955. On file at Historic Annapolis, Inc., Annapolis, Maryland, 1983.

Visual Aesthetics for Five Senses and Four Dimensions: An Ethnographic Approach to Aesthetic Objects

John Forrest

In this paper Forrest presents a tantalizing and elusive approach to how complicated an evaluation of the esthetics of an object can be. He demonstrates how a quilt is almost alive in seeming to undergo chameleon-like changes as a result of the way it is perceived in the five senses of different individuals in different dynamic settings. In other words, properly perceived in the total setting any object takes on a kaleidoscope of esthetic beauties and meanings. Forrest asks for a symbiotic blending of all possible appreciations: "I therefore plead for an adequate and comprehensive ethnography of aesthetic objects. What could be more potent than a form that bridges the world of the senses, links spatio-temporal dimensions, and joins the two; a form that acts as mediator between felt experience and cognitive appreciation—and what could be more human?" And what could be more useful for the student of popular culture?

One ought, every day at least, to hear a little song, read a good poem, see a fine picture and, if it be possible, speak a few reasonable words.—Goethe, *Wilhelm Meister's Apprenticeship*

Several years ago a student friend of mine looked away puzzled from a large display of Amish quilts and asked "Why is it that the Amish live such drab lives yet make such colorful quilts?" The fact that the quilts were hung on plain walls and stripped of their normal cultural environment had allowed this student to divorce "life" from "quilt"— assigning the title "drab" to the first and "colorful" to the second. But anyone seeing an Amish quilt on an Amish bed in an Amish house is forced to fuse the categories of life and quilt and confess that some aspects of Amish life are bold and colorful.

Making a similar kind of mistake was a turning point for me in my early days as an apprentice anthropologist. I was casting around for field projects in the coastal regions of the American South, and in the process fetched up on Chincoteague Island in Virginia. I had scarcely been there a day when, for the first time in my life, I saw an American traditional quilt. I had seen plenty of slides shown to me by fieldworkers, but this was the real thing. However, it was not draped carelessly over a hand crafted bed or pinned artfully to a museum wall; it was being used by a local woman to carry a load of oysters to a beach party. My initial reaction as a stranger both to America and to quilts was utter horror, followed by a desire to rescue this beautiful thing from such a sacrilegious use and to restore it to its "proper" use as an artistic wall hanging or bed covering. It finally dawned on me a good deal later that proper usage was being defined for me by the actions of a native informant. This woman—the quilt's maker, in fact—was showing me that hauling bulky and awkwardly handled food items was a legitimate local use for a quilt (of a certain type), and that if I wished to explore its aesthetic qualities I should take this fact into account.

Both of these anecdotes point to the need for finding appropriate and appropriately detailed contexts within which to describe objects that have aesthetic qualities. It is all too seductive to take an object with prominent visual qualities and confine analysis to the object-as-image. Participant observation fieldwork, long regarded as the hallmark of cultural anthropology, could well reveal a different story. I have shown elsewhere (Forrest 1988), for example, that certain quilts in a North Carolina community are rarely seen by anyone but their makers and certain others are stored so as to be seen by *no one*—ever. A quilt-as-image analysis of these quilts would, in the latter case, be contextually inappropriate, and, in the former, myopic.

One of the primary strengths of the ethnographic method is its ability to place entities, which otherwise we might naively consider to be discrete and autonomous, in ever widening social and cultural contexts thereby deepening our comprehension of their significance (Douglas 1970; Turner 1966, 1967). Yet the kinds of contexts that satisfy the ritual or kinship specialist may not be immediately relevant to an ethnographic exploration of aesthetics, even if in the long run they can effectively be called into play.

I wish to advocate the use of the five human senses and the four dimensions of spacetime as primary contexts within which to begin the ethnographic elaboration of aesthetic forms. And, I hope to demonstrate that such an approach can be enriching to those theorists in popular culture (and related fields), who habitually use aesthetic objects as primary data.

I have selected the five human senses and four dimensions of spacetime as starting points for contextualizing aesthetic objects not because they, in themselves, provide for complete descriptions, but because they allow us to move outward to more general social and cultural contexts in a balanced and well informed manner. What follows is by no means meant to circumscribe the ethnography of aesthetic objects, but simply to sketch the limits of what I call the first *shell of significance* (see Forrest 1990). Then one may broaden out to aesthetic contexts, symbolic contexts, economic contexts, and so forth.

The initial justification for considering sensory perception as a primary context of aesthetic objects is the very meaning of the word "aesthetic." Although the word has accumulated a host of meanings, and a great deal of philosophical baggage, some of its root meaning from classical Greek is preserved. For Plato the distinction between the *aestheta* (things as perceived with the senses) and the *noeta* (things known to the mind) was fundamental. We may no longer agree with the dichotomy, but the legacy, nonetheless, has been to associate the aesthetic with the senses (see Forrest 1988 and 1990 for a complete discussion).

To assist the exploration of sensory and spatio-temporal contexts I am going to focus on one type of aesthetic object—the traditional quilt— but it must be borne in mind that this substantive narrowing is for demonstration purposes only. What I have to say could equally well apply to a range of aesthetic objects, and is meant primarily to stir the imagination.

Because of our Western taboos against touching museum objects let me begin with touch. Touch is a complex sense (see Montagu 1971), but even without going into great detail you can understand that there are a multitude of ways to be in physical contact with an object. You can run your fingers across a quilt, hold it up to your face, lie on it or under it, or wrap it completely around you. Even if we say it feels warm under all these conditions what we feel and what we mean are decidedly distinct in each case.

Because of the distinctness yet connectedness of visual and tactile perception it is possible for a quilter to play one off against the other. Think, for example, of a warm *feeling* quilt made in cool *looking* colors. Admittedly the aesthetic and symbolic understanding of such an object must go beyond the observation of simple sensations to analyze the semantic domains of "warm" and "cool," but, nonetheless, it is clear that touching an object as well as looking as it can increase our awareness of its aesthetic potentialities. (I might also mention in this regard the possibility of creating objects that, say, *look* hard but *feel* soft and, therefore, require both looking and touching to get the joke—and don't forget the seemingly irresistible urge to touch a glossy newly painted surface to see—that is, feel—whether it is wet.)

When you snug down in bed and pull a quilt up around your face you cannot help but smell it. It may smell fresh from being laundered and hung in the sun, or as if that's what needs to happen to it. Or it could be redolent of storage—pouring forth fragrances of must, cedar, or camphor. At one time there were even more pungent possibilities as Verna Mae Slone reports in *What My Heart Wants to Tell*:

My father's generation had no glass jars, so they did not can fruits or vegetables. They filled large crocks or churns with applebutter. When boiled down very stiff and sweetened with molasses, it would keep fresh for many weeks. Big barrels were filled with smoked apples; a few holes were made in the bottom of the barrel so the juice would run out, then filled up a few inches with apples that had been pared and sliced, with the core removed. On top of these a dish was placed in which a small amount of sulfur was slowly burned by placing a heated piece of iron beside the dish. A quilt over the top kept the smoke for escaping. Next day, another layer of apples and more sulfur was burned and so on, until the barrel was full. The sulfur gave the apples an 'off' flavor that took a little getting used to, but was supposed to be good for you. (Slone 1979: 63-64)

It didn't make the quilt smell like a bed of roses either. In fact certain smells like this, or the smell of the oysters carried by the Chincoteague woman, mark these quilts off as no longer suited for use as bed covers. As I will explain a little later, a quilt has to *look* a certain way—that is, ragged and tattered, or faded and worn—before it is acceptable to allow it to smell a certain way. If it looks suitable as a bed covering it may not smell offensive.

In the normal course of things you may not taste a quilt, although I have certainly seen many babies have a good go at it. But what they taste of, or rather do *not* taste of it closely allied to particular uses. Verna Mae Slone describes shelling corn into a clean quilt as a kind of giant improvised sack prior to scooping the grains into more permanent containers (1979: 109-111). In this case the quilt used was one reserved for guest beds because it would be clean and therefore, not impart an unwanted taste to the food held in it. (And, reciprocally, dried corn grains are clean and therefore leave no residue on the quilt).

As a sidelight I should also note that during the Depression it was not uncommon to make quilts out of cotton sacks that food items—especially flour and sugar—were sold in. The manufacturers to encourage women to buy their products printed the bags with attractive floral prints, thus giving them the edge on competitors who offered their wares in plain white wrappings. This may seem a special case of the relationship between food, taste, and quilts, but quilts designated specifically as "flour sack" or "sugar bag" quilts show up with regularity as well defined objects, and with a little practice they can be identified by the look of the prints and the coarse texture of the cloth.

Quilts relate to the sense of hearing in two ways: via the sounds they make of themselves and those they transmit and filter from other sources. When you move under them they make characteristic soft, rustling, crumpling sounds produced by surface textures rubbing against one another and by friction between the quilt and other bedclothes or surfaces. When they are shaken out or hung on a line they make a dull, thumping flap associated with their thickness, mass, shape, and size.

Since quilts, particularly ragged and tattered ones, are frequently used as window and door coverings or temporary room dividers, their thickness and mass play a part in their ability to screen out or keep in sounds. As might be expected, they are not especially effective acoustic barriers, yet sounds heard through them are somewhat muffled and distorted. What is more, a room using quilts as doors, window, floor, and bed coverings—as was, and is, usual in country attics and lofts used in bedrooms—has noticeably diminished echo and reverberation.

Issues involving the sense of sight are so enmeshed with those having to do with the spatio-temporal dimensions that I will deal with them all together. I will very quickly pass over dealing with quilts as two-dimensional objects since this is the context that museums, books, slides and other common methods of presentation place them in, and it is precisely this limited approach that I seek to move beyond. Besides I have dealt at great length with issues of two-dimensional design, such as the juxtaposition of shapes, hues, and values, elsewhere (Forrest 1988). (This is also why there are no images accompanying this text. If you want to follow my analysis more actively, go out and find a quilt and involve yourself with it using all your senses.)

Although glossy, picture book images of quilts in two dimensions may be appealing in certain ways, they tell but a limited story; for as every quilter knows, a quilt is, at the very least, a three dimensional object. A quilt is made by first constructing a top and then assembling a three layer sandwich of top, batting, and backing. All three are then sewn together, with the functional aim of preventing the batting from moving about inside the package. In addition the quilting stitch multiplies the object's aesthetic complexity. The effect is to sculpt the two dimensional top into a three dimensional array of swirling and spiraling hills and vales, or into specific motifs that frequently provide a curvilinear counterpoint to the more rectilinear designs on the pieced top. The changing locations of light and shadow caused by the three dimensionality of the quilting stitch are an essential aspect of viewing quilts in their habitual contexts.

Quilts might also be said to be sculpted onto the beds they cover and this aspect of their three dimensionality influences the way they are conceived and fabricated. When a quilt drapes over a bed, some of the designs are displayed horizontally, some vertically, and some are curved over the edge or around pillows. In addition not all of the quilt can be seen at one time and it is necessary to move around the room to get a sense of the whole, thus combining seeing with physical motion and proprioception. These results are not accidental, but planned as the quilt is assembled. Quilters often lay out unfinished tops on beds to get a sense of how the designs will look there and how they could be augmented.

The visual effects of three dimensionality become yet more elaborate when we add the fourth dimension: time. If you hang a painting in a windowless gallery under even lighting it will look pretty much the same from day to day. But quilts live in rooms with windows where light quality and direction change hour by hour, day by day, and month by month. Dramatically different light qualities radically change colors and shades. Furthermore, the look of the quilt changes when it is naturally brought into contact with other objects, animate and inanimate, and when it is moved around as part of its general utility.

We must also consider longer ranges of time and understand that a quilt has a definable life span through which it will undergo predictable changes. Again, I have dealt with these issues at length elsewhere (Forrest 1988) so I will simply epitomize a few key themes. The way a quilt looks when it is made may determine, as is the case in coastal North Carolina, which of two kinds of life courses it is destined to follow. Best quilts, that is, those made from store bought materials, are used sparingly for special guests and public display, and, in consequence, rarely need washing. Because they are made from new materials and because they are delicately handled, they endure in much the same condition for long periods of time. When finally they begin to show signs of wear they are carefully stored away and preserved as heirlooms. Scrap quilts are made from oddments of fabric, or material that has been used before in items of clothing. They are constantly used and washed until the fabric fades, softens, and tears. Up to a point these transformations may be considered aesthetic enhancements of the original object. Quilters lovingly run their hands across a quilt softened with many washings, and sometimes differential fading and bleeding of dyes produce dramatic results.

It is most often the tearing of the much washed top fabric that marks a turning point in a quilt's life cycle. Then it is removed from bed duty and pressed into a variety of harsh uses that ultimately destroy it. This transformation may alter not only its functional contexts, but its sensual ones as well. I have already alluded to a quilt's possible tasks that make it smell offensive, but the way it is seen may change too.

Only ripped and torn quilts are used as window covers, because they are pinned or nailed in such a way that damages the cloth. Now as day fades into night the quilt—like stained glass—goes from translucent to opaque, and as the day returns the images shine again in the morning light. Age and wear determine new ways to see old quilts.

This rapid tour through the multisensory and multidimensional contexts of the aesthetic object leads to a number of conclusions—methodological and theoretical. To begin with, it is clearly past time to develop comprehensive field methods for the documentation of aesthetic objects. Taking one or two photographs and calling it quits is not adequate. That approach is the simplest avenue to the object-as-image kind of analysis. Following the object on its daily and yearly round not only sensitizes the analyst to its many facets, but also provides rich opportunities for interaction with informants that should eventually move into deeper areas of affective sensibility.

This demonstration ought to teach us to move away from a monolithic interest in the image alone as the be all and end all of expressiveness in the aesthetic object. No doubt it is satisfying to contemplate an image by pulling layer after layer of meaning, noting metaphoric and metonymic relations between them, ambiguities and contradictions, condensations of vast epistemological domains, puzzles and riddles that tumble forth: even if we cannot agree on the foundations of interpretation—for some, like Nelson Goodman (1968), the image is language-like in its symbolic structures, for others, like Suzanne Langer (Langer 1953), it is a symbolic form quite unlike language.

One of the truisms of symbolic and structural analysis is that symbols mean according to contexts. As Wittgenstein (1953) suggests, it is relatively fruitless to attempt to discover what a symbol, such as a word, means in any kind of absolute and definitive sense. What, instead, you must do is to see the word structured into sentences, and infer the rules that apply to its usage. In this way you move away from unitary and unchanging meanings to elaborately constellated domains of significance that account for new and creative linking of familiar symbols, and also for the possibility of shifts in meaning over time as possible contexts change.

But there is an important lesson to be grasped here for aesthetic analysis. Words not only have a syntactic or symbolic context, they also have a sound context, so that words whose rules for application are quite different can merge and exchange meanings because of overlaps in the ways of sound. The English words "jaw" and "jowl," for example, were at one time quite distinct—the first commonly used to signify the jawbone and the second, the skin around the neck (Partridge 1958: 318, 323). Over time the sound associations, as well as symbolic relations have confused the two terms so that they can be used interchangeably in many contexts.

What I have tried to show here is that images have a variety of sensual and dimensional contexts analogous to the sound contexts of words, and capable of asserting like force on meaning. A quilt made in cool colors does not have unambiguous meaning. We cannot analyze images in blue and green by themselves without addressing the fact that the quilt feels warm.

The aesthetic object provides tremendous possibility for ambiguity and interaction (first) between sense (second) between dimensions, and (third) between sense and dimension. As I have made clear, how a quilt looks is intimately related to how it feels, smells, tastes, and sounds. And, furthermore, once normal relations between the senses and dimensions have been established in a culture, there is scope for manipulation. Quilts made in satins and silks, for example, feel cool to the fingertips, but feel warm if you lie under them.

One of the key steps to exploring how sense context and meaning are related is to consider the physical natures of the different senses and how each works to exploit sameness, likeness, and difference. Tasting shares certain physical attributes with touch, for example, in that the objects so sensed are brought in direct physical contact with the sensory organ. If you don't like to touch soft, squishy things chances are you are not a connoisseur of sea cucumber or lamb's brains. But taste is also intimately linked to smell, such that most tasting—besides the crude differentiation of salt, sour, bitter, sweet—is smelling. In this way taste mediates between touch and smell. Hearing, sight, and smell can be thought of as senses at a distance in that we do not need to bring objects directly in contact with our ears, eyes, and nostrils to sense them. But analogues exist to unite the contiguous and distant senses. We can touch with our eyes, and taste with our noses. The sensory context of all aesthetic objects is therefore, of necessity richly synaesthetic. That is, we don't have to touch every quilt to know what it feels like, but we do have to experience some that way to train our eyes; and it is a mistake to think that because sometimes we only look we are not engaging all the other senses.

Except under special circumstances we naturally engage with visual objects through all four spatio-temporal dimensions as well, and, like the senses, they create ambiguities and interconnections. A quilt top made up of squares can be called rectilinear in two dimensions. When it is made up using a swirling quilting stitch we may call in curvilinear in three dimensions. The fourth dimension—time—separates and mixes these contradictory positions. Early in the day when the sun is low and casting long shadows the three dimensional images dominate, but when the sun is stark overhead, the shadows disappear and the two dimensional forms emerge. Between times the two fade back and forth.

This dimensionality may also interact with the senses. A top made in silks is, in two dimension, smooth to the eye and to the touch. But it could be very tightly quilted in three dimensions, making it rough to eye and touch. that is, dimensionality introduces *scale* to the senses. The silk is still smooth on a *small* scale but rough on a *large* scale. The addition of dimensionality requires motion between two scales and makes the synaesthetics of sight and touch ambiguous.

Beyond this ground is the vast area of the relations between cognition and affect which I have tangentially alluded to several times. The quilt that looks cool and feels warm is as much cutting across cognition and affect as across sight and sound. The coolness of blue is based on cognitive associations between things that are blue and cool, and since not everything that is blue is cool—nor everything that is red is warm— these color symbols are conventional and standardized categories. Although the warmth of the touch of the quilt may also have cognitive associations it need not—it can be directly affecting regardless of potential symbolic elaboration.

Let me stress that I am not trying to equate affect and certain kinds of sensation. As Dan Sperber notes (1975: 115-118) we in the West have a very poor vocabulary for talking about smells. Most of our expressions in common language refer to the smell's cause—the smell of a rose— or its effects—a nauseating smell. Even though there does exist a neutral and well defined smell vocabulary akin to color terms—there is even an olfactory wheel—used by flavorists and perfumers, it has yet to find its way into everyday speech (Amoore 1982). Part of the reason may be the desire to *avoid* the imposition of cognitive categories over a sense that we like to reserve for affect. If I tell you, for example, that the smells of coffee and of skunks share certain mercaptans you may find a skunk in your next cup, or a pot of mountain grown crossing your path. When I assert that touch and smell are directly affecting, therefore, I am suggesting this is *culturally* so, not a neurophysiological constant.

So the ambiguity between the warm feel and cool look of a quilt is an ambiguity only insofar as our culture ascribes affect and cognition to the different senses—and suggests ways in which the focus on aesthetics ethnographically can probe the natures of the affective and cognitive domains cross-culturally.

I therefore plead for an adequate and comprehensive ethnography of aesthetic objects. What could be more potent than a form that bridges the world of the senses, links the spatio-temporal dimensions, and joins the two; a form that acts as mediator between felt experience and cognitive appreciation—and what could be more human?

Works Cited

Amoore, John E. "Odor Theory and Odor Classification." In Ernst T. Theimer (ed.) *Fragrance Chemistry: The Science of the Sense of Smell.* New York, 1982.

Douglas, Mary. *Natural Symbols: Explorations in Cosmology,* London, 1970.

Forrest, John. *Lord I'm Coming Home: Everyday Aesthetics in Tidewater North Carolina,* Ithaca, New York, 1988.

———— "Analyzing Aesthetic Forms through Appropriate Contexts: A West African Example: *Studies in Third World Society* (forthcoming), 1990.

Goodman, Nelson. *Languages of Art: An Approach to a Theory of Symbols,* Indianapolis, IN., 1968.

Langer, Susanne K. *Feeling and Form: A Theory of Art,* New York, 1953.

Montagu, Ashley. *Touching: The Human Significance of the Skin,* New York, 1971.

Partridge, Eric. *Origins: A Short Etymological Dictionary of Modern English*, New York, 1958.

Slone, Verna Mae. *What My Heart Wants to Tell*, Washington D.C., 1979.

Sperber, Dan. *Rethinking Symbolism*, Alice Morton, trans. Cambridge, 1975.

Turner, Victor. *The Ritual Process: Structure and Antistructure*, Chicago, IL., 1966.

———— *The Forest Of Symbols*, Ithaca, NY: 1967.

Wittgenstein, Ludwig. *Philosophical Investigations*, Oxford, 1953.

Maya Popular Culture

Malcolm K. Shuman

In this paper Shuman presents a fascinating study which demonstrates how in certain aspects of contemporary Mayan popular culture one can see through a time warp and view Mayan popular culture of a thousand years ago. Interestingly it is the popular culture instead of the elite culture which because it is diffuse and at times invisible and seemingly unimportant that has survived change through the ages. But the unchanging popular culture has been folk culture in Mayan civilization. Present day popular culture as we know it outside Mayan culture is having a dramatic effect on that Mayan culture. If it is now possible to see early Mayan culture through its popular culture, it will soon be difficult or impossible as changes ensue. This dramatic change can tell us much about the effect of electronic popular culture on less sophisticated forms as it dramatically impacts on underdeveloped cultures. Students interested in historical and comparative popular culture have much to read out of Shuman's essay.

Introduction

Anthropologists have long been familiar with the problems posed by culture change, even if they have been less than entirely successful in determining how and why these changes occur. Translated to the subfield of archaeology, the issue often resolves itself into the question of determining the extent of cultural continuity between contemporary peoples and their ancestors. Obviously, if there were a perfect correspondence, archaeological work would be unnecessary. Just as obviously, in such a case cultures would be static and cultural evolution could not occur.

Thus, any attempt to detail correspondences between living and extinct members of the same general culture requires a careful consideration of many factors, some of the most important of which are technological innovation and environmental change. It is gratuitous to remark that culture is a system, whose parts are articulated to varying extents, but it is only from such a perspective that any comparison between the living and the extinct can be appreciated.

Finally, it must be realized that in comparing a contemporary group with its forebears, we are mixing two levels of interpretation. One, of course, is that of personal observation and experience. The living can be seen, their words recorded, their daily activities and works photographed and described in minute detail. With the dead, however, the only evidence we possess is, in many cases, inferential, based on archaeological excavation. While we can know what a contemporary Maya farmer thinks of the cosmos by asking him, his ancient ancestor leaves us no record, unless we resort to the glyphs, which reflect an elite view of the world. Thus, in the following consideration of resemblances between current Maya popular culture and the popular culture of the pre-Columbian Maya, it must be borne in mind that the way is hazardous, and conclusions not always certain.

The Ancient Maya: The Maya are a diverse cultural group, and this was as true in ancient times as it is today. Though linguistic evidence (Vogt 1969) would suggest a proto-Mayan community of as few as 5,000 people in northwestern Guatemala around 2,600 B.C., these original Mayans had, by 1,000 B.C., managed to spread as far north as the Yucatan peninsula, and as far south as northern Honduras. By the Classic Era (A.D. 300-900) they were a thriving concern in the highland Chiapas state, Mexico; Belize; El Salvador; the highlands and lowlands of Guatemala; and both the east and west coasts of Yucatan (Figure 1).

While the languages of these various groups differed there were, nevertheless, certain elements that bound the group together (and it must be said that many of these elements were also shared by other high cultures of Mesoamerica, such as the Teotihuacanos, Toltecs, Aztecs, Olmecs, and Mixtecs). Chief among these traits were a subsistence based on slash-and-burn agriculture (although recent evidence has tended to indicate that irrigation was practiced on a larger scale than previously thought); a stratified society of hereditary priests and rulers; a sophisticated network of trade and commerce; and a religion combining a number of elements, such as a reverence of the sun (*kin*), and pantheon of similar dieties (Thompson 1970). But perhaps the most outstanding of the Maya characteristics that archaeology has brought to light is the ability to write and to reckon time in a sophisticated vigesimal number system. Much of the glyphic record consists of astrological predictions entered in the three surviving codices, but many texts also relate to the subject of specific kings, and are found on the stone stelae that dot Maya sites of the Classic period. Maya Kings, it develops were as vainglorious as any other temporal rulers known to history, and their monuments were sometimes erected as frequently as at five year intervals throughout their reigns. It goes almost without saying that the ability to write in glyphs

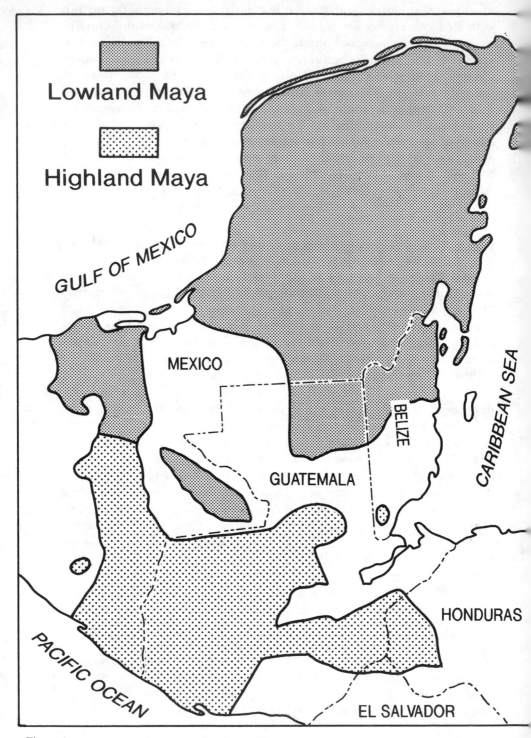

Figure 1. Maya Indian Area (Map by Mary Lee Eggart)

and reckon time by use of several intermeshing calendars must have been restricted to the elite.

Like any other dynamic civilization, however, that of the Maya was subject to continual disruption, from both within and without. While the relationship between the early Maya and the shadowy Olmec remains unclear, the influence of the Valley of Mexico is well known, especially in the Maya highlands of Guatemala. So strong is this influence that it seems likely that the site of Kaminaljuyu, on the outskirts of contemporary Guatemala City, was the home for an imported group of Teotihuacan priests. Likewise, Teotihuacan influence is found in the pyramid of Acanceh, in central Yucatan. By the end of the first millenium, Teotihuacan was a memory, but a train of other events not yet fully understood resulted in the complete collapse of the old Maya elite. Volumes have been written on the subject (e.g., Culbert 1974), and there is space here only to say that the event (or events) seem linked to influxes of people from the Gulf Coast and perhaps soil exhaustion in the central Guatemalan Peten. Some centers, such as Tikal and Uaxactun, were deserted at this time, but in Yucatan, to the north, life continued under a group of foreign Toltec lords from central Mexico. Two hundred years later a new group of invaders came northward from the Gulf Coast and established their own hegemony, which soon collapsed into factionalism, and two hundred years afterwards, when the Spanish arrived, Yucatan was a collection of warring principalities. The Spanish took stern measures to suppress both Maya independence and the ancient religion. In neither case were they entirely successful and one Maya group, the Itza of Guatemala, resisted until 1699. The Maya religion survived by absorbing Christianity and accepting the Catholic saints as Maya Gods with new names. When the last great Maya revolt occurred, in 1847, it was as part of a syncretistic cult whose icon was a Talking Cross, reflecting both an indigenous and a European component.

Throughout this history of triumphs and disaster, invasion and dispersal, certain things appear to have remained relatively unchanged, while other traits have become extinct. Unsurprisingly, what has remained is primarily the folk culture, while it is the elite culture that was ruthlessly oppressed by the Spanish, and, possibly, by preceding groups. Consequently, the popular culture of today's Maya stands a better chance of telling us something about the popular culture of past Maya than it does of the culture of the hierarchs who engineered and controlled Maya civilization.

What, then is the popular culture of contemporary Maya?

Contemporary Maya Culture: Today's Maya are one of the largest linguistic groups of Mesoamerica (i.e., Southern Mexico, Guatemala, Belize and parts of Honduras and El Salvador), with Maya speakers numbering in the neighborhood of one and a half million people. Comprising some eleven linguistic subgroups, the Maya inhabit areas as diverse as rain forest, karst plain, and mountain highland. Probably the least acculturated are some of the groups of Chiapas State, Mexico (Vogt 1969). This would include, specifically, the Tojolabals and to some extent the Lacandons, though the latter have been strongly affected by Protestant missionary groups. Guatemalan Maya have been affected by the almost continual civil strife that has taken place in that country over the last ten years, but indigenous culture traits are still fairly plentiful. The Yucatec Maya were listed as among the most acculturated in Tax's famous work (Tax 1952), almost forty years ago. This subgroup is itself comprised of two divisions, the Maya of the corn belt, south and east of the capital city of Merida, and the Maya of the henequen growing zone around the capital city. The writer is familiar with both groups but the present discussion will be largely limited to the former.

Popular Culture of the Yucatec Maya: The Yucatec Maya were participants in the ancient Maya civilization. Those of the extreme eastern forests, near what is now the city of Felipe Carrillo Puerto, were largely left alone by Europeans until the first part of the last century. When, in the middle of the nineteenth century, the Europeans turned to the cultivation of sugar cane, and began to encroach on Maya lands and impress the Indians as laborers, the Maya rose up in a bloody revolt and drove all the way to the gates of Merida (Strickon 1965). This revolt, though it incorporated elements of Christianity and European technology (the chief weapon of the rebels was the steel machete), preserved many aspects of the Maya heritage, and these traits are to be encountered today, although often in an attenuated form. The Maya language, for instance, continues to be spoken, though the lexicon includes an increasing number of Spanish words. The tourist development at Cancun has converted many Maya farmers into day laborers and even tourists guides, but most Maya still keep gardens. More, the influx of tourists has augmented the craving for modern technology. Still, there are many who continue to adhere to the old way, as corn farmers, and it is these who can give us some view of the culture of their forefathers. Indeed, it is precisely because these are the less aggressive, ambitious and wealthy of the contemporary Maya that they have retained the old ways, and it is to them that we must look for any traces of culture as it existed among the common man in ancient times. Let us consider this popular culture as it exists today and examine what it can tell us of the past.

Today's Yucatec Maya, the group with which the author is most familiar, are spread fairly evenly throughout the Yucatan peninsula. In this arid, karst plain around Merida, the small Maya villages are formed into *ejidos*, or cooperative, land-holding polities which sow and harvest henequen or sisal, from which rope is made. The henequen industry is a complex bureaucracy, involving a government-sponsored bank that provides credit, and a government-owned henequen processing and exporting organization (Cordemex). In effect, the villagers are employees of the government, which supports them not only with wages, but with a federal medical system and other benefits. This group of Maya, because they are so close to the urban center of Merida, were the very ones who were exploited as hacienda laborers in the last century, under the dictatorship of Porfirio Diaz. Thus, their exposure to the European world has been profound and of long-duration. This has not, however, prevented them from maintaining many of the old customs, such as folk medical beliefs, some crop ritual, and typically Maya world view. Their material culture has been a mixture of the old (e.g., thatched houses) and the new (e.g., televisions). Their language has suffered greatly as the children learn to read and write Spanish in the schools. From a language with an increasingly Spanish lexicon, Maya will soon become an idiom that is no longer spoken. In the corn-growing zone, located in the richer soils to the east and south, the Maya villagers have been relatively more isolated, though electrification has by now reached almost every hamlet, and even the most remote settlement boasts a government-built basketball court. The Maya language is less adulterated, the houses pole—rather than stone—sided (although in both zones more and more people are opting for cinder-block houses with corrugated metal roofs). Certainly the belief system is more intact and folk medical remedies still practiced (though usually in conjunction with modern cures). Most important of all, in this area the Maya peasant is a corn farmer, like his ancestors, and it is this activity and the associated rituals that invest his life with meaning.

From this brief sketch, let us go into more detail about those traits that seem to have remained since earlier times and those which appear European in derivation.

Contemporary Versus Ancient Maya Popular Culture

In this section, today's Maya popular culture will be subdivided into six domains, ranging from those that have changed least to those that have been most affected by modernization.

A. *Kinship, residence and family.* Today's Maya family is probably very similar to the Maya family of five hundred years ago, in terms of family size and residence, but kinship reckoning has changed considerably. The Maya were originally organized into a series of exogamous, patrilineal clans, but today they reckon kinship bilaterally (Villa Rojas). Still, some terms reflecting the old kinship system remain, as do the old clan names, which now serve as patronymics. Residence after marriage is with, or near, the residence of the groom's parents, although availability of house plots in a given village may cause the newlyweds to live further away. Marriage is monogamous, although in ancient times it is probable that this was through economic necessity rather than through any absolute prohibition, for the elite certainly practiced polygyny. The author is aware of a case of polygyny that existed in a fairly remote village in the 1970s. Interestingly, the husband was a *h-men* or shaman, who terrified the other villagers with his sorcery, and it is tempting to speculate that his action was a continuation of marriage patterns from a time when there was an organized Maya priesthood. Family size seems to have remained steady, at between five and six persons per household.

The life-cycle appears relatively stable, with marriage, parenthood, old age, and death occurring at roughly the same age as previously. The difference is that there has been an overlay of European customs, such as Catholic baptism, in addition to the traditional Maya custom of *hetz-mek*; a formal period of government-mandated schooling (usually one to four years); occasional recourse to a physician for difficult births; and utilization of modern medicine as well a traditional remedies for the ailments of old age.

B. *Ideology and cognition*: In this area, too, one can probably speak of something like a "basic Maya world view" and a "Maya psychology" that has not changed greatly through the centuries. The complication is that in many respects the Maya psychological makeup is similar to that of the Spanish. Maya fatalism, for instance, is complimentary to the Spanish sense of destiny (*destino*). In both, there is a tendency to view events as preordained and the individual as relatively helpless. The Maya tends to be stoic and uncomplaining, with death and hardship viewed as a necessary part of life. Certainly this would appear to be an almost necessary psychic component of any peasant's outlook, in view of the history of exploitation suffered by peasant people the world over (Wolf 1966). This does not mean that the Maya cannot show emotion; indeed, I have seen grown Maya men break down in tears upon leave-taking.

In the use of alcohol there has been marked change since the arrival of Europeans. Whereas, originally, alcohol seems to have been restricted to ritual contexts, its use today is general, in some locales approaching the epidemic. In general, it may probably be said that alcohol abuse, as opposed to use, is most frequent in towns closest to Merida, and less encountered in the more remote areas.

Religion, as previously mentioned, is an extremely important component of Maya life. The European religion, which is generally Catholicism (although in recent years Protestants evangelical religions have made many inroads), is generally left in the hands of the women, while the old religion, even if strongly syncretized, is the domain of the men. Thus, the rain ceremony, or *Cha-chaak*, will still be practiced, with the only concession to Christianity being the four wind gods are now identified with the archangels and given their names. Likewise, there is a pantheon of nature spirits or guardians, who protect the fields and crops and who own the land. There are also elfin pranksters (*aluxoob*) who bedevil people who venture too close to the ruins, and who whistle at people at night. There is a lively belief in sorcery, although many of its elements are combined with those of Spanish folk belief, which also emphasizes witchcraft. Medicine is founded upon an extensive ethnobotany (Roys 1931), but today many of the herbs are augmented by modern patent cures, ranging from aspirin to tonics. Healing often involves recourse to both physicians and shamans (*h-menoob*), reflecting a pragmatic way of dealing with health management. Some illnesses, however, seem particularly folk (if not necessarily Maya) in origin, such as *susto*, a sort of neurasthenia whereby the victim wastes away, and this illness is particularly responsive to a folk cure. Many elements of this folk cure are purely Maya and probably are of considerable antiquity. The author, for instance, has "made the rounds" with a Maya healer, and noted that one sufferer was closely questioned as to when he had last made ritual offerings to the guardians of the fields. When he ruefully admitted that he had been remiss, such a ceremony was prescribed to set things right. Finally, the Maya believe in a single, all-powerful God, today called *Dios* (God), but previously known as *Hunab-Ku* (the one God). In pre-Columbian times, this deity apparently ruled a hoard of lesser dieties. Today's Maya have amalgamated the Christian and pagan concepts to arrive at a single deity who rules over the saints, who equate with the inferior gods of former times. The concept of the Trinity is a cloudy one which has little place in today's cosmology, although the Virgin thrives. The Virgin, however, is seen not so much as a single person, the mother of Christ, as she is a plethora of virgins (or manifestations), each of whom is patron of a particular locality. Thus, at ruins which contain stelae or carved monuments, local Maya may consider the sculpted stone a "Virgin" and light candles there in veneration. At one such *virgin* the first fruits of the hunt are brought. These are certainly pre-Columbian customs with a thin Christian veneer and it is all but certain that these virgins are but thinly disguised versions of ancient female dieties, such as *X-chel*, the goddess of childbirth.

Finally, the standard pagan field ceremonies for sowing, rain, and the first fruits are still practiced, sometimes by the individual (i.e., on sowing) but more often through the employment of a ritual specialist. At such times, people gather to reaffirm social ties and tell stories that have been handed down for generations.

C. *Language.* As previously mentioned, one of the great constants in Maya culture is language. It seems to possess the capacity to absorb the lexicons of invaders while maintaining its structure relatively intact. For instance the Mexican invaders of pre-Columbian times left such words as *ak*, or "reed," and *xiu*, or "grass." Today, the Maya lexicon contains a number of Spanish words, one of the most notable being *dios* (God) in place of the original *ku*. Thus, the expression for "thank you" is today *dios bootic tech*, or "God pay you." Other Spanish words frequently employed are those for which there are no Maya equivalents, such as *amigo*, or "friend." The closest equivalent would be *et-meyah* or "co-worker," which does not carry the same meaning. Other Spanish words frequently inserted into Maya sentences are those denoting time (*año*, "year"), government (*municipio*, "county") and words related to the Catholic faith (*misa*, "mass"), although the word for "baptism" is *ok ha?*, or, literally, "enter water." Basically, the creolization process is sufficiently far along that almost any Spanish words may be inserted into Maya sentence structure and understood.

The syntax of the language remains far more stable, although it has, of course, changed over time, as can be readily seen by comparing such turn of the century grammars as that of Lopez Otero (1968; orig. 1914) with the language spoken today in the villages. Many usages that reflect ancient concepts are still employed. For example, the Maya preoccupation with the carrying of firewood and other burdens, and their construction of raised ceremonial roads (*zacbeoob*) finds a counterpart in the still used expression *Biix a bel*, or "How is your road?", which may be transliterated as "How goes it?" More ominous is the word for marriage; a man who has married has "finished his road" (*dzocaan u bel*). Doubtless, a Whorfian could read much into the Maya view of the universe through an analysis of linguistic forms.

D. *Economy.* In the field of economy, there has been considerable change in the last thirty years, and the change has accelerated in the last ten. While the traditional Maya peasant was a slash-and-burn corn farmer, today's Maya work in the henequen fields, previously mentioned; they work as wage laborers in the cities of Merida and Valladolid; and they work in the tourist industry, headquartered at Cancun. Even those who practice agriculture take advantage of modern innovations, such as gasoline powered pumps, and they enroll in government plans which involve the planting of citrus fruits. Nevertheless, there are still Maya who farm in the old way; who find a field that has been fallow for fifteen years; go through the time-honored process of measuring its boundaries (*ppizil col*); who honor the lords of the field when burning; and who call upon a ritual specialist to make a rain ceremony (*cha-chaak*) and first harvest rite (*u uail col*). In fact, it may be said that this traditional agricultural ritual is the essence of what is thought of as "Maya" and that its antiquity extends for two to three thousand years.

E. *Political Organization*: Obviously, the destruction of the Maya political hierarchy by the Spanish was epochal in its effects. Nonetheless, it is easy to oversimplify the matter. That is, the European Conquest at one level began a series of widespread political upheavals, in which the Maya (and other indigenous peoples) were ruled successively by the Spanish Crown; by the Mexican governments; and by a number of regimes within the Mexican government. Each change brought slightly different ways of dealing with subject peoples. At the more immediate level (that is, from the viewpoint of the Indians), however, the advent of the Europeans began a period of what was nominally ended by the Mexican Revolution of 1910, but whose vestiges still remain. Put another way, changes in Mexico City were often attentuated by the time they reached Yucatan. But what of the period before the Conquest? Politically speaking, the changes may have been fewer than one might imagine. The peasant farmers of Yucatan have always been subject to the whims of externally imposed rule. Early in the Classic period (AD 300-900) there was a strong influence from the powerful central Mexican state of Teotihuacan. By AD 1000, the influence came from the Toltecs, who left their architecture and gods at Chichen Itza, though their capital was north of Mexico City. At a time not yet well documented there was an influx of foreigners called the Itza, and in 1400 a new group arrived from the Gulf Coast, calling themselves the Xiu, or "grass people."

What must the effect of these many incursions have been on the Maya commonfolk? Surely there must have been bloodlettings and dislocations. Indeed, the Maya view of history, divided as it was into 256 year periods, singled out one 20 year epoch or *Katun* from the 13 that composed the calendar, as the time of lamentations and gnashing of teeth. The Maya, based on bitter experience, positively *expected* disaster in this time period (or *katun*), and it may not be accidental that when the last Maya were subjugated by the Spanish, in 1699, it was, in fact, in the unlucky *katun*. None of this is to minimize the qualitative differences that distinguished the Spanish from previous conquests; the introduction of new diseases was devastating in every way. Still, it is easy to project onto the ancient Maya peasant some of the same political attitudes voiced by those today. No doubt the construction of pyramids was as onerous a task as working on government projects today. No doubt the same cynicism about the leadership prevailed then as it does now. The gore-smeared priests who called for human sacrifice were doubtless respected but avoided, just as, to a lesser extent, the Catholic priest is today. Taxes, inflation, and broken promises: Has the common man's litany against government ever been different?

F. *Material Culture*: It is, of course, in the realm of material culture that Maya life is changing the most. Even remote villages have received electricity; roads have been paved; and bus and cargo truck service connect virtually all settlements. In 1977 the first video games were introduced and televisions have become fairly commonplace. While women have traditionally dressed in the Maya *hipil* or smock, with embroidered collar, today more and more women are eschewing this for the dress. Men, however, still wear sandals, which are by far the most practical footwear available, and some of the figures in ancient Maya sculptures show sandals.

Housing has changed, too. Originally, the Maya commoner lived in a thatched, pole sided hut with a single (front) door. The Spanish conquest rearranged the layout of Maya villages, using the traditional grid pattern employed in Spain, and Maya houses soon came to have two doors (Kurjack 1974). At the same time, the elite had constructed elaborate stone residences, commonly referred to as palaces or range structures. Today, after centuries of life in the modified peasant hut, many Maya seem to be again opting for stone houses, these usually of cinder block, with corrugated metal roofs. It is the common man who remains unchanged, living in his thatched structure. It is ironic that many Maya temples, such as those at Palenque, are but stone versions of the original humble hut, with stylized features representing what was once a functional component of the hut (Figure 2). In a real sense, one may say that, "In the beginning was the hut!" It is probable that as time goes on the huts will vanish, being replaced by a homogeneous kind of stone, peasant house.

Finally, diet focuses on the time-honored staples of corn, beans and squash, with the addition since European times of pork and occasional beef, but here, too, mechanization has entered and in many villages there is now a mechanical *tortilleria* which produces tortillas from the grain brought by the village women. In short, what we see is a new way to maintain an old diet!

Conclusions

From the foregoing, it may be seen that there are certain continuities between the contemporary Maya peasant and his ancient counterpart, but it would be dangerous to assume a one-to-one correlation.

Further, today's popular culture is becoming more and more of an amalgam of modern Mexican culture and the indigenous, and the tide is irreversibly against the latter. Television and radio have served to deluge the Maya peasant with stimuli from the outside world and it is increasingly to this world that the Maya turns.

Figure 2. Classic Period Maya Temple with Stylized Elements of Thatched Hut.

And yet this trait-list approach to culture perhaps obscures the fact that shared human behavior is more than simply an assemblage of acts or even of domains. The Maya peasant can no more be gridded and figuratively sliced than anyone else; to do so would ignore the multilayered and intermeshed aspects of culture and behavior. It might, therefore, be more accurate to say that in certain situations the observer of the contemporary Maya peasant would get virtually no insight into the Maya peasant of long ago. But in other situations, time might also seem telescoped, so that one is afforded a sudden glimpse into the world that was.

In a cornfield, with the sun sending heat waves off the exposed limestone rock; before a small shrine set in jumbled ruins, where a hunter stops to light a votive candle; at night, in the fellowship of the rain ceremony, when men drink and regale the young with folk-tales handed down from time immemorial: These are when the outsider is privileged to glimpse the Maya world as it might have been in 1450, on the eve of the European arrival, or even in 1000, at the end of the Classic Era. But it is a glimpse that saddens as well as enlightens, for the windows into that remote epoch are fast closing and soon the only memories of these times will be in museum exhibits and in the archives of anthropologists.

Works Cited

Culbert, T. Patrick. *The Classic Maya Collapse.* Albuquerque: University of New Mexico Press, 1974.

Kurjack, Edward B. *Prehistoric Lowland Maya Community and Social Organization: A Case Study at Dzibilchaltún, Yucatan, Mexico.* Publication 38. Middle American Research Institute, New Orleans: Tulane University. 1974.

López Otero, Daniel. *Gramatica Maya, por el Pbro. Daniel López Otero* (Original 1914). (Ed. Paulino Novelo Erosa). Segunda Edición. Mérida: Zamná Press, 1968.

Roys, Ralph L. *Ethnobotany of the Maya.* Publication 2, Middle American Research Institute, New Orleans, Tulane University, 1931.

Strickon, Arnold. Hacienda and Plantation in Yucatán: an historical-ecological consideration of the folk-urban continuum in Yucatan. *América Indígena* 25: 35-63, 1965.

Tax, Sol. *Heritage of Conquest: The Ethnology of Middle America.* New York: Macmillan, 1952.

Thompson, J. Eric S. *Maya History and Religion.* Norman: University of Oklahoma Press, 1970.

Villa Rojas, Alfonso. The Maya of Yucatán. In E.Z. Vogt (Ed.), *Handbook of Middle American Indians,* Vol. II, pp. 244-275. Austin: University of Texas Press, 1969.

Vogt, Evon Z. The Maya: Introduction. In E.Z. Vogt (Ed.), *Handbook of Middle American Indians,* Vol. VII, Pt. 1, pp. 21-29. Austin: University of Texas Press, 1969.

Wolf, Eric. *Peasants.* Englewood Cliffs, N.J.: Prentice Hall, 1966.

Towards a Methodology of Disasters:
The Case of the *Princess Sophia*

K.S. Coates and W.R. Morrison

This essay raises a point in scholars' search for what we ought to be interested in and want to know, and raises even more interesting questions of whether the general public is wiser in its interests in popular culture than scholars. If disasters are of more interest to the general public than to scholarly researchers, does that tell us something about the scholars that perhaps they should correct? The essay is particularly important in this volume because it points out three ways that disasters might be studied—through society at the time of the disaster, through reconstruction of the disaster, and through the manner in which society copes with the disaster.

All the world seems to love a good historical thriller; histories of scandals, crimes, wars, controversies, and other examples of human frailty are the stock in trade of best-selling non-fiction writers. At or near the top of any such list is the genre of disasters, a favorite subject of novelists, songwriters, and poets, as well as amateur and non-academic historians. But the subject has traditionally attracted few from the ranks of the professional historians, especially in Canada, where the profession has turned its back on research tainted by association with the marketplace in favor of more scholarly unremunerative tasks.

Why should this be so? Why have such major disasters as the Winnipeg flood, the Vancouver fire, the Halifax explosions, to take three famous Canadian examples, not attracted academic historians? In many cases, such events have entered into the popular culture of city, region or nation, have become an integral part of collective folk memory, and have become food for a variety of writers, from novelists (Hugh Maclennan's *Barometer Rising*) to poets (E.J. Pratt's work on the *Titanic*) to journalists and antiquarians. And yet these episodes, many of them not only dramatic but of pivotal importance to their region or to the nation, have remained essentially unstudied by historians. Can it be that there is nothing of interest to the historian in these dramatic and sad events?

The sinking of the *Princess Sophia* is an excellent case in point. The ship, owned by a subsidiary of the Canadian Pacific Railway Company, operated during the First World War carrying passengers and freight on the inside passage route between Vancouver and Skagway, Alaska. In late October 1918, at the height of one of the largest out-migrations from the Yukon River valley since the end of the Klondike gold rush, the *Princess Sophia* left Skagway, ran aground on Vanderbilt Reef in the Lynn Canal about 20 miles north of Juneau, and after 40 hours on the rocks, sank in a driving blizzard. All 353 passengers and crew on board died in what was acknowledged to be the worst maritime disaster in the history of the Pacific northwest.

As with most other catastrophes, the significance of the sinking of the *Princess Sophia* rests in the social context of the episode rather than with the mechanical details of the sinking, or with the human interest narratives that accompanied it. The passengers on board the ship represented a cross-section of northern society (or at least the non-Native segment of it): businessmen and workers, community leaders, miners, and entire families, most of whom were either abandoning the north forever or participating in an annual migration to a wintering home in the south. The episode provides what is probably the most valuable single source for prosopographical analysis in the region's history. Yet it has been more than unstudied by historians of the region; it has been almost completely ignored. The major surveys of the Canadian north[1] and of Alaska[2] offer not a word on the *Princess Sophia* episode, the worst calamity to strike the white population of the northwest in its history.[3] This can be seen as part of a larger pattern in which the history of the north is neglected: a recent survey text in post-Confederation Canadian history does not once mention the Yukon.[4]

While ignored by academics, the *Princess Sophia* disaster has been kept alive in the memory of maritime enthusiasts and journalists, most of whom have got important details of the episode wrong and have kept alive the various unsubstantiated rumors that swirled for years about the events at Vanderbilt Reef. In an attempt to recreate the disaster "as it happened" and to give it its proper place in the history of the far northwest,[5] we recently published a book on the episode.[6] Through extensive use of court and Royal Commission records, we were able to describe the events leading up to the disaster, to reconstruct biographies for many of the passengers and crew, and recapture the urgency, the pathos and ultimately the despair which gripped the northwest in the late autumn of 1918. In so doing, we have tried to rescue the disaster from the popularizers, particularly the newspaper columnists who, perhaps because of the exigencies of their trade, have misunderstood and distorted it.

In the course of writing the book we became puzzled by the absence of professional interest in disasters, both specifically and as a subject in general, and we have written this paper in an attempt to draw attention to what we see as an unfortunate gap in our discipline, drawing on our experience with the book to offer an historiographical analysis of the study of disasters. We believe that events such as the sinking of the *Princess Sophia* offer historical and historiographical opportunities that historians have been unwise to neglect, for in such events, historians can find a unique and penetrating insight into the nature of the society upon which the calamity has fallen.

While historians have ignored disasters, the general public has maintained an enduring fascination with them. In the immediate aftermath of a disaster there is typically intense public interest, which often does not wane, but sustains knowledge of the incident (however inaccurately) until it passes into folk memory. The sinking of the *Titanic* is the century's best example of the process, and there can be few literate speakers of English who are not familiar with the name of the ill-fated ship. The same is true to a lesser degree of incidents such as the *Hindenburg* crash, the San Francisco earthquake, and similar occurrences. Recent examples are the *Challenger* spacecraft explosion and the destruction of the Pan-Am flight over Lockerby, Scotland, though it remains to be seen if these two become part of common folklore; one suspects not, particularly for the plane crash, since such incidents lamentably have become all too common in the last part of this century.

A great deal of public interest in these disasters is at root essentially voyeuristic, a feeling that "there but for the grace of God go I"—airline disasters are particularly fascinating because of the thought that a similar incident might well strike closer to home. But there are other explanations for this interest: there is tremendous curiosity about the manner in which people act under stress, whether they become heroes or cowards; again, the unasked question is "how would I behave under similar circumstances?" The immediate causes of disasters are also of great interest: simple awe at the raw power of nature, on display in floods, tornadoes, earthquakes, and hurricanes. The irony of life or death depending on being in a particular place at a particular time is also a subject of perennial fascination.

But there is a limit to this interest. We seem especially fascinated with those that strike close to home, either physically or socially. Natural disasters that hit North America, or to a lesser extent Central America, attract far more attention than, say, a storm in Europe, an earthquake in Turkey, or a typhoon in Bangladesh. Though the last may elicit an outpouring of sympathy and assistance, there is little of the intense interest attached to those calamities that strike closer to home in an ethnic or cultural sense. The exception is an incident like the Ethiopian famine, which was gruesomely prolonged, and which benefitted from an extremely effective publicity campaign. There may be class-based ramifications as well. Dozens die in a coal-mine explosion, scores in a fire in an Hispanic nightclub, but these events do not linger like the image of the doomed, bejewelled first-class passengers on the *Titanic*.

The *Titanic* in fact is perhaps the best example of the reasons why a disaster passes into common folklore. In the first place, it falls into the subcategory of disasters in which people are trapped by a failure of technology over which they have no control. It must partly be because such fear is a commonplace of modern society that the *Titanic*, the *Hindenburg*, the *Challenger* spacecraft, and PanAm flight 103 over Lockerby linger in the public memory. Secondly, the *Titanic* was a catastrophe at sea, a genre which has a remarkable following, not only among maritime buffs but among the general public. The sinking of the *Titanic* has been recorded in dozens of survivors' memoirs and a very large number of books and articles. It has been described in poems, songs, movies, and on television, and the ship's carcass has recently been the object of a widely publicized and successful undersea search.

The timing of the sinking of the *Titanic* was exactly right (as that of the *Princess Sophia* was exactly wrong) for it to become fixed in popular memory. It sank in the golden summer of the Edwardian age, after a century of relative peace among the great powers (colonial and other minor wars notwithstanding), and shocked the European world in the same way that the assassination of President Kennedy shocked the American world half a century later: it seemed to be the end of an age of innocence. The *Princess Sophia*, on the other hand, was swallowed in the holocaust of World War I, when mass death had become commonplace. There are parallels; how many now remember the *Athenia*?

The *Titanic* disaster also fulfills a fourth requirement for immortality; it feeds the voyeurism that sustains public fascination with historical events and personalities. Popular histories of this event have revolved around the alleged failings of the ship's builders, owners, and crew, and the behavior, noble and otherwise, of the passengers. They emphasize several standard emotional philosophical elements: the ironies of life (the idea that the *Titanic* was unsinkable,[7] the events that cause one person to purchase passage on the ship and another to wait for a later sailing), the belief that wealth and status are no protection against the vagaries of natural catastrophes (though a first class ticket did help to a considerable degree on the *Titanic*). Acceptance of the fraility of human life is central to our understanding of the human condition, and it is likely that the fascination with disasters represents one important way in which people attempt to deal with the uncertainties of life and the absence of guarantees about the future. Following the history of catastrophes is, therefore, a significant means of dealing with the prospect of our own sudden death.

The very suddenness of most disasters is a major reason for the public fascination with them, and is also an important reason why many of them are worth studying. They often strike society in the midst of its normal routine; as a result, the season, cycles of work, travel and leisure activities—the routines of everyday life—play a crucial role in determining how people react to them and how they are affected by them. People often have little time to prepare for a disaster; it catches them like a flashbulb exploding in the dark, illuminating a slice of their lives. It is the essential normality of the moment—the victims are on a business trip, on a holiday, travelling to work—that helps to generate popular interest and makes the incident so useful to the historian.

Academics in disciplines other than history have not, of course, ignored disasters, particularly those caused by the forces of nature. There are a number of centres for the study of disasters, most with a strong natural or social science orientation, but rarely, if ever, do historical considerations enter into their deliberations. One reason for this is that most of this research is forward looking, seeking to analyze recent events to see how similar catastrophes might be avoided or better managed in the future.[8]

There is, for instance, a sizeable literature on natural disasters in Australia, a country which seems to experience the ravages of nature on a more regular basis than does Canada.[9] Cyclone "Tracy," which hit Darwin on Christmas Day 1974, destroying most of the town, has a permanent place in the historical memory of the town, the region, and the nation.[10] There have, consequently, been a variety of academic efforts to study the effects of and to plan for such events, but again, historians do not participate in these discussions. A major conference on the subject, the proceedings of which where published as *Response to Danger*, included 20 papers by specialists in the area of disaster studies, including geographers, behavioral scientists, engineers, military planners, and Red Cross officials. Most of the papers were historical, though dealing only with the recent past, using contemporary experiences as a guide to future planning—yet no historians took part. The words of the conference organizer might be taken as a call to historians to consider the phenomenon of disasters:

Disasters involve people. This means that the cultural systems and economic structures of communities and the attitudes of individuals must be considered. Those human characteristics of a hazard-threatened area influence significantly the sort of impact a disaster may have, how vulnerable the area is and the choice of an appropriate response.[11]

But this advice was ignored, and the planners continued to plan, as they have so often done, in a virtual historical vacuum.

This indifference to history—it might be called "ignore-ance"—is fairly general in the study of disasters. Events beyond the immediate past are considered irrelevant to planning for present and future dangers. When historical data is included in studies of disasters, it generally appears as a catalogue of past events, designed to show the scale of the danger, or to indicate an increasing incidence of disasters, with no attempt at analysis and no effort to learn from the specific response of a human population to a natural catastrophe.[12] This is true, for instance, of one of the more important books in the field—*Disasters: The Anatomy of Environmental Hazards*, a geographical text in which historical references are generally limited to the dates of major events which provide evidence for the global pervasiveness of disasters.[13]

There is, then, a gap at two levels. The first is the tendency of historians to ignore disasters, both as a formulative influence on an area under investigation or as a means of studying the social, economic, and cultural basis of the society being studied (which is the approach we took with the *Princess Sophia*). Secondly, in the broader and more varied literature on the human response to disasters, there is little evidence of an historical consciousness, or of any sense that the experience of the past might speak to the concerns of the present. It is an interesting conjunction: lack of interest on the part of historians, and, perhaps partly because of this lack, a virtual absence of historical understanding on the part of those most anxious to understand the process by which society responds to natural or man-made disasters.[14]

It is tempting at this point to take a leap of faith into the social sciences for confirmation that history is the path of scientific or theoretical validity. A popular path for such a leap is in the direction of Clifford Geertz, though one must bear in mind the comment of Ronald G. Walters that "the elegance of Geertz makes it possible to use him as window dressing, embellishing points an historian was going to make anyway."[15] This caveat aside, Geertz does offer some useful perspective in studying events that are generally ignored by historians. His advocacy of "deep description," of getting "inside" an event and exploring its full social and economic ramifications and implications, is worth keeping in mind. At the superficial level, disasters are of interest to journalists, popularizers, and—if there are survivors with harrowing tales or if someone dies nobly—to the *Reader's Digest*.[16] Only by moving beyond the headlines and rummaging about more vigorously in the debris of disaster, can more useful evidence and insight be found.

There is a remarkable range of sources available for the historical study of disasters. By their very nature, such events generate a diverse and detailed set of documentary sources which permit a detailed analysis of a society in crisis. Documentation exists at a variety of levels. Using the sinking of the *Princess Sophia* as an example, it is possible to see how the record permits a full investigation and analysis of the social, cultural, and economic significance of the disaster.

Our research into the sinking of the *Princess Sophia* began in a traditional historian's fashion. We examined the newspaper accounts of the day, and, allowing for the remarkably inaccurate reports of details and tremendous confusion over passenger lists and other data, gained a general impression of the episode. Here we were helped by the contemporary newsworthiness and complexity of the disaster, for it was followed for weeks in the national press and in intense detail by newspapers in the cities especially touched by it: Juneau, Skagway, Dawson City, Whitehorse, Fairbanks, Vancouver, Victoria, Anchorage, Seattle. These provided the basic details of the episode (though often conflicting), and evidence of the regional and national response to it.

The first logical archival source was that of the *Princess Sophia*'s owners, the Canadian Pacific Railway Company, but this proved a dead end when the archivist informed us that the company had no records relating to the disaster—an unfortunate circumstance, and one that somewhat strained our credulity. We soon, however, found other, and ample sources. In the case of the *Princess Sophia*, as is common in disasters, government moved to investigate the circumstances and to assign (or perhaps to diffuse) blame. Ottawa set up a commission of inquiry, under Mr. Justice Aulay Morrison, which met in Victoria, Vancouver and Juneau, interviewing dozens of witnesses, including the men involved in an unsuccessful rescue attempt as the ship sat stranded on Vanderbilt Reef. The transcript of this commission, which ran to about 770 pages, in conjunction with newspaper accounts, permitted a careful and detailed reconstruction of events of the sinking; it also provided a means of assessing the rumors and gossip that engulfed the wreck of the *Princess Sophia* in 1918 and for many years thereafter.

However, this data, which was mostly technical, did not permit a full social and economic assessment of the disaster. To accomplish this, we required details on the individual passengers and crew members, particularly as concerned their relationship to the northwest. Here again the newspapers proved useful, for several of them (particularly the *Dawson Daily News*) printed detailed, though generally eulogistic, obituaries of the victims. This information often permitted us to track down at least one additional obituary, usually in a person's home town. The major primary source for an analysis of the passengers, however, came with the happy discovery that relatives of over 200 of the passengers had launched a suit for damages against the C.P.R. in a Seattle court.[17] Part of the voluminous court records, which ran to over 8,000 published and manuscript pages, involved a detailed biography of each victim—a treasure for an historian.

This personal data, combined with details from the press accounts, provided a solid core of prosopographical information, and the raw material for a broader social and economic assessment of the disaster. Following a statistical analysis of the material, we were able to reach a variety of conclusions about the transient nature of northern society (the number of passengers who went "outside" every year and had never spent a winter in the north, those who did so on occasion, those who had never been outside since they first arrived in the region), about investment practices of the northern business community (those who took their annual profits south for investment), about relations between the far northwest (the Yukon River basin) and the Pacific Northwest, patterns of mobility in the post-gold rush era, and about a variety of other themes. The data, in sum, provided a glimpse into the personal lives of a cross-section of northern society, and provided a unique opportunity to examine some of the most central themes in the region's history in the early part of this century.

Our research extended in several directions beyond these major sources: to the memoirs of people living in the north at the time (Laura Berton's autobiography[18] is a noteworthy example), to government, church, and personal correspondence, all of which provided insights into community reaction to the disaster, to additional statistical material (including probate records from the Alaska State Archives which supplemented our personal data), employers' records (particularly the personnel files of the White Pass and Yukon Route, which provided details on the careers of the WPYR workers),[19] and to a variety of legal and court records.

Armed with this data, we ventured into the uncertain waters of oral history. We placed advertisements in newspapers throughout the Pacific Northwest, the Yukon, and Alaska, and received dozens of offers of information (though interestingly, virtually none from the north), some of which supplemented, clarified, or corrected the information coming from other sources.

We would not claim, of course, that the sheer weight of documentation alone makes the sinking of the *Princess Sophia* historically significant, only that it made a book-length treatment of the subject possible. Much of the disaster's historical importance lies in the particular combination of social, economic, and political forces which surround it. But with the episode placed in such a context, and armed with copious statistical and biographical information, we were able to reach a variety of conclusions as to the impact of the sinking, and more significantly, about the post-gold rush reorientation and general collapse of society in the far northwest.

It proved to be fairly easy to judge the broad social and economic significance of the *Princess Sophia* disaster to the far northwest; what was more difficult was to assess its short and long-term effect. How, for instance, does one assess the psychological impact of such an event on the region most affected by it? There were a variety of contemporary comments made by northern residents, most of them impressionistic and inconclusive, on the devastation wrought by the disaster. But these occurred mostly soon after the sinking, when people were mourning the loss of close personal friends—often dozens of them. There is almost no evidence from later years, when one would have expected memorials to be built,[20] references made during church services or on the anniversaries of the disaster, or other such examples of community mourning. Such lack of evidence suggests that the transient nature of the community in the far northwest meant that the disaster was largely forgotten and its significance lost to the region.

Much the same is true on the social and economic front. While it is fairly easy to tally the total human capital represented on the boat— a dehumanizing process that occupied lawyers and the courts for many months—it is hard to assess what the actual loss to the north might have been. Many of the wealthier people on the *Princess Sophia*—the mining promoter and operator Captain Alexander and his wife, for example—were almost certainly leaving the north forever. Can their deaths properly be chalked up as an additional loss to the territory? It is virtually impossible to judge how many businesses closed, how much steamer traffic declined on the Yukon River, how much additional cost employers incurred in finding suitable replacement workers because 8 percent or more of the white population of the Yukon Territory died that October evening in 1918. The deaths of those people, though a terrible loss to their friends, can be viewed from an economic perspective as little more than an acceleration of the process which was occurring in the region in any case.

It seems best then not to claim too much about the immediate social and economic impact of the *Princess Sophia* disaster, and better to concentrate on the relation between the episode and the broader social and economic decline of the far northwest after the Klondike gold rush. Such an approach is, of course, specific to this particular disaster. In other cases the evidence gathered, the biographies of victims, the harm to the region, businesses closed, communities uprooted, might well provide more solid and telling evidence of the impact of the disaster. Just as each disaster follows its own unpredictable course, so much each historical investigation seek its own direction.

We have argued, in our book and elsewhere,[21] that the sinking of the *Princess Sophia* is of vital importance in understanding the history of the Canadian north. We believe that this applies to a variety of other disasters—natural and man-made—which, if properly studied, will provide a unique and fortuitous window into the society in which they occurred. Because of the human and environmental devastation associated with catastrophes, we discover a great deal about the social and economic relationships between people, business, and governments. By studying societies at their weakest and most vulnerable points we can gain insights into their priorities, attitudes and values. The study of disasters provides the opportunity to judge the degree to which people come to terms with their environment, or to which they believe—like people in San Francisco, along the Malibu coast, in Darwin, Australia, or in any of the hundreds of other places where societies live under the threat of natural hazards— that they are either immune to disaster or powerless to deal with it.

In conclusion, we offer some suggestions on how a disaster might be studied, recognizing that such advice must be very general, allowing for considerable variation. We suggest that the following stages of investigation, as well as others that no doubt will fit particular cases, might well form the basis of an historiographical typology for the study of disasters.

Stage one: Society at the time of the disaster—Social and economic relationships and trends; the physical distribution of the population at risk (either within a community or a region), activities underway at the time of the disaster. The events disrupted by disaster, as for example the annual migration from the northwest in 1918, often reveal a great deal about the values, attitudes, and behavior of the communities affected, or, as in the case of the *Titanic*, they may reveal broader social and cultural patterns.

Stage two: Disaster—Reconstruction of the disaster, with particular emphasis on the disruption of social and economic patterns in the community. Although this is of course the area highlighted by non-academic investigators, detailed analysis is needed to learn as much as possible from events. Does the crisis say anything about gender relationships and expectations? Is there a class division evident in the disaster—are the rich spared while the poor suffer? Does the community's response to disaster suggest anything about the norms of social control and the law—is there looting and further destruction of property, or do people co-operate and assist the victims?

Stage three: Dealing with the disaster—the manner in which society deals with disaster can be extremely useful in identifying broader social and economic patterns. In the immediate aftermath, who is cared for and who left to suffer? Which segments of society respond to the personal, communal or physical devastation, and what does this reveal about society's broader ambitions and goals?

These are only a few of the possible questions and themes raised by disaster and mass tragedy. It is likely that as a professional literature in the field emerges, new questions, methodologies, and comparative issues will emerge. One can think of many subjects that lend themselves to study through an examination of disasters: the nature of heroism and courage, of mourning and mass death, of journalism and public information about disasters, of the effectiveness of institutional response to catastrophe (police and fire departments, local governments, regional and national administrations, religious organizations, social and fraternal clubs, and so forth), of business and the remobilization of capital in the aftermath of catastrophe, of changes to the environment brought about by human and natural causes.

These are questions of central importance to society, for it is in its response to disaster that a community's mechanisms for protection, self-renewal, mourning, consensus, and generosity are most severely tested. And it is in the aftermath of disaster, as a town, region or nation attempts to rebuild for the future that one finds, perhaps, the clearest evidence of a social, economic, and political agenda—or as in the case of the *Princess Sophia*, the absence of such an agenda. By tackling the subject of disasters seriously and systematically, academic historians can recapture a share of the field from the popularizers, and place it firmly in the mainstream of the serious reconstruction of the past.

In advocating the broader study of disasters, we hope that we are doing more than simply offering a post facto justification for a work complete. We suggest that it is imperative that academic historians speak to the general reading public—in fact, this is one central characteristic that sets the discipline of history apart from most fields of academic endeavor. Historians have the advantage that they need not always wait for the intellectual trickle-down effect, in which scholarly ideas formulated by academics are introduced to the general public by popular historians, journalists, or schoolteachers. Unlike most of their academic colleagues, they have the chance to write for two audiences at once— the scholarly and the interested public; the study of disaster provides an excellent opportunity for doing so.

Notes

[1]Morris Zaslow, *The Northward Expansion of Canada, 1914-1967* (Toronto: McClelland and Stewart, 1988).

[2]Claus-M. Naske and Herman E. Slotkin, *Alaska: A History of the 49th State*, 2nd ed. (Norman: University of Oklahoma Press, 1987).

[3]The Native population had experienced the catastrophe of devastating epidemics which had done far more damage to them than the *Princess Sophia* did to the white population.

There was only one Native person on board the *Princess Sophia* when she sank—Walter Harper, son of Frank Harper of Bonanza fame and a Native mother.

[4]J.L. Granatstein et al., *Nation: Canada Since Confederation* 3rd ed., (Toronto: McGraw-Hill Ryerson, 1990).

[5]Defined as the Yukon Territory and the interior of Alaska.

[6]*The Sinking of the Princess Sophia: Taking the North Down With Her* (Toronto: Oxford, 1990).

[7]This apparently was not true. According to a recent account, neither its builders nor its owners ever claimed that the *Titanic* was unsinkable—the story is a folk myth. Michael Davie, *The Titanic: The Full Story of a Tragedy* (London: Bodley Head, 1986), p. 215.

[8]A good example is R.L. Heathcote and B. Thom, *Natural Hazards in Australia* (Canberra: Australian Academy of Science, 1979), particularly the articles by Cheny, Denham, Oliver, Douglas, and Douglas and Hobbs.

[9]For a chatty assessment of the significance of natural disasters in Australia, see Eve Pownall, *Elements of Danger* (Sydney: Collins, 1976).

[10]For a journalistic account of the Darwin disaster, see Keith Cole, *Winds of Fury: The Full True Story of the Great Darwin Disaster* (Adelaide: Rigby, 1977).

[11]John Oliver, "The Disaster Potential," in J. Oliver, ed. *Response to Disaster* (Townsville: Centre for Disaster Studies, 1980). See also Heathcote and Thom, *Natural Hazards* and G. Pickup, ed., *Natural Hazards Management in North Australia* (Darwin: North Australian Research Unit, 1978), both of which are collections of conference proceedings.

[12]See for example Ian Burton, et. al., *The Environment of Hazard* (New York: Oxford University Press, 1978).

[13]John Whitlow, *Disasters: The Anatomy of Environmental Hazards* (Athens: University of Georgia Press, 1979).

[14]This observation is, however, not universally true. One of the most impressive works of scholarship on a disaster, Kai T. Erikson's *Everything in Its Path* (Touchstone Books, 1978), examines the social and psychological impact of a devastating flood. The author was aided in his research by the fact that many people survived the disaster and that he was able to get quickly to the scene to interview them. As a direct result of this research technique, he was able to put together a masterful assessment of the social, economic, and environmental context of the disaster, focussing on a critical assessment of the mining operations that helped cause it, and an examination of the unique social fabric of the region under investigation. For a similar, though less successful assessment of the Cyclone "Tracy" disaster, see E.R. Chamberlain, et.al., *The Experience of Cyclone Tracy* (Canberra: Australian Government Publishing Service, 1981).

[15]R.G. Walters, "Signs of the Times: Clifford Geertz and Historians," *Social Research*, 47 (1980).

[16]The *Princess Sophia* incident has been described in many popular articles and publications, including the following: Nancy Barr, "The *Princess Sophia* Revisited," *Alaska Magazine*, July 1976: B. Bowman, "All Lost when 'Sofia' [*sic*] Sank," Nanaimo *Daily Free Press*, 22 October 1966; Richard W. Cooper, "293 Prayed as the Gale Raged," Victoria *Times-Colonist*, 22 October 1989; A. Cottrell, "But Listen," *Vancouver Province* 2 November 1951; N. Hacking, "Divers Probe Old Wreck," *Vancouver Province*, 26 November 1976; Jim Nesbitt, "The West Coast's Worst Disaster," *Maclean's*, 15 October 1951; T.W. Paterson, "Sophia Disaster," *Victoria Daily Colonist*, 27 October 1963; T.W. Paterson, "B.C.'s Greatest Marine Tragedy," *Victoria Daily Colonist*, 28 November 1976; "S.S. Princess Sophia,"

The Skipper, August 1959; A.H. Wells, "The Ship of Sorrow," *Victoria Daily Colonist*, 5 March 1971.

[17]The suit did not have a happy ending for the relatives of the passengers, however, for after the case had been before the courts for 13 years, the C.P.R. won and they got nothing. The relatives of the crew were compensated by the B.C. Workmen's Compensation Board, thus negating their right to sue.

[18]Laura Berton, *I Married the Klondike* (Toronto: Little, Brown, 1954)

[19]The *Princess Sophia* was carrying a number of WPYR river steamer crews, leaving the north as the Yukon froze in the late fall.

[20]There are no fewer than five memorials to the crew of the *Titanic* in Southampton England, where many of them lived. There are no memorials anywhere to the victims of the *Princess Sophia* except the tombstones of those whose bodies were recovered.

[21]In, for instance, "The Sinking of the SS Princess Sophia: A Missing Element in the Cultural History of the Far Northwest," *Northwest Folklore* 7, no. 2 (Spring 1989).

His Very Silence Speaks:
The Horse Who Survived Custer's Last Stand

Elizabeth A. Lawrence

Lawrence's paper is a delightful and informative example of how research in museums and among animals can cast light on the surrounding and supporting civilization. Few better examples could be found than Comanche, the horse that was the "sole" U.S. Army survivor of Custer's battle at the Little Big Horn. Comanche became and remains a symbol behind which a large slice of America can be read. This essay should provide stimulation and a model for more such studies on animal symbols and "spokesanimals."

No man of the immediate command of Lieutenant Colonel (Brevet Major General) George A. Custer survived to describe the dramatic clash between Seventh U.S. Cavalrymen and Sioux and Cheyenne warriors which became known as "Custer's Last Stand." Fought on a Montana hillside on June 25, 1876, the conflict in which approximately 210 cavalrymen lost their lives has evoked extraordinary interest not only in the minds of Americans but even on a worldwide scale. Although the Custer Battle was part of a larger two-day military engagement, the Battle of the Little Big Horn, it is the "Last Stand" that has exerted such a profound influence on people's imagination. The image of Custer's men, outnumbered and surrounded, fighting to the death against overwhelming odds is a perennially fascinating image deeply etched into human consciousness and often expressed through popular culture.

Much of the appeal of Custer's Last Stand is rooted in the mystery that surrounds the event and the many questions about it that even a single soldier who lived through the battle might have clarified. But the one being who became famous as a survivor was mute. Almost incredibly, two days following the battle a cavalry horse from Custer's command was found alive—Comanche, the mount who had belonged to Captain Myles W. Keogh of Troop I. Seldom in history have people wished so fervently that an animal could speak and illuminate the unknown elements of the battle and the actions and motivations of its controversial leader. Although other Seventh Cavalry horses survived, and, of course, the Seventh Cavalrymen not detailed with Custer as well as great numbers of victorious Indians lived through the battle, Comanche

84

became widely known as the "sole survivor" of Custer's Last Stand. This designation has been an inextricable part of his fame—molding his life and legend from the time of the battle even through the present day.

Following his discovery, the badly wounded horse was rescued from the battlefield, nursed back to health, and maintained as an honored member of the Seventh Cavalry until his death in 1891. Though he did not have the capacity for speech, Comanche communicated in other ways. For, as a heroic survivor, he was invested with deep significance, and he assumed a powerful symbolic role in American culture. When he died, his body was preserved and mounted as a museum specimen that continues to be a very popular exhibit at the University of Kansas in Lawrence. Over the years, Comanche has become even more articulate as he has taken on diverse meanings at different times and for various groups of people.

Seldom in history has there been a more cherished relic of a battle than the surviving cavalry horse—both in life and after death. Great value was attributed to the wounded mount from the very moment of his discovery following the battle. As a living creature found by soldiers at the scene of so much death and destruction, Comanche represented the only element of hope in the face of shock and despair. Viewed as the last living tie to Custer and his men, Comanche became a kind of surrogate for the annihilated battalion. Instantaneous sentiments on the part of the men who found him spared Comanche the merciful death routinely meted out to suffering war horses. Against the dictates of practicality and custom, the mount was treated for his injuries and conveyed back to Fort Lincoln with the same care due a wounded soldier.

News of the Seventh Cavalry's overwhelming defeat at the hands of Indians was keenly felt by the young country celebrating its one-hundredth anniversary as a nation in July of 1876. Not only was the victory of an untrained and so-called "savage" foe at the Little Big Horn perceived as a national disgrace, but there was also a sense of loss and grief for the death of the flamboyant General Custer and his command of soldiers who reportedly had been "massacred" to the last man. These cavalrymen, most of whom had been killed in the prime of life in this unexpected defeat, were generally regarded as heroes who died bravely fighting for their country. When Comanche was discovered among the dead near the battle site, his wounds had made him a comrade-in-arms of the fallen troopers. From the cavalrymen he represented, Comanche took on the mantle of heroism. The horse soon became a link between the living and the dead. His endurance and invincibility were symbols for survival in the face of overwhelming odds. The wounded horse became the focus for various emotions—the bitter anger of defeat, sorrow for the dead cavalrymen, and vengeance toward the Indians.

Comanche lived for fifteen-and-a-half years following the Little Big Horn battle, and became the most famous of American military horses. As the "lone survivor," he earned his own place in history through fortitude, and conferred fame upon his rider. The strong bond between Captain Keogh and his horse, which may well have actually existed, soon took on legendary proportions and was purported to be the reason for the animal's unlikely survival. Accounts of Comanche during the two days prior to his rescue depicted the wounded horse standing guard over the dead Keogh, trying to awaken the beloved master he hoped was only sleeping (Luce 1939:64). It was widely believed that Keogh was unwilling to shoot his mount for use as breastworks as the other cavalrymen did. This view is upheld by Indian testimony that Keogh (or someone fitting his description) did indeed remain with his horse until the end, kneeling between the animal's front legs and shooting from under his breast. Little Soldier, a Sioux who fought in the Battle of the Little Big Horn, explained Comanche's survival by reference to the relationship between horse and rider. Keogh, he said, died gripping his mount's bridle reins tightly in his hands. No matter how badly in need of a horse, no Indian would take the mount of a dead man who still held the horse's reins (Charles 1941:4). Reality and legend are often inextricable, for men of the burial party determined from the nature of Keogh's and Comanche's wounds that the same bullet hit them both and man and horse went down together (Luce 1939:60). Thus Comanche became known not only as a paragon of endurance, but of faithfulness as well. The horse's bond to his rider became a symbolic expression of humankind's ancient dream of unity with the animal world.

Under the assiduous care of the Seventh Cavalry, Comanche ultimately regained his health. He is undoubtedly unique among horses as the subject of a remarkable set of military injunctions known as "General Orders No. 7." Proclaimed by Colonel Samuel D. Sturgis at Fort Abraham Lincoln on April 10, 1878, these orders clearly documented the symbolic meaning of the horse whose "very silence speaks in terms more eloquent than words of the desperate struggle against overwhelming odds, of the hopeless conflict, and heroic manner in which all went down that day." The horse's special care, retirement status, and ceremonial role within the regiment were established (Luce 1939:67). To understand the genesis of these orders, it is necessary to acknowledge not only the significance of the horse to the nation, but his special meaning to Colonel Sturgis, commander of the regiment. For the officer's only son, a lieutenant newly graduated from West Point, had been killed with Custer's battalion. Recent studies by scholars from various disciplines have shown that animals can play a healing role for people in times of grief, and the veteran war horse who had been present with Custer's men, had suffered with them, and somehow survived to become their surrogate, served as an instrument of solace for a father's sorrow and a nation's pain.

During his retirement, Comanche was not only an honored soldier referred to as the "second commanding officer" of his regiment, but a pampered pet as well. Reportedly, he was allowed to roam free on the grounds of his assigned post to "graze and frolic as he wished" (Luce 1939:66). Many visitors traveled to see the celebrated equine survivor who was often regarded with near-veneration and whose fame became widespread. Comanche remained with his regiment during his lifetime and following his recuperation at Fort Lincoln he was stationed at various military posts including Fort Totten, Fort Meade, and Fort Riley. On solemn occasions, especially on the anniversary of the Battle of the Little Big Horn, Comanche, draped in mourning with a pair of boots facing backward in the saddle, represented the honored dead in ceremonial parades.

Throughout his life, Comanche stood for the honor of the defeated men who had died for their country and for the shame and anger the nation felt at the Indians' victory. As the years unfolded, the horse was also embued with broader meanings, for the United States was undergoing an era of dramatic change. Comanche's life as an Indian fighter came full circle, spanning the time from the great Indian victory at the Little Big Horn through the Indians' total defeat at Wounded Knee in 1890 (an engagement often referred to as "the Seventh's revenge"). In that same year, the American frontier had been declared officially closed. For all practical purposes, the wild continent, including the Indians who had attempted to resist white encroachment upon their land, was now tamed, and Manifest Destiny was fulfilled. Honor and glory was accrued to those who had a part in the "winning of the West," and foremost among these were frontier heroes like Custer and his Seventh Cavalrymen—and their mounts. Horses indeed were the instruments that had made possible the conquest and settlement of the new continent, and it was fitting that the courageous and enduring mount, Comanche, who had participated in the struggle, received the honor due his kind.

For many people, Comanche was a symbol of patriotism. One writer noted of the "gallant steed" that he served his country well, and "from his back many brave blows were struck for the preservation of the lives and homes of frontier settlers" (Old Comanche Dead 1891). Barron Brown, the earliest biographer of the horse, expressed the idea that "Comanche belongs...to the whole country and is identified with all that is best in our military annals and the conquest of our West." He revealed that "My researches, and the long and close study of the famous horse...have made a better man and a better American of me. I wish that I and a lot of other people had the same self-possession, devotion to duty, courage, sense of obedience, and as few faults as had the noble animal" (UK

Archives). Brown extols Comanche as a "personification of faithfulness and fearlessness, a symbol of the conquest of a great continent," who "will always live as long as valor and the dreams of high achievement live in the hearts of men" (1935:16,77). Comanche's image as a teacher of patriotic values is sustained by the inclusion of the horse's story, along with other national heroes, in a seventh grade reader on American freedom used for the moral instruction of Catholic school children (Perpetua et al 1959:173-79).

When Comanche died at Fort Riley in 1891, his deep meaning to his regiment and to the nation was recognized. His remains were preserved and mounted by Lewis L. Dyche of the Natural History Museum at the University of Kansas, where he is still displayed. One of the conditions of Dyche's agreement with the Seventh Cavalry was that he could exhibit the stuffed horse along with his other zoological specimens at the World's Columbian Exposition at Chicago in 1893. Thus Comanche's posthumous role began as an oddity—a domestic animal standing among wild species—an incongruous attraction for throngs of people who attended the fair. As one source reported, "The period saw no harm in mixing the scientific with the purely sentimental and historic" (More of the Story 1932). The purpose of the Exposition was to commemorate the four-hundredth anniversary of the landing of Columbus by celebrating American progress. Yankee ingenuity and hard work had carved a nation out of the wilderness, and 1893 was a time to take pride in the accomplishments of expansion and the final conquest of a once wild continent, which many people construed as the victory of "civilization over savagery." The ambience of the Exposition was dominated by the evolutionary view of humanity that presumed progression upward from the barbarity of native life to the lofty achievements of Euro-American culture (see Rydell 1984:38-71).

America was entering the machine age, and the end of the horse era that was represented by the cavalry horse was fast approaching. Comanche was an extremely popular attraction at the Chicago Fair, and it was reported that "thousands of people came to the Kansas building for the express purpose of seeing what is still in existence of this memorable and historic horse." In describing Dyche's display of wild fauna among which the horse stood, anthropomorphism and racism were often combined. For example, two wolverines were said to be "meditating upon some kind of meanness," and so were referred to as "Indian devils." It is noteworthy that Comanche, "the old war horse," was designated as "the only surviving horse of the Custer massacre" (Report of the Kansas Board 1894:36). Comanche, like other elements associated with Custer's Last Stand, became inextricably identified with the term "massacre," an inappropriate word since the battle involved armed fighting forces on both sides. Well into the middle of the twentieth century, the designation "Custer massacre" was routine. It is still used. For example, in 1987, a Kansas newspaper referred to the famous horse as the "survivor of the Little Big Horn Massacre" (Lawrence's Year 1987:C1). Incredibly, the 1989 Spring and Summer University of Oklahoma Press catalog begins the description of one new book with the phrase "Ever since the Custer massacre."

Little information has come to light regarding Comanche's first few decades as a museum specimen, which presumably began in 1902 when he was placed in the newly constructed Dyche Hall at the University of Kansas. In 1931, Major General Hugh Scott, who remembered caring for the wounded horse after the battle, paid a visit to him in the museum (An Old Friend 1931). From 1934 until 1941, the building which housed him was closed and Comanche was stored in the basement of a university auditorium. There, neglect of the stuffed mount allegedly caused deterioration—a factor used later by those who wished to transfer the specimen elsewhere.

Comanche's significance and the value he embodies as a relic for many people are reflected by the numerous requests to obtain him— either as a loan or permanent possession—that have been and still are received by the University of Kansas. For example, a movement spearheaded by General Jonathan Wainwright in 1947 sought to transfer Comanche to the U.S. Cavalry Museum at Fort Riley. Later, South Dakota claimed the horse for Fort Meade, and North Dakota also put in a bid. Numerous owners of museums in the West sought to purchase him, and Comanche was in demand for a publisher's autograph party, for various frontier days and state anniversary celebrations, and for display at a race track (UK Archives).

Beginning in about 1938, and continuing sporadically through the Little Big Horn Centennial in 1976 and into the present, the greatest number of requests have involved relocating Comanche at the Custer Battlefield National Monument Museum. Edward S. Luce, one of the horse's main biographers, who was the first superintendent of the Custer Battlefield, was an active proponent of this transfer, and many present day Little Big Horn buffs still favor the move. In general, National Park officials and Custer Battlefield personnel have opposed transferring Comanche to the battle site (even if it were possible), arguing that the horse would overshadow other displays used to interpret the battle. Their responses reveal much about the horse's image and popularity as a relic and their failure to take into account some of the most meaningful factors underlying the profound appeal of the Last Stand and Comanche's role in it. One regional director, for example, considered the horse "not essential to the proper interpretation of the battle," stating that "if we retrieved the horse, it would be entirely on sentimental grounds." He added that though the horse would exert "a potent spell" upon students of the battle as well as the average visitor, it would not "enlighten him on the historical background, the tactics and maneuvers that make the story so fascinating." Thus, the horse would make the visitor "goggle and exclaim" rather than understand. One official even asserted that Comanche's main value was as "an interesting example of the techniques of taxidermy in transition," and was not among the "genuine historical objects interpreting the Custer Battlefield story" (CBNM Files). Recently, a former Custer Battlefield historian summed up the objections more succinctly: "We don't want Comanche here. The horse would become more important than the battle."

Undoubtedly, many visitors would disagree with the National Park officials' position, but the argument is purely philosophical. For, from the beginning and with increasing vehemence, the University of Kansas has resisted all proposals for transferring its prized possession. As pointed out by the exhibits director at the Dyche Museum, after his death "Comanche has been the object of more battles than he was in." Verbal wars raged between the university and those agencies that would claim Comanche, though often tinged with humor, have consistently evidenced absolute unwillingness to part with the famous exhibit, whose value only grows greater with time. Whereas for those who want him at Fort Riley Comanche epitomizes the glory of cavalry life, and for those who would move him to Montana he is an inseparable part of the battle that made him immortal, for the University of Kansas he represents cherished tradition. It is noteworthy that virtually never in the university community (or elsewhere) has Comanche been referred to as "it." He is fondly personified by students, alumni, and all who are associated with the institution. As the university chancellor who resisted the army's onslaught explained, Comanche is "quite unconcerned and calm about the hullabaloo which has been blowing about his ears. He seems to want to stay right where he is very much indeed and I am confident that he will remain there." Later, during one of the arguments over returning the horse to the battlefield, letters were published purportedly written by Comanche and another mount expressing preference for the climate and conditions in either Kansas or Montana.

To insure Comanche's retention at the university, graduates wrote letters insisting that their alma mater "hold that line" against any attempt to remove him, for they remembered the horse as an essential part of college life, the "battle-scarred old 'Faithful' " who "was 'our silent partner' and in our hearts became a real part of the University." Because of Comanche's courage and endurance, students would rub Comanche's nose or steal a strand of his tail hair to bring luck in exams (before he was encased in glass). As alumni they looked forward to returning to be greeted by "the old boy" in the museum. An alumnus who called

Comanche a "stout hearted hero," was "sure he would prefer to remain [in] his present 'Happy Hunting Grounds' " (UK Archives).

And so Comanche has stayed, secure in his special humidified glass "stall" at the University of Kansas. Prior to 1970, there was a brief label outlining the horse's history beside the exhibit. The first sentence stated: "Comanche was the sole survivor of the Custer Massacre at the Battle of the Little Big Horn on June 25, 1876." Over the years, no one seems to have objected to this wording, but in 1970, the idea of Comanche as "sole survivor" and the inaccuracy of "massacre" for what was in reality a battle took on new significance. Times were favorable in that year not only for the questioning of deeply entrenched assumptions but for action. American Indian students at the university took up the challenge that, for them, was embodied by the display and interpretation of the cavalry horse in the museum. As a result of this different kind of onslaught, Comanche's image would be transformed to accommodate new meanings for the modern era.

Calling the Comanche exhibit a "racist symbol," a group of native American university students protested that the horse perpetuated the stereotype of Custer and his troops being "massacred" by "savage" Indians who were in the wrong. And since in reality large numbers of Indians lived through the battle, the students were distressed over the designation of the horse as the sole survivor of the Little Big Horn. As a faculty member who championed their cause wrote in the university newspaper,

What does this make of the Indians who won the battle—sticks? rocks? vegetables? non-persons? The children of those Indians are today's American citizens, and the Battle of the Little Big Horn is part of their history and ours....The Sioux that he [Custer] pursued were acting lawfully and peaceably, but he was intent on a battle and he got one. History does not offer many such simple stories in which evil receives its just desserts, but the Battle of the Little Big Horn was such an instance, and if the Museum of Natural History is to display an exhibit about that battle, then the history should be full and accurate.

As a cavalry mount, Comanche was not responsible for Custer's morals; and, as a symbol of a great battle, he merits the popular attention that he receives. But a university museum should exhibit truth rather than comfortable prejudice. (Wax 1971)

Even the protesting Indians, with their tradition of profound respect for horses, placed no blame on Comanche himself, but rather expressed anger at the way the exhibit had been used and interpreted. A committee representing the native American students met with the museum director and asked that the Comanche exhibit be closed until a more accurate label was written. The director and other officials complied, listened to the Indians' grievances, provided total cooperation, and came to understand feelings and viewpoints they had never before considered. Recalling those events, the museum director told me, "Comanche was one of the greatest learning experiences of my life." In November 1971, a celebration sponsored by both Indians and whites accompanied the reopening of the Comanche exhibit. There was now a long text that began by explaining that the horse stands "as a symbol of the conflict between the United States Army and the Indian tribes of the Great Plains that resulted from the government's policy of confinement of Indians on reservations and extermination of those Indians who refused to be confined," and detailed the Indians' struggle to retain their land and way of life. The Battle of the Little Big Horn was designated as an Indian victory, and the 1890 engagement was accurately termed "the Massacre of Wounded Knee Creek."

Although the Indians had first wanted the horse permanently removed from the museum, they compromised and wisely decided Comanche could be a "learning tool" for both sides. Thus he was transformed from an object representing a federal defeat to a subject articulating the Indian peoples' way of life and struggle for existence. As a museum official told me,

The protest over Comanche was a sign of the times, and similar things went on throughout the country. That was a bad label, anyway. It was slanted toward the army's viewpoint and didn't tell the real story. The display has great value to the museum, but it was misrepresented for so long, and was used to idealize cavalry life.

Comanche once symbolized a terrible loss to Americans, but now he stands for the conflict between Indians and whites. The horse symbolizes one of the few and the greatest of all victories the Indians ever had, and the terrible mistake made by whites. For Indians, he's a symbol of victory; everyone likes to ride a winner!

The Kansas University protest accomplished a great deal, representing "a victory for the Indians seeking to tell their viewpoint of American history." One writer explained, "The horse that once angered Indians" now "allows them to raise their heads in the pride of telling their side of the story. . . . They were able to change the horse Comanche from the battle's 'lone survivor' into a symbol of the Indians' perseverance against government policy that sought to push them from their ancestral lands." Now, the horse was not just "a symbol of the Indians' past victories," but "what modern Indians can accomplish" (Comanche Once Angered 1978).

Indeed Comanche, in his new role, led the way for further beneficial changes within the museum. To dispel implications that angered the native Americans, Indian exhibits were disassociated from those dealing with "primitive man." Native American religious objects, previously appearing as "curios," were labelled in a more respectful manner or removed. The whole idea of how best to exhibit cultural relics and artifacts for educational purposes was re-examined and addressed. Indians themselves realized they needed to know more about their heritage in order to interpret it for others. Comanche's influence in raising consciousness about Indians took on even broader aspects, as courses in native American studies were set up at the university and Indian students were recruited for admission. One of Comanche's most astounding accomplishments was to bring together the Indians at the University of Kansas and in neighboring communities. As the protestors expressed this unique phenomenon, "Comanche helped in uniting us. He was a positive thing that gave us hope. Although it's generally hard to get Indians to agree, they agreed on Comanche. We were all from different backgrounds. I thought we would all go our own way and not get organized; I expected we would be factionalized and individualistic, but I was thrilled when we acted together. It was one of the few times different Indian people agreed."

During the last two decades, Comanche has continued to be a highlight for the 120,000 annual visitors to the Dyche Museum, many of whom travel long distances specifically to see him. He attracted increased attention at the time of the Little Big Horn Centennial in 1976, when some new interpretive displays about the battle were added and a pamphlet about him was published by the university. In 1986, when Comanche was damaged by accidental flooding, news of the disaster was flashed nationwide. No effort was spared in his repair, and museum experts agree he is now in better shape than ever.

Although artifacts such as guns and arrows whose provenance can be traced to the Little Big Horn are highly valued and objects from archaeological digs at the site are eagerly sought, Comanche still surpasses all battle relics. As a once-living creature whose posthumous existence is even more meaningful than his cavalry career, and as a member of a species with a long history of close alliance with humankind, he has an image of courage and endurance with which people continue to identify, adapting it to their own ethos and times. Beyond his capacity to lend a sense of immediacy to Custer's Last Stand, Comanche is a focus for the empathetic responses commonly evoked by that event— an affective process that transcends the significance of weapons and battle tactics.

Comanche faces into the twenty-first century appearing peaceful, as horses are known to be except when ridden into battles not of their making. He stands as a symbolic bridge between the living and the dead, between Indian and white, between civilization and the untamed, between humankind and the animal world, and between the mute and the voiced, and links the horse era with the machine age. Freed now from any label identifying him in time and place, he continues to instruct in silence and hopefully will come to be seen in a larger context than Custer's Last Stand. More than a battle relic from a bygone era, "his very silence speaks in terms more eloquent than words," articulating a timeless message protesting humankind's aggressive domination of nature, the oppression of the weak by the strong, and even the universal barbarity of war.

Works Cited

Charles, Tom. "Why Comanche Survived," *The Graduate Magazine*, December: 4, 1941.

"Comanche Once Angered Indians," *Olathe Daily News*, January 10, 1978.

Custer Battlefield National Monument Files, Crow Agency, Montana.

"Lawrence's Year in Review," *Lawrence Journal-World*, January 1: Cl, 1987.

Luce, Edward S. *Keogh, Comanche and Custer*. Privately Printed, 1939.

"More of the Story of Comanche, Survivor of Custer Battle," *Lawrence Journal-World*, January 13: 10, c. 1-5, 1932.

"Old Comanche Dead," *Junction City Union*, November 14:3, 1891.

"An Old Friend of Comanche Finds Him in K.U. Museum," *Kansas City Star*, April 30, 1931.

Perpetua, Sister M., R.S.M., Mary Synon, L.L.D., and Katherine Rankin. *These Are Our Freedoms*, Boston: Ginn & Company, 1959.

Report of the Kansas Board of World's Fair Managers, Topeka: Hamilton Printing Co., 1894.

Rydell, Robert W. *All the World's A Fair*. Chicago: University of Chicago Press, 1984.

Archives of the University of Kansas, Lawrence, Kansas.

Wax, Murray. "Comanche's Stand: To the Editor," *University Daily Kansan*, October 15, 1971.

The City and the Circus:
Engagement, Symbol and Drama in the
Adelaide Grand Prix

Ade Peace

Often we are likely to study outdoor entertainment as entertainment events unto themselves—the internal structure, dynamics, esthetics contained therein. But there are many more ramifications. In this essay an anthropologist turns to the "social and symbolic properties of the Grand Prix," now held annually in Adelaide, Australia, "which allow it to transform the social face of an Australian city and to engage the collective gaze of an urban population" and tens of millions throughout the world who witness the event on television. The impact on Adelaide is real. This anatomization of an event in a city is an excellent case study which may well serve as a model for other studies in popular culture.

In the following pages, I provide a preliminary sketch of the narrative structure which emerges as Adelaide, South Australia's capital city, hosts an international circus, the Grand Prix. Inasmuch as this major event involves a capital investment of millions of dollars, requires a cast of several hundred central actors and many thousands of supporting ones, transforms for a brief period of time a city with a population of almost one million, and is beamed by satellite to tens of millions of homes throughout the globe, so any anthropological account can but modestly penetrate its complexities. This paper does not even claim to do that: its central concern is more to pose the problem than to answer it. What are the social and symbolic properties of the Grand Prix which allow it to transform the social face of an Australian city and to engage the collective gaze of an urban population? On just four occasions now, for no more than four days in the months of October or November, this gargantuan spectacle has been hosted by Adelaide. By general consent of the citizenry, its impact has been enormous and inescapable: even its detractors—and there have been a good many—have readily conceded this point. How then is this urban transformation effected, what are the processes which combine to effect the focussing and the engagement of the population of an entire city? The perspective adopted here is that the relationship between the city and the circus brings into being and progressively elaborates an unfolding narrative order which is constituted at different levels and therefore has the capacity to differentially engage the population at large. This narrative structure is neither centrally orchestrated nor rendered internally coherent. It is rather a composite or an amalgam of a number of discrete narrative themes emergent from the city-circus relationship: these engaging narrative themes together constitute a series of meta-statements about the form and content of Adelaide society and the wider system of relations which encompass it.

Although a dominant theme of this analysis is that the intertextual character of the city-circus relation is essentially and critically an uncoordinated process of emergence, it warrants initial emphasis that the four-day event itself is highly orchestrated. A wide range of activities is coordinated in such a way as to culminate climactically in the two hours of the Sunday afternoon when the Formula One race is run. Some twenty-six cars hurtle over eighty-two laps of a track through the parklands and race course which immediately abut the commercial heart of Adelaide. The vast green area bounded by the track is taken up by huge stands overlooking the course, and by a multitude of tents and more permanent constructions from which spectators can purchase specifically-produced merchandise, a wide range of foodstuffs, and above all alcohol since, this being a male dominated event, the many beer tents are well occupied throughout. From these varied locations it is possible to watch *inter alia* fashion displays, Guinness Book of Records competitions, vintage car parades, parachute jumps, aerobatic displays, plus ear-shattering low-level flypasts by the fastest and most modern fighter planes of the Royal Australian Air Force. In addition to the Formula One race on the fourth day, formula two and touring car competitions, as well as a celebrity race, fill the first three days along with untimed practice runs and qualifying sessions for the major event. It is, as numerous advertising brochures repeatedly affirm, 'an action filled four day program,' not least because of numerous off-course activities such as special music and entertainment sessions in clubs and pubs, and street parties over two nights in Adelaide's (rather modest) redlight district.

The greater part of these activities are orchestrated by the commercial firm which now controls the Grand Prix in conjunction with the State Government of South Australia under whose auspices the event was initially launched. The overall organization of the Grand Prix would assuredly merit analysis in its own right not least because the state first assumed the major entrepreneurial role and later entered into partnership with the private sector. The concerns of this paper however lie elsewhere. I am more concerned with the processes of engagement and the production of social meanings which are more generally emergent from the conjuncture between the city and the circus, for these surface in the main without conscious intervention or any controlling agency. From the vantage point of the anthropologist it is the latent and sustained properties of the city-circus conjuncture which provide the more interesting avenues for exploration and analysis.

Consumer Society, Metropolitan World

The imperative and consistent backdrop against which the city-circus relation is emergent is that of high consumerism, since for a period of approximately two months, it seems that little escapes being represented and re-packaged with a Grand Prix motif. In this fashion, the pending event becomes a celebration of consumerism and becomes firmly embedded in the material fabric of everyday life. Unlike any other 'international' event to which it might be compared, the advent of the Grand Prix permeates the popular consciousness through the most mundane of contexts and the most mediocre of commodities. The cheap goods of Woolworth's supermarkets become 'Pit Stop Specials,' advertisements proclaim 'Target's Grand Prix Savings,' modern shopping centres announce 'Grand Prix Trading Hours.' The goods consumed by the average household on a daily basis—milk, bread, cereals, or anything else with a wrapping—increasingly concentrate attention on the imminence of this secular drama. And not only what is consumed but also what is worn on a more or less daily basis,—T-shirts, sweaters, jackets and ties—, bear the same message. Certain companies take a lead in this re-presenting process. There are for example some one hundred officially licensed products which, in the advertising jargon of the Official Program, allow one to 'gear up for the Grand Prix.' These range from peaked caps, diaries, bottles of wine and ties, through tankards, cigarette lighters, cans of beer and watches, to quilt covers, pillow cases, rugby tops, and sunglasses. Others display remarkable ingenuity, as when Liquorland proclaims the 'Grand Prix Survival Kit' comprising a six pack of South Australian stubbies, a cooler bag, GP cap, T-shirt, and stubbie holder—all 'fine value at $19.99 only.'

The growing avalanche of advertising cast in these terms constitutes the initial sensitizing of most people on an annual basis. As the event draws nearer, not only does the appeal to particular markets intensify, so too does its resonance with the customary hierarchicalization and differentiation of consumption patterns. 'Special editions' of particular makes of cars appear on the market whilst in 1986 one enterprising estate agent offered 'Grand Prix Town Houses,' the upper floors of which overlooked the racing circuit. The advertisement for comparatively expensive Benetton sportswear reads 'chic, sleek, Italian fashion, ideal for lounging near the pits.' Australia Post offers '4 Special Australia

Post Grand Prix Souvenir Envelopes' which are claimed to be 'not just Grand Prix Souvenirs—but Collectors' Items.' And the notion that amongst all of this teeming rubbish there are some quality commodities is elaborated by a regular consumer column in Adelaide's most popular midday newspaper, *The News* (Tuesday, October 21, 1986):

> While many prefer to avoid memorabilia, classifying it all as 'junk,' those who look a little closer will find many of the stores stock novelties which deserve upper crust souvenir billing.
>
> And for visitors and Adelaide locals alike, that means a chance to collect a cache of memorabilia worth storing.

Faced then with this veritable flood of 'new' commodities, the discerning purchaser can practice her customary expertise: this too is the general message from Adelaide's most prestigious department stores. In such ways is this 'exceptional' event progressively assimilated into the 'normal' world of intense consumerism, with the particular target being those who are expected to organize patterns of household consumption.

A more striking and singular interpretive process centres upon and engages the relation between the parochial city and the metropolitan circus.

It is central to the collective self imagery of Adelaide that it is a parochial place: the city's style and ambience is not that of a major metropolis but more of a large country town. This is what gives it its cultural integrity, its distinctiveness, within the semi-peripheral status of Australian society more generally. There are two levels of contrast at work here: the first emphasizes the spatial and social distance between Australia and the global centres of economic and political power, chiefly North America and Western Europe; the second is the relative peripherality inside Australia of Adelaide by contrast with the metropolitan centres of Sydney and Melbourne. With a population of slightly under one million, a spatial layout which has remained more or less intact for well over a century, a commercial heart of modest proportions, and a plethora of parks, gardens and leafy bungalow-dominated suburbs, it is terms such as 'relaxed,' 'leisurely' and 'easy-going' with which the residents typify their city. It is, in short, a city for residence rather than a city of industry; and this in the popular imagination is its strength rather than its weakness when compared with cosmopolitan yet crime-ridden Sydney and metropolitan yet motor-dominated Melbourne. Adelaide is exceptional amongst Australia's cities in understating its metropolitan-ness and adhering with alacrity and pride to the self-selected labels of 'provincial' and 'parochial'. The tourist-generating industry has added further dimensions to this image of parochialism: but the notion that Adelaide is a relatively slow-moving city built around the meandering Torrens river is as much a part of the popular imagery as it is a fiction of tourist brochures. When one of Adelaide's leading journalists deploys such terms as 'sedate,' 'prim,' 'orderly' and 'fiercely parochial', and typifies it as 'a city that's grown up to become a town...(while)...the neighbourliness of the village survives' (this is in the 1987 official Media Guide), then such characterizations are ones which many residents would accord with.

To this extent, the customary images of Adelaide as the capital city of 'the driest state on the driest continent' could scarcely constitute a more striking point of contrast as the Grand Prix circus leaps into its interpretive domain, for the truly parochial is being brought into a highly symbolic relation with the archetypally international. Contemporaneously a number of occupational and quasi-occupational domains readily symbolize the global character of modern popular culture: film stars and rock stars are the obvious cases in point, tennis players and golfers are others. On a somewhat different plane, the more pre-eminent in music and drama are as internationally itinerant as those who purvey the artifacts of popular culture. In its very itinerancy then, the Grand Prix circus is little untoward. What is exceptional is the sheer scale of the enterprise, its spectacular character, and its ability to link together major metropolitan centres of the global system in order to highlight its own internationalism. This is the Grand Prix's circus quality, its ability to connect, for by the time of its arrival in Adelaide, the last stop on the annual circuit, 'the greatest show on earth' has passed through Brazil, Spain, San Marino, Monaco, Belgium, Canada, U.S.A., England, Germany, Hungary, Austria, Italy, Portugal and Mexico.

In the weeks which immediately precede the Grand Prix, then, the conceptual dichotomy which emerges is that of, on the one hand, the normal, provincial and parochial world of Adelaide, and the extraordinary, cosmopolitan and international world of Formula One racing, on the other. The contrast is a forceful one, especially when compounded by the prevalent belief that the migrant circus has the ability and the potential to transform the semi-peripheral status of the city,— to locate Adelaide on the international map, to effectively site it on the world globe. This extraordinary power has been from the start quite pivotal to the selling of the Grand Prix to the ordinary citizens of Adelaide: from the moment it was announced that Adelaide was to join the Grand Prix circuit, its political and business elites emphasized that Adelaide would henceforth be known and be recognized outside Australia. 'This will put Adelaide on the international map. From now on everyone in the world will know exactly where Adelaide is' proclaimed the state premier in 1985. On Friday October 24, 1986, the South Australian *Advertiser* commented that:

...running as it does through the heart of our small, beautiful, in many ways insular city, the Grand Prix looks like becoming the annual festival for which Adelaide will become best known.

A young shop assistant who denounced the pollution generated by the racing nevertheless had to concede that 'On the whole, its a good thing though. I mean, before the Grand Prix came, most people outside of Australia had probably only heard of Sydney. Now Adelaide is right on the map.' Finally, in similar vein, an international reporter, Frank Keating of the *Guardian* 'reports from Mexico' on October 19, 1986:

Mansell goes to Adelaide still heading the championship. If he finishes third or higher, he takes the title no matter what his two rivals, Piquet or Prost, do. It all makes for an awesomely charged couple of hours to enliven that normally gentle and snoozy old riverside city.

As the Grand Prix provides further impetus to the wheels of high consumerism in a modern urban context, the distinctive narrative thread to unfold concerns the transformative capacity of the Grand Prix circus. The city is to have its collective identity transformed from that of a minor semi-peripheral urban place to one which can realize international recognition and prestige. It is to be thrust into the international limelight and accorded a perhaps fleeting prominence in an integrated global order. For the most part of course the sense of peripherality is not of much consequence for the residents of Adelaide: it is an assumed and an accommodated part of everyday life. What is telling then about the advent of the Grand Prix is that its imminence renders up for reflection some part of the taken-for-granted everyday world. Precisely because the modern circus is so evidently international and cosmopolitan, it serves to heighten in mirror-like fashion what Adelaide is not. But backed up as it is by the enormous technological armory of modern communications systems, the coming of the Grand Prix signals what the city can become—the focus of the global gaze in a modern world system linked together by instantaneous television and radio transmission. There are two types of power at work here: the power of the Grand Prix to focus this international gaze, the power of the technological media to satiate it.

Urban Space, Circus Time

As months shorten into weeks, this sense of imminence is progressively transformed into more concrete manifestations of the Grand Prix event. The restructuring of urban space is a major chord and the recasting of time as a minor one take further the process of engagement.

Apropos of time, the fact that the Grand Prix is an annual event ensures that it can be readily incorporated into a calendrical cycle characteristically punctuated by mass festivals and large scale celebratory activity. In addition to Christmas and the New Year, the Australian calendar exhibits numerous high points of mass celebration, some of which are nationwide such as the Melbourne Cup race day, some of which are specific to particular states, such as in South Australia the Adelaide Royal Show. More particularly, in imitation of the count-down process which characteristically sets in motion any competitive sport or game, mass media presentations become replete with such phrases as 'ten (eight or six) days to the Grand Prix,' just as they attempt to stimulate a sense of pending climax at Christmas. This shift of emphasis from a general sense of imminence to a highly specific timetable assumes a distinctive impact amongst the population at large.

On a more substantial plane, the progressive colonization of major urban space for the Grand Prix represents one of the most important physical transformations of Adelaide; for this constitutes—sometimes in literally concrete terms—the process whereby facets of normal everyday life are disrupted and displaced in order to accommodate the abnormal and the spectacular. Adelaide's is a street circuit, and this was quite critical in the first instance in bringing the Grand Prix to Adelaide. Most other Formula One venues (the exceptions are Monaco and Monte Carlo) are purpose built race circuits; but these lack much of the excitement of street circuits, and so the proposal from Adelaide in the mid-80s was well received. The symbolic consequences of this consideration are inescapable since the appropriation of urban space is ramified. In addition to major routeways being gradually sealed off for repairs and, in some instances, total closure, extended lines of huge concrete blocks (to protect the crowds against accidents) increasingly disfigure the low-level city landscape. High mesh wires, overhead walkways, and the extended banks of terraced seating are assembled in large quantities. The city horse-race course is reconstructed into an open air stadium within which will be concentrated most of the ancillary activities which surround the major event. Substantial tracts of parkland— the green belt which is so pivotal to the social construction of Adelaide's urban identity—disappear from view.

Under such circumstances, it is hardly surprising that the event now begins to generate a disputatious discourse:

Your correspondent, R.J. Armstrong, talks of two months each year when the parklands are transformed 'into a venue of energy and excitement.'

In fact, the time span of the Grand Prix invasion is four months when Victoria Park, Dequetteville Terrace and the Eastern Parklands become venues of ugliness, inconvenience, harassment and blatant advertising. (Letter to the Editor, *The Advertiser*, October 19, 1987)

More generally, recurrent conversational themes concern the myriad ways in which people deploy their familiarity and intimacy with the urban milieu in order to minimize the disruption to their daily lives.

This general tendency to accommodation is seized upon by city administrators who elaborate an appeal for cooperation in order to enhance international status. In a widely distributed full page advertisement which details traffic restrictions for motor vehicles and re-routed bus ways, the headline reads: 'How you can help turn a city into a circuit': this is followed by 'Grand Prix 86 is almost here. Once again the eyes of the world will be on the streets of Adelaide': and finally the warning that 'work on assembling the spectacular has been in process for some weeks, but this will intensify dramatically as the big week draws closer.' The message here is easy to decode: international standing can only be bought at a price and by all. But whatever the particular response and whatever the particular reading placed upon such messages as these, the point remains that, as everyday urban space is surrendered to this singular event, a closer identification is being forged between the circus and the city. As people arrive late for work, as they exchange their local knowledge to minimize disruption to their lives, and as they begin to positively evaluate or comment with hostility upon the changing character of street architecture, a symbiosis is being effected between this local population and this metropolitan elite.

Ordinary Man, Superman

With such processes in motion, the stage is well set for the arrival of the central actors and the imported supporting cast. To use the term in the loosest possible, lay sense, this 'invasion of the megastars' (to use one radio commentator's phrase) has all the qualities of a modern cargo cult as drivers and their supporters, engineers and mechanics, vehicles and spare parts, all descend from their specially chartered aeroplanes.

The collective role of the city's population is to be impressed by the sheer scale of the enterprise as captured by some elementary statistics. They are informed for example that the Formula One circus involves a combined investment of some $200 million: that a single team of engineers and mechanics may number between thirty and one hundred: that some 900 media representatives are registered (in 1986); and that whilst a sell-out crowd will (in 1986) number 120,000 (by contrast with 100,000 in the previous year), some 850 million people throughout the world will see Adelaide on their television screens. The population at large is not, of course, intended to assimilate these particular statistics, as is evidenced by their presentation in blitz-like fashion from a diversity of sources. But they assuredly acquire a sense of the vast capital, labor and technology resources here on display. In isolation, the fact that one hundred tons of equipment are being shipped in is, for most people, beyond meaning: in normal life there are few standards by which to make sense of this, and many other, particular facts. It is generalized impressions which are being transmitted, and they are truly awesome. Here is a substantial but highly elite metropolitan clan (see below), descending with its physical and symbolic cargo, into the now somewhat transformed life-worlds of ordinary urban citizens.

Much of this is by way of preliminary to the emergence of multiple narratives concerning the individual drivers and the relations between them. Henceforth, if the city of Adelaide is the focus of the international gaze, it is the drivers who are accorded close scrutiny by the city.

Before their arrival, at least the names of the leading drivers are widely known even beyond the ranks of racing *afficionados*: in the emergent process whereby a face becomes attached to a name, a critical part is played in this culturally heterogeneous setting by the appropriation of social stereotypes from the society at large. Indeed, so pervasive are such stereotypes that a minor cultural map of the Prix's leading figures is spelled out via the combined effects of the mass media. In 1986 for example (drawing here on several newspaper and television sources), Nigel Mansell, the leading British driver, is considered to be 'cool, calm and in control,' whilst the Frenchman Alain Prost bears 'a perpetual Gallic grin.' Another Frenchman, Patrick Tambay, is 'handsome, debonair, and dashing': and Alan Jones, the sole Australian member of this metropolitan elite is dubbed to be 'the true Aussie battler...the dogged Aussie who despite endless technical problems battles on.' So this is a narrative frame constituted out of popular stereotypes, and within this frame even inversions (perhaps, especially inversions) can be readily accommodated. Thus for example the Italian driver Teo Fabi by virtue of being 'tiny and balding' is considered 'one of the most unlikely-looking GP drivers' whilst Stefan Johansson's nickname of 'the smiling Swede' assumes a particular significance since, as everyone well knows, Swedes are a dour lot. The introduction to clan nicknames is an especial feature: by virtue of their being the distinguishing mark of insiderness, outsiders are on the one hand being allowed a privileged insight while on the other extreme social distance is being highlighted. Through them some access is being permitted to the elite's inner refinements—as well as the internal differentiations which identify the cream of this occupational elite. Thus in 1986, Mansell, Prost, Senna, Piquet and Rosberg were known as 'The Gang of Five' since the Formula One world championship was being fought out amongst these men alone.

In the course of this narrative web being spun around the drivers and their closest associates, descriptive flesh is being hung on a hitherto bare skeleton of elementary information. Not only are individual characters rounded out into complex personae, the wider audience is introduced to the code of interpersonal relations which guides and circumscribes their performance on the track and elsewhere.

Notwithstanding how the situation might appear to the uninformed observer, a recurrent theme is that there is constantly at work a distinctive occupational code, a morality which tempers and contains the ambitions of these supermen. It is emphasized for example that close teamwork is essential to company success, and accordingly the individual must subordinate his ambition to the interests of the whole. From this commercial imperative one can acquire a number of practical rules: towards the end of the season, for example, should two men from the same team be in the lead as the end of the race draws near, the driver with the best chance of becoming world champion is allowed to surge forward—and thus bring glory to the entire team. In rather more pedestrian order, it is learned that cars which are being lapped by the race leaders must always give way by maintaining a steady course, whether or not they are part of the same team. Wherever possible, even the most intense of rivals are expected to warn one another of suddenly emergent hazards, such as a broken down vehicle or oil patch round a 'blind' bend. One acquires the knowledge that whilst a flying start allows any driver to gain a critical competitive edge especially on a street circuit, the initial few seconds of any race are amongst the most hazardous: gaining that edge is not to be realized by creating 'a shunt'—insider parlance for an accident. Last but by no means least, at the end of the day gentlemanly rules apply: the clan code is that whatever has transpired throughout the race, those in first, second and third place shake hands on the winners' podium in full public view before spraying the assembled multitude with champagne.

I emphasize at this juncture that the range and the depth of knowledge thus acquired is hugely variable: for present purposes the critical consideration is that members of the urban audience at large acquire some facility for exchanging opinions about the Grand Prix. It also merits note that the audience does not in the main learn the rules of the Grand Prix circus in this itemized fashion. Rather they are acquired by media reference to particular personae whose calibre as moral actors is being described. In 1986 for example Mansell was frequently referred to as 'a gentleman of the track', an individual who closely adhered to 'the rules': on an earlier occasion having unwittingly created 'a shunt' he readily admitted his error and apologized to those who progress he had hindered. Alternatively, the attentive observer acquires an insight into the rules through accounts of incidents where they have been unambiguously breached; for whilst there are heroic figures on 'the circuit', it has its (necessary) villains too. In 1986, the role of the villain was undoubtedly filled by Ayrton Senna of Brazil (a man with—no coincidence here—'a glacial stare'): not only was Senna a member of 'The Gang of Five,' he was also the current *enfant terrible* of the Formula One circus. His reputation substantially hinged on a major incident in Rio de Janeiro when in the first lap he forced Mansell off the track. The result is described in the Grand Prix Official Programme as follows:

> That was in Rio, and when they had arrived at the next race in Jerez you had to search hard for a Grand Prix driver with a good word for Ayrton. 'A fantastic talent' they chorused 'but a man with Formula Three manners. A dangerous driver.' Nigel, Alain, Nelson, Keke, Michele...they all told the same tale. They admired the ability, disliked the man.
>
> Senna has never made any bones about it: he considers he was put on this earth to drive race cars, and more specifically, to be world champion. Nothing—not his relationships, friends, even his marriage—is allowed to stand between him and his ambition.

In 1986 however Senna had no monopoly on the role of the villain: another leading driver, Nelson Piquet, shared the role—although in his case it was poetic justice which finally played its part. In 1985 the rivalry between Piquet and Mansell became so intense that major rules were breached:

> In defeat, Piquet was scarcely magnanimous, and in victory (at Hockenheim two weeks later) he was no more gracious. Nigel held out his hand and Nelson looked the other way.
>
> The difference between the two this year is that Mansell has been a fighter, always as competitive as his car allowed. Piquet, by contrast, was no less than pathetic at Monaco, and in his anxiety to respond to Mansell at Detroit crashed twice.

Not only does this elite brotherhood have its heroes and villains who can become increasingly identified with, as with all clans it has its own patriarchs too. Over the four year span at Adelaide, the patriarchs which have come to the fore are Stirling Moss, Juan Fangio, Sir Jack Brabham and Jackie Stewart. Virtually by definition, patriarchs are not only those who exemplify the normative code of behavior which should be adhered to by all, they also attempt to impose that code on those most inclined to undermine it. The first consideration is pointed up in the following account of how 'Fangio leads cavalcade of legends' in the orchestrated build up to the major race:

> Fangio! Just the mere mention of that name was enough to strike fear into the hearts of drivers and their teams during the halcyon days of motor racing...
>
> Fangio, now a frail but lively 75, is coming to Adelaide for the Grand Prix and will 'duel' one last time with his 1950s *arch-rival, friend and one time team mate* Stirling Moss.

The second consideration—that by virtue of exemplifying codes for conduct this gives them leverage over the present young stars—was signalled in a television commentary in 1986 by the Scot, Jackie Stewart. On this widely broadcast occasion, Stewart remarked how 'I and a few others like me (i.e. patriarchs) have had a few words with Ayrton (Senna) about the way he's been carrying on' since, as we have already seen, Senna's ambition was putting at hazard the well being of the other members of 'The Gang of Five.' Clearly the message here being baldly transmitted is that Senna's behavior is beyond the pale: not only are the patriarchs actively engaged in sanctioning him, Senna's miscreancy is so unacceptable that it merits being put on display entirely beyond the narrow social boundary of the clan brotherhood.

Front Stage, Back Stage

The crucial consideration to emerge from the above narrative themes is that the form and content of the circus is one of marked contrast. On the one hand, the Grand Prix's central actors constitute an elite enjoying wealth, glamour, and high prestige. Living in such a rarefied atmosphere has its manifest drawbacks: it is, as one driver remarked in a television interview, 'a gypsy life' in which 'you wake up each morning wondering which city you're in today' (and) 'live out of suitcases, never having a home to relax in, only another hotel room that looks just like the last.' The compensations however are substantial by the standards of ordinary folk—annual incomes beyond their wildest dreams, houses in the more prestigious corners of the globe, the ability to purchase the finest of consumer commodities, and with all of this ready access to the privileged domains of other international elites. On the other hand, the recurrent counterpoint to this narrative theme is one which powerfully resonates with the world of the ordinary man—and implies that this is not such an entirely rarefied world at all. Here are interpersonal relations of sustained friendships and enduring partnerships, and relations of envy and outright hostility. Here are men who have struggled to prominence through a competitive apprenticeship system while others have fallen by the wayside. Here too are father-figures who provide a controlling hand vis-à-vis those inclined to excess, for even in this highly competitive milieu it is possible to be too ambitious, too ruthless. So even if these are megastars with exceptional qualities, their daily lives are nevertheless informed by the natural passions of affection, respect, camaraderie, envy and jealousy: in brief, under the skin the behavior of these men is informed by the same sentiments as those whom they entertain. To this extent, the Otherness of this elite domain is constituted in such a way as to be made resonant with, and assimilable into, the commonplace lifeworlds of the urban citizenry. These are the elements of the small narratives which emerge from privileged glimpses behind the front stage façade.

Considerably more can be made of this elementary, dramatic analogy. For just as in everyday life those on the front stage can only realize merit and privilege through the sustained efforts of those unrecognized in the rear, so there is an entire and unassuming backstage to 'the greatest modern show on earth.' And this backstage is heavily populated by many hewers of wood and drawers of water. Television news items comprise one major source of such information. In the days immediately prior to the four day event, increasing attention is drawn to the transformation of urban space by (to use a much employed phrase) 'the army of workers' erecting scaffolding, banks of seats, wire mesh and concrete blocks. More discretely 'hidden away' is the staff of the central coordinating office; and by virtue of their being discrete, so more interpretive work is called for. Thus in *The News* (October 21, 1986) appears an article headed 'Behind the Scenes: a year long race to be ready', the initial emphasis of which is the sheer brevity of the Grand Prix as such:

But for the energetic staff in the Grand Prix office it is a year long race against the clock.

The clock started ticking for the 1986 race when the chequered flag fell (in 1985) on the formidable Keke Rosberg and his Williams car.

According to assistant Publicity Manager, Jacqueline Drewer, the hard working Grand Prix Staff Office met for a debriefing session that exciting November evening before joining the post race celebrations.

In short, these are utterly committed back stage actors and there are many more besides such as 'a legion of workers (who) transformed Adelaide's streets and parklands into an arena for the world's fastest cars and drivers' and the 'major medical back up operations' which range from 'a professor of neurosurgery to the St. John's Ambulance major contingent of 520 paid and volunteer workers' (*The News* October, 24, 1986).

So, just as the circus is internally differentiated, so too is the numerically substantial domain of the backstage. Furthermore, by virtue of some being able to move from the dimly lit rear to the bright lights of the frontstage, not only is the boundary between the two embellished and reinforced as salient: interpretive opportunities are also being created for making linkages between specific individual careers and generalized ideological currents at work in Australian society. Central to this process is the Grand Prix's Executive Director, Dr. Mal Hemmerling, for around this man in particular has emerged a mythical persona of considerable weight. In the early 1980s when the South Australian Government first made its bid to put Adelaide on the international Formula One circuit, Hemmerling was a senior public servant quite out of the public eye. But as the Grand Prix event took off in 1985 and was transformed from a state enterprise into a private company, so the Director's meteoric career trajectory became inseparable from the rise to prominence of the event itself. Throughout this period, Hemmerling has been defined by the mass media as 'the mastermind' behind the Grand Prix: but by 1987 he was unquestionably a prominent actor centre stage (as indicated by the fact that he figured prominently in Telecom's advertising campaign for cellular mobile phones: 'The Phone for Those Who Live in the Fast Lane', 'Do it because to win in business these days, you have to go flat out. Just ask Mal Hemmerling.') The way in which Hemmerling was presented, and indeed presents himself, is however particularly striking; this persistently emphasizes his own provincialism—a concern which, as we have seen, is resonant elsewhere. In an article in 1986 (*The News* October 23) bearing the characteristically alliterative headline 'Why Hemmerling may quit as guru of the Grand Prix,' he is asked what motivates him to endure the pressures of high executive office:

'I am South Australian through and through' he said. 'Money is not my motivation. For me to bring this event to S.A. and to make Adelaide one of the Grand Prix venues of the world is my motivational force.

'I believe Grand Prix racing is just starting in S.A. and is nowhere near its full potential...

'People now know that it is their race, not Mal Hemmerling's, not the Government's, but their race.'

On the one hand then, here is a man who emphasizes his provincial roots, on the other he is evidently a man of energy, drive and imagination. To this extent, it seems plausible to argue that the reason why he (of all previously backstage actors) has captured the public eye is that what is known of his career is readily decodable as a metaphor for the possibilities for individual advancement in an economically expanding society which (in numerous quarters) is considered to be classless. As the U.S.A. now so patently lacks the capacity to epitomize the open frontier in the late twentieth century, increasingly Australia—the lucky country, land of opportunity and Crocodile Dundee—has appropriated that symbolic ensemble. The narrative myth surrounding the Executive Director of the Grand Prix not only trades on that ideology but also reproduces it, the more so as this particular successful South Australian becomes linked in the public image via advertisements, news photos and television programs, with other 'high achievers' who have made good—not so much despite, as because of, their humble origins.

Super Men, Super Tech

While the Grand Prix Formula One circus is in many ways constituted as a different and distanced Other world, an elite domain which bears only the most limited resemblance to that of most Adelaide residents, as its inner complexities unfold it becomes mediated and assimilated into the economic and social arena of everyday lifeworlds. Over time and in diverse ways the Grand Prix circus comes to comprise a meta-social commentary on the content and character of city life. The juxtaposition of the city and the circus is a composite of separation and unity, of differentness and association. In the phase of dramatic climax, these dual themes are elaborated and embellished further as another emergent narrative focussing upon the relation between supermen and super technology, is increasingly developed.

In the week or so before the peak of the four day event, media coverage of all types assumes the dimensions of a flood. Television and radio commentaries—for example, 'Grand Prix Updates'—are increasingly presented in fast, slick, breathless form in such a way as to heighten the sense of climactic imminence. It is however in this mounting media blitz that the leading drivers are presented to the wider audience as, above all other considerations, men of consummate technological skill and total occupational professionalism. As they appear in the pits on the city racecourse which has been transformed into the physical hub of the event, the previous concern with their personalities and their social lives is accorded secondary status. In 'live interviews from the track' their comments are increasingly invited on the condition of the route, the mechanical facilities available, the technical problems which they have faced or which they now anticipate, the prospects concerning themselves and others vis-à-vis the world championship, and so forth. These considerations are now raised and the details unpacked not by local or regional newsmen but by the cosmopolitan commentators who follow the circus throughout its global itinerary. Some of these become leading personae in their own right such as Murray Walker who is presented as the doyen of this cohort, 'the voice behind the big race roar' (*News* October 24, 1986). Whether the drivers are single, divorced, or married, whether they live in Monaco or the Isle of Man, are earlier concerns which tend to be downplayed as they are paraded across the screen as an occupational elite of technological supremos.

To some extent the ground for the consolidation of this salient image has already been laid down: but motoring magazines, special glossy publications, and the like are in the main for *afficionados*. Immediately before the major event however the media focus becomes so intense that some specialist knowledge seeps through to a wider audience. We, as consumers of this media attention, are increasingly made aware of the variable factors which might affect the final outcome between Them. It now becomes evident for example that the apparently modest variable of the weather is much more than that: certain cars—previously much of a muchness—respond well to dry conditions whilst others thrive under more adverse ones: particular drivers favor, and are favored by, the one rather than the other. Again, much is made of the calibre of the different pit-stop teams who service the vehicles during the course of the race: their importance is driven home by reference to particular foul-ups where a tire change has taken twenty seconds rather than the ideal target of six or seven. We are introduced to some of the more important and refined products of the high technology on which Their success or failure will crucially hinge. For example, one recurrent message is that the racing car tires bear only the most superficial resemblance to those on the family car: they are produced at exceptional cost and incorporate endless technological refinements; and besides lacking treads, they have a short life which cannot be accurately predicted. It is this kind of modest acquired knowledge which allows the audience at large, no doubt in hugely variable degree, to make on-going sense of particular twists and turns prior to 'the big race' and during it. This is knowledge which We can deploy as moments of high drama emerge either as directly observed or as mediated by the screen. Even if in only elementary fashion, We can now make sense of, in the 1986 race for example, the blow-out of Mansell's rear tire. This proved to be quite the most spectacular development in the Grand Prix so far since it occurred in an open stretch of track at high speed and produced a huge shower of sparks. But We were already sensitized to the reasons as to why this might happen and its ramifications: tires, We have been informed, render vulnerable the ambitions of even the most skillful drivers; and with this particular instance taking place in front of our eyes (and endlessly replayed subsequently), We were also aware that the ambitions of the man best placed hitherto to win the world championship now lay in ruins.

It is doubtless the case that as the climax of the Formula One race takes place, its own properties of high drama, of men 'dicing with death' and similar rhetorical imagery, exercise their full force. On the other hand, *the race* is better comprehended if we are to fully appreciate its potential for engagement as the final thread of an unfolding and on-going narrative in which men have to triumph over technology in order to compete successfully with one another. By this stage, the audience is reasonably aware that certain drivers and their vehicles have but the most limited chances of coming out on top. Its shared knowledge is sufficient to make sense of the significance of, for example, one driver giving way to another, the likely consequences of an unduly extended pit-stop. And the audience at large can recognize and give meaning to the manifestations of personal enmities as these are occurring out on the track. Yet at a more profound level, We can sense that the triumph of one superman over another is entirely contingent upon his ability to master the high technology in his hands. There is an ordering of power relationships here in which that between man and technology assumes an inescapable determinacy over that between man and man. In full public view, the final outcome rests upon the command which these members of an elite coterie have over technology in order to realize their mastery over one another. Realizing the technological potential of their racing cars is the means of creating hierarchy within their own ranks. One might suggest therefore that in this iconography is embedded the ultimate fascination of the Grand Prix, the race's own potential for engagement. For while the ostensible story line centres upon the contest on the track between Alain, Ayrton, Nigel and Nelson, the more profound narrative theme draws upon and symbolically represents the power relation which underpins the rise of modern society. The immediate contest between exceptional men and exceptional technologies serves as a symbolic synchronic metaphor for the material diachronic emergence of modern industrial society.

Gender and Power, Grand Prix and Society

The general argument advanced here then is that the impact of the Grand Prix derives from its being variously grounded in the sites, processes, and structures of everyday life in Adelaide. The symbolic import of the race as climax derives from its serving as a powerful metaphorical statement about the conditions under which society in general has emerged. In conclusion we again bring to the fore what is a latent yet nevertheless consistent undercurrent to the Adelaide Grand Prix, namely the form and content of gender relations since these too are so constituted as to reflect and reinforce certain ever-present aspects of Australian society.

There are a number of evident ways in which the Grand Prix is a male affair. The drivers are all men, so too are their support teams, the leading media commentators, the more prominent organizers, and the majority of spectators. At the same time, women do figure as, so to speak, a submerged narrative thread in the Grand Prix in the sense that their collective status is neither especially prominent nor particularly public. To return to an early point of departure, the initial identity as constructed by much advertising is that of woman as household provider. Her assumed role is to provision others with basic requirements in the private domestic domain: she is a responsive and innovative purchaser but only in a subordinate capacity to her menfolk. Thus in a regular cooking feature in *The News*, the resident female columnist writes:

The big race warms up tomorrow and Adelaide comes alive. Quick, convenient, easy to prepare dinners and lunches will be necessary over this busy weekend.

The headline to this reads 'Fast food for quick Grand Prix stops': the message is that the woman is ever innovative yet ever subordinate also. Not so much by way of alternative as by way of extension, if the woman appears in an independent capacity on this scenario it is as a female acutely concerned with matters of personal appearance and contemporary fashion. Thus daily consumer columns in newspapers or occasional radio and television commentaries are concerned with what might be worn to the Grand Prix or to major supporting events such as the Grand Prix Ball, increasingly a major social event on the elite calendar. What men are wearing is never of consequence: how women dress themselves consistently is. So in the 'Image' (sic) column of *The News* (October 21, 1986) appears a full page spread with the heading 'Our Celebrity belles of the Grand Prix circuit':

> The News asked our best known female celebrities to model their fashion choices for this exclusive preview of what the fashion leaders will be wearing on and off the circuit.
>
> Looking cool and casual for relaxing around the circuit or gorgeously glamorous for a myriad of social functions at this time, our local ladies are doing us proud.

These words are surrounded by several photographs of 'Channel 7's lovely newsreader,' 'Channel 2 weathergirl,' 'Channel 7's stunning Wheel of Fortune hostess' and 'Channel 10's charming Touch of Elegance hostess.'

The third role in which women are cast is that of 'the dolly bird' ranging from the bikini-clad models in chain store and supermarket brochures to those selling or giving away free samples in spectators' enclosures around the race circuit. In the medium of glossy motor car publications, they are draped across vehicle bodies or photographed in the laps of ace drivers: in 1987 a publicity innovation involved 'grid girls' who would 'perform a dance routine before the start of the great race,' 'keep their traditional role of protecting anxious Formula One drivers from the blazing sun,' whilst 'their body-hugging Speedo costumes are bound to give record crowd a big lift' (*News* October 30, 1987). Finally, even where particular women come to the fore by dint of their being members of the cosmopolitan and international elite drawn from overseas to this provincial place, their secondary and subordinate status is confirmed. For these women appear as the dedicated, endlessly supportive, long suffering wives of the leading drivers: the pathos of their condition is powerfully contrasted with the excitement and high repute enjoyed by their husbands. Typical of this theme is the Adelaide *News* article (October 28, 1986) entitled 'Grand Prix Wives: the terror at track's edge':

> The drivers' wives share a special bond, whether they are friends or mere acquaintances.
>
> Only they know the terror and pain of watching their men defy death during every race on the circuit.
>
> Even when all goes well, and hubby takes the checkered flag without a hitch, their nerves are still raw and ragged for days afterwards.
>
> ...The saying 'behind every great man is a great woman,' is especially applicable to the wives and girlfriends of these dare devil men...
>
> For many drivers and their wives, Sunday meant an end to months of living on the edge and a return to family life for a little while at least.

Alternatively consider the article in the same newspaper (October 21, 1986) where a half portrait photograph of 'Beautiful Sina Rosberg' is followed by this commentary:

> Since her marriage to the ace driver, she has lived through the tension of high speed tracks and race days.
>
> But on Sunday, after the Formula One Grand Prix, the worry will end—Keke will retire...
>
> Whether he wins or not, for Sina the trauma will finally be over.

Even the 'prominent' women therefore are cast in an ancillary role: they suffer, they are traumatized, they know pain—but they are consistently supportive. Elsewhere in the social scale, they are subordinate purveyors of Grand Prix commodities; or they are more widely exhorted to innovate within their customary consumer-provisioner role in the private domain of the household. By default, as it were, their concerns are not the concerns of their menfolk: they are the secondary characters in a multiplicity of staged performances dominated and controlled by those of the opposite sex.

To this extent the roles played out by women during the Grand Prix, or those accorded to them by those who order the images purveyed by the mass media, not only reflect but also reproduce the characteristic divisions of labor on gender lines which are encountered in Australian society at large. More generally, the crucial point to be emphasized is that whilst the Grand Prix can be said to transform certain aspects of Adelaide urban society, its overall character is such as to reproduce intact and therefore reinforce the patterns of social differentiation and inequalities of power which are customarily embedded in this modern urban milieu. While the advent of the Grand Prix provides a near-infinite range of novel prospects for selling mass merchandise, the characteristically inegalitarian patterns of commodity purchasing remain unchanged. While the residents of Adelaide may ephemerally savour the focus of international attention generated by the Grand Prix, its semi-peripheral status—with all the disadvantages which this brings in a modern global order—is essentially reproduced. The arrival and brief sojourn of the metropolitan megastars assuredly provides entertainment and excitement for those who witness it at first hand or through the mass media: yet ultimately the material inequalities between cosmopolitans and locals are as pronounced as ever. Finally, while at one level, the contest for prestige and privilege between men centres upon their ability to control the products of modern technology, at another level the lines of social differentiation between male and female are not so much contested as wholly taken for granted.

At this juncture it should be clearly acknowledged that the lines of social differentiation and social inequalities of which I have made mention are indeed diverse. At first glance they do not appear to be comparable and to associate them together in this fashion may seem idiosyncratic. But this diversity is precisely the consideration which, I propose, needs to be brought to the fore in the anthropological analysis of major processes and events in contemporary Australian society, for inequalities of power are as much a property of interpersonal relations as they are of the global order, social differentiation is as much a characteristic of gender associations as it is of relations between cosmopolitans and locals, and the reproduction of inegalitarianism in the consumer domain is as much a feature of extraordinary events as it is part and parcel of everyday life. Unless we recognize the especially diffuse, diverse and discrete character of power relations in present-day Australian society, then we are likely to remove from anthropological view precisely those key attributes which render power relations opaque and miasmic to those whose lives are encompassed by them.

Thus the final generalized property of Adelaide's Grand Prix which merits emphasis is that the diffuse and diverse character of the power relations which permeate it, is rendered especially opaque by virtue of the event's seemingly non-political quality as a secular urban performance. Inasmuch as the varied narrative themes which engage the population at large are ostensibly lacking in overt and recognizable political significance, so the mass event in its entirety can be entered into in a spirit of entertainment, fun, relaxation and leisure: this is, in short, time-out from the routines and rigors of everyday life. The event has all the appearance of being apolitical from the early phrase in which the circus is heralded as being on its way, through to the finale at which the winners spray the assembled crowd with champagne. Without question this apparently apolitical character is the most crucial property of the Adelaide Grand Prix in that while its ostensible status is that of pure entertainment, a ludic event which can be savored by the mass in leisured fashion either from the grandstand or in the domestic setting, as a secular urban celebration it is wholly confirmatory of the sources of political inequality which permeate everyday life. Its narrative, iconic themes ephemerally engage whilst the structures of society which give meaning to such narratives persistently and permanently encompass.

Works Cited

(For two reasons this paper contains no specific reference to other literature. First this is a preliminary analysis arising from the dominant themes of the event itself rather than any particular theoretical perspective. Second the Grand Prix cannot be effectively categorized as a festival, fair, secular event or carnival as these have been defined in the anthropological literature previously. But I have benefitted from reading some of this literature and it is the more germane of the anthropological studies which are listed below).

Alomes, Stephen. "Parades of Meaning: The Moomba Festival and Contemporary Culture," *Journal of Australian Studies* 17, pp. 3-17, 1985.

Barthes, Roland. *Mythologiques*, Paladin, London, 1980.

Blonsky, Marshall (ed). *On Signs: A Semiotics Reader*, Blackwell, London, 1985.

Brass, Tom. 'Cargos and Conflict: The Fiesta System and Capitalist Development in Eastern Peru,' *Journal of Peasant Studies*, 13:45-62, 1986.

Cohen, Abner. 'A Polyethnic Carnival as Contested Cultural Performance,' *Racial and Ethnic Studies*, vol. 5, no. 1. pp. 23-41, 1982.

Coward, Rosalind and John Ellis. *Language and Materialism: Developments in Semiology and the Theory of the Subject*, Routledge & Kegan Paul, London, 1982.

da Matta, Roberto. 'Constraint and License: A Preliminary Study of Two Brazilian National Rituals' in Sally F. Moore and Barbara Meyerhoff (eds) *Secular Ritual*, Van Gorcum, Amsterdam, 1977.

Falassi, Alessandro (ed). *Time out of Time: Essays on the Festival*, University of New Mexico Press, Albuquerque, 1987.

Gottdiener, M. and A.P. Lagopoulos. *The City and the Sign: An Introduction to Urban Semiotics*, Columbia University Press, New York, 1987.

Lasch, Christopher. *The Minimal Self: Psychic Survival in Troubled Times*, Picador, London, 1984.

Lavenda, Robert H. 'The Festival of Progress: The Globalizing World System and the Transformation of the Caracas Carnival' *Journal of Popular Culture*, vol. 14, no. 3. pp. 465-75, 1980.

Manning, Frank E. 'Cosmos and Chaos: Celebration in the Modern World,' in Frank E. Manning (ed) *The Celebration of Society: Perspectives on Contemporary Cultural Performance*, Bowling Green University Popular Press, Bowling Green, Ohio, 1983.

—— 'Carnival and the West Indian Diaspora' in Gerald Gold (ed) *Minorities and Mother Country Imagery*, Institute of Economic and Social Research, Memorial University of Newfoundland, 1984.

Mewett, Peter. "Darwin's 'Beercan Regatta': Masculinity, Frontier and Festival in North Australia," *Social Analysis* No. 23, pp. 3-37, 1988.

Meyerhoff, Barbara and Stephen Mongulla. "The Los Angeles Jews' 'Walk for Solidarity':" Parade, Festival, Pilgrimage" in Henri Varenne (ed) *Symbolizing America*, University of Nebraska Press, Nebraska, 1986.

Moore, Sally Falk and Barbara Meyerhoff (eds) *Symbol and Politics in Communal Ideology: Cases and Questions*, Cornell University Press, Ithaca, 1975.

Truth and Goodness, Mirrors and Masks: A Sociology of Beauty and the Face

Anthony Synnott

The importance of the human body in society is undeniable. Body language and face language (as well as head language, in such manifestations as ears and hair) speak, as we say, volumes. We read the face with our eyes, and if we are blind we read the Braille of the face with our sensitive finger tips—and read characters, emotion, intentions and philosophy with our eyes and fingers. The most powerful part of the face is, of course, the eyes, which shine forth in dozens of expressions, from tenderness to thunder. Study of the body and face is undoubtedly as old as the earliest humanoid's recognition of the separateness yet associativeness of two bodies. There has always been a need for an anthropology and sociology of the body and face. This present detailed study demonstrates how there could be such sociologies of other artifacts and phenomena of human existence.

What is the face? The face, as unique, physical, malleable and public is the prime symbol of the self. It is unique, for no two faces are identical, and it is in the face that we recognize each other, and identify ourselves. Pictures of our faces grace our passports and identification papers. The face is physical, and therefore personal and intimate, yet the face is also "made up," "put on" and subject to fashion. And, malleable, with its eighty mimetic muscles, the face is capable of over 7,000 expressions.

Furthermore, the face indicates the age, gender and race of the self with varying degrees of accuracy, also our health and socio-economic status, our moods and emotions, even perhaps our character and personality. The face is also the site of four of our five senses: sight, taste, smell and hearing, and the site for our intakes of food, drink and air. It is also the source of verbal communication, and an important source for non-verbal communication. Gloria Swanson once said: "We didn't need dialogue. We had faces." Moreover the face is also the principal determinant in the perception of our individual beauty or ugliness, and

Reprinted in slightly different format from that printed in the *British Journal of Sociology*, December 1989 and March 1990, with permission of the author and Routledge Press.

all that these perceptions imply for self-esteem and life-chances. The face indeed symbolizes the self, and part of the body, we identify the face as *me* or *you*. Nothing indicates the significance of the face more than the failure to recognize faces and facial expressions. Dr. Sacks has described one such person, a victim of Korsakov's syndrome who, during the medical examination, apparently mistook his wife for a hat, and tried to, literally, pick her up to put on his head; not surprisingly, he could not recognize facial expressions either. Yet another patient, horrifyingly, could not recognize his own face in a mirror (1987: 11-13, 21).

The face, however, and indeed beauty and the physical body also, have been largely ignored by mainstream sociology, at least until relatively recently. Indeed only Simmel (1901/1965) and Veblen (1899/1953) among the early sociologists and later Mauss (1936) and Mead (1949) concerned themselves seriously with this area which we now refer to as the sociology of the body (Douglas, 1973; Polhemus, 1975; Turner, 1984; Berthelot et al, 1985; Synnott, 1987).

In the last few years, however, beauty, attractiveness and the face have been researched by historians (Freedman, 1986; Banner, 1983, Steele, 1985), feminists (Lakoff and Scherr, 1984), journalists (Baker, 1984), anthropologists (Boone, 1986; Brain, 1979; Ebin, 1979), social psychologists (Berscheid and Walster, 1978), sociologists (Patzer, 1985), photographers (Fisher, 1984; Kirk, 1981; Virel, 1980), art historians (Thevoz, 1981; Clark, 1980)—just to mention books, not articles, and only those within the last ten years. Evidently these matters are increasingly being considered important, and from many perspectives.

Physically, psychologically and socially, the face is hard to ignore, and its significance in the acquisition of a self and in social interaction can hardly be overestimated. In this paper, however, we consider first the equations of beauty as goodness and goodness as beauty. The beauty mystique, as I call this equation, dates back to Plato, and perhaps to Homer, and has had profound implications for the beautiful, as well as for the physically handicapped and the ugly, in Graeco-Roman cultures. We then consider the face, and particularly the belief that the face reflects the character of the individual; this facism, as I call it, ascribes a special quality to the face, and dates back to Aristotle and again perhaps to Homer. In practice, however, the beauty mystique and facism are conceptually linked, since beauty is perceived as residing principally in the face. These twin beliefs are then traced from the Greeks and the Romans, through Christianity to the Renaissance and up to modern times.

The face may be a *mask*, however, for it is malleable: expressions like masks can be interchanged. This matter is discussed next, followed by the face as *art*, including both make-up and cosmetic surgery. Both topics relate to the presentation of the self and impression-management. Yet beauty and make-up are controversial; the face is therefore a *battle-field*.

The immense and increasing social significance of beauty in general and the face in particular can be seen in economic terms. In the United States sales of beauty aids have increased from $40 million in 1914, for a per capita expenditure of 40 cents per annum, to about $17 *billion* in 1985, for a per capita expenditure of about $70 per annum. The industry achieved a 10% earnings gain over the previous year and the cosmetics stock price index rose 29% in 1986, as compared with a 15% gain for the market as a whole (Raines, 1974; Standard and Poor, 1988: H34-5). Comparable data for the United Kingdom are not available, but evidently beauty is big business, and getting bigger. The beauty mystique is growing stronger rather than weaker.

The first modern beauty contest, apart from the judgement of Paris in Greek mythology, was conducted by Phineas T. Barnum in the United States in 1854, with the people as judges.[1] The Miss America contest was staged in 1921 and was followed by Miss World (1951) and Miss Universe (1952). Quite apart from the thousands of local competitions, in municipalities, universities, football teams, etc., the national pageants in the United States now include Miss Black America, Miss Teen U.S.A., Little Miss America, Mrs. America, Miss Wheelchair America, Miss Pork Queen (sponsored by the Pork Industry), Miss Nude World, the World's Most Beautiful Tattooed Lady and Miss Man Made (for transsexuals). There are relatively few beauty competitions for men, but these include Mr. Olympia, won by Arnold Schwarzenegger seven times, and Mr. Gay America (Burwell and Bowles, 1987; 3-14; Russell, 1986: 20,168; Banner, 1983: 249-70). In the United Kingdom, the competitions include the "Face of the Eighties," Miss Lovely Legs, Long is Lovely (for hair), English Rose and Miss Pears (soap).

In 1983 Poland was the first Eastern block country to send a contestant to the Miss World competition. In 1985 the first beauty contests were held in Hungary and China. And in 1988, under the auspices of Glasnost, Moscow had its first beauty contest. Only Muslim countries do not hold such contests. Thus the beauty mystique is increasingly being institutionalized around the world.

The high value set on beauty is indicated by data from France, where the majority of the people believe it is better to be lucky than beautiful, but the majority also believe it is better to be beautiful than rich (Bourdieu, 1984: 204). Beauty nonetheless remains controversial. In 1984 it was expected that one-third of the population of the United States would watch the Miss America beauty contest on television; but in that same year in the Old World, the BBC decided to stop televising beauty contests, deeming them "anachronistic and almost offensive" (*New York Times*, 11.9.84; 25.11.84).

The most conclusive evidence of the socio-economic significance of beauty and ugliness is presented by Kaczorowski (1988), in his study of the Canadian Quality of Life panel survey of 4,000 full-time workers conducted by York University in 1977, 1979, and 1981. Kaczorowski has shown that good looks and high incomes are highly correlated. Thus in 1977 the "good-looking" (37% of the sample) earned 75%, i.e. about $6,000, more than the "ugly," and the "ugly," with average incomes of $8,000, only earned 57% of the average incomes of the good-looking. This relationship holds even with such intervening variables held constant as age, years of education, unionization, number of years with company, and so on. Furthermore, Kaczorowski has shown that good looks determine wealth, rather than vice versa, as might have been expected. One explanation for the difference is the applicability of the halo/horns effects: the good-looking were much more likely to be judged sincere in their responses by the trained interviewers; 81% of the good-looking were said to be sincere compared to only 59% of the ugly; conversely 41% of the ugly were deemed to be insincere compared to only 18% of the good-looking. Evidently looks do matter. Although there has been some research on the socio-economic and legal dimensions of such related areas as height (Keyes, 1980; Miller, 1987), obesity (Millman, 1981; Baker, 1982), and physical handicaps (Murphy, 1987), this is the first national study on aesthetic inequality, and indicates the immense importance of beauty and the face.

Various caveats must be entered here. First, the face as physical is of course part of the body; for the purposes of this discussion, however, it is necessary to keep the two topics conceptually separate despite the obvious overlaps. Second, the roles of the face in non-verbal communication and emotional expression have been so extensively researched and reviewed (Darwin 1955; Morris, 1977; Knapp, 1980; and others) that they are not presented here in detail. Also, the fashions of facial beauty, which have changed over the years, have to be omitted for reasons of space (see Brophy, 1963; Liggett, 1974; Freedman, 1986; Banner, 1983; Steele, 1985). The most recent developments here have been the emergence of the protest faces of the Skinheads, with safety pins or other objects through the cheeks, nose or earlobes, foreheads and lips tattooed, sometimes with obscenities, and the unconventional hair styles of both the Skins and the Punks (Synnott, 1987). The practical matter of the role of beauty in social mobility ("My face is my fortune, sir, she said") also has to be omitted; but the literature in empirical sociology is reviewed by Maruyama and Miller (1981), Berscheid and Gangestad (1982), Cash and Janda (1984), and Patzer (1985). The differential significance of physical appearance for men and women is also not considered here. Our principal concern here is the semiotics of beauty, especially facial beauty, however defined.

Beauty is defined by the Concise Oxford as "Combination of qualities, as shape, proportion, colour, in human face or form, or in other objects, that delights the sight." This reflects the earlier definitions of beauty by Aristotle and Aquinas, as we shall see; but such definitions do not and cannot de-code the full significance of beauty and, by implication, the human face and body. Their significance is immense, psychological and sociological, economic and literary, philosophical and even theological; they are entwined with non-verbal communication, mood and character assessment, social mobility, helping behavior of all sorts, sexuality and a wide range of personal and moral qualities; furthermore beauty may be seen as physical or spiritual, inner or outer, natural or artificial, subjective or objective, positive or even negative. Beauty is therefore a rich and powerful phenomenon, with many meanings at different levels or in different dimensions at different frequencies. These themes and textures weave in and out of one another over time, appearing and re-appearing, perhaps with subtly different implications. I try, however, to tie these themes together in a sociology of the body in the conclusion.

The Good: Plato and Beauty

The beauty mystique, in its simplest form, is the belief that the beautiful is good, and the ugly is evil; and conversely that the morally good is physically beautiful (or "good-looking") and the evil is ugly. Thus the physical and the metaphysical, body and soul, appearance and reality, inner and outer, are one. Each mirrors the other.

The belief is most ancient. In *The Iliad*, Homer equated evil and ugliness in his description of the loathed Therstis (Bk. 2; 1983: 45):

He was the ugliest man that had come to Illium. He had a game foot and was bandy-legged. His rounded shoulders almost met across his chest; and above them rose an egg-shaped head, which sprouted a few short hairs.

He looked like the villain he was, and not unlike a Fleming villain. Similarly in *The Odyssey*, the only villain, apart from Penelope's suitors, was the one-eyed giant, Cyclops. Odysseus, on the other hand, was "radiant with comeliness and grace" (1981:108). These are the first indications of the identification of the good and the beautiful, the evil and the ugly.

Plato, however, established the beauty mystique on a metaphysical base which is now an intrinsic part of Western culture. In the *Greater Hippias* (206-304) he argues that beauty is good and the good is beautiful: the two are identical (1963:1549-58; cf *Lysis* 216). But he made the point most clearly in the *Symposium* (211) where he provided the philosophical ground not only for Plotinus, Augustine and Aquinas, but also for the moderns. In this dialogue several of the literary celebrities of Athenian society make speeches in praise of love. Sexual, specifically homosexual love, is the topic; but in Socrates' speech, Plato shifts ground to develop his theory of beauty as the object of love, and to describe the increasingly abstract or ideal types of beauty which ultimately culminate in pure or absolute beauty, transcending sex, sensuality and "mere" physical beauty. Here Diotima instructs Socrates that there is a scale of perfection ranging from individual, physical beauty up the "heavenly ladder" to Absolute beauty (1963: 562-3):

Starting from individual beauties, the quest for the universal beauty must find [the candidate] ever mounting the heavenly ladder, stepping from rung to rung—that is from one to two, and from two to every lovely body, from bodily beauty to the beauty of institutions, from institutions to learning, and from learning in general to the special lore that pertains to nothing but the beautiful itself—until at last he comes to know what beauty is.

Now this vision of the beautiful subsists "by itself in an eternal oneness, while every lovely thing partakes of it in such sort that, however much the parts may wax and wane, it will be neither more nor less, but still the same inviolable whole." This absolute beauty, she concludes, is Love, and Socrates adds that "all my life I shall pay the power and the might of Love such homage as I can" (*Symposium* 211-2; 1963: 562-3).

Thus beauty, in Plato's philosophy, is not an isolated quality— it is identical with good and it is the object of Love; it is also identical with happiness, for happiness is possessing the good and the contemplation of beauty (*Symposium*); it is connected also to wisdom, for "Wisdom is the most beautiful, and ignorance the most shameful of all things" (*Greater Hippias* 296; 1963: 1549). Wisdom, which is the pursuit of knowledge and truth, in turn leads to happiness (*Meno* 88c; 1963: 373), and is the characteristic of the guardians, the rulers of the city (*Republic* 4, 428; 1963: 670).[2] Thus the soul rises on its wings to "the plain of Truth," to "the region where the gods dwell" or "by ugliness and evil, it is wasted and destroyed" (*Phaedrus* 246-8; 1963: 493-5).

Beauty is therefore a central idea in the philosophy and politics of Plato. His equations can be expressed schematically as follows:

beauty	:	ugliness
goodness	:	evil
wisdom	:	ignorance
truth	:	lies
love	:	hate
happiness	:	unhappiness
God	:	waste and destruction

This metaphysic of beauty has a corollary, however. The ranking of spiritual and moral beauty above physical implied, as Diotima warned, that "the beauty of the body is not, after all, of so great moment"; furthermore, "once you have seen [this vision of the very soul of beauty] you will never be seduced again by the charms of gold, of dress, of comely boys, or lads just ripening to manhood" (*Symposium* 210-11; 1963: 562-3). This was, of course, a clear challenge to the Greek love of beauty, particularly physical beauty. That this challenge was not a coincidence is reinforced later in the evening by Alcibiades' drunken confession that he had tried to seduce Socrates, unsuccessfully, "because, you know, he doesn't really care a row of pins about good looks—on the contrary, you can't think how much he despises them—or money, or any of the honors that most people care about" (*Symposium* 216; 1963: 568). Physical beauty and moral beauty, sex and the good, are clearly polarized.

Plato's ascetic attitude to beauty and the body was strongly influenced by the Orphic doctrine of *soma—sema*: body—tomb. In *Phaedo* (65c-67d), Socrates explains that the body is an "impediment," and "imperfection," "interrupting, disturbing, distracting and preventing us from getting a glimpse of the truth"; it is impure and infects, contaminates, enslaves and shackles us. Indeed it is a source of evil (1963: 48-50). Again, it is a prison (*Phaedo*, 82; *Phaedrus*, 250; 1963: 66,497); an enemy (*Timaeus*, 70e; 1963: 1194); and perhaps a tomb, as the Orphics believed (*Cratylus*, 400c; *Gorgias*, 493a; 1963: 437,275). The range of metaphors is startling, but the dualism is clear. Body and soul are not only separate and unequal but opposed as inferior to superior.

This contrast is clearest when Socrates advises: "let us seek the *true* beauty, not asking whether a face is fair, or anything of that sort, for all such things appear to be in a flux" (*Cratylus*, 439d; 1963: 473). And praying to Pan, Socrates asks: "grant that I may become fair *within*" (*Phaedrus* 279d; 1963: 525). Thus although physical beauty may lead to the absolute, the body, beautiful or otherwise, is not only inferior to the soul, but even an enemy, a tomb, a prison of the soul.

The Greeks loved beauty, as their architecture, statuary, pottery, coins and mosaics show; and they loved the beauty and power of the male body competing, nude, in the Olympic Games for a thousand years. Aristotle even said that beauty is "the gift of God" (Laertius, 1972: 461), which surely implied that ugliness is, or may be, a punishment from God.[3] If the one is positive, the other is negative. This asceticism in the thought, and the life, of Socrates was therefore extremely unpopular in the hedonist climate of Greece; nonetheless Plato's philosophy exerted enormous influence in Christianity, particularly through Plotinus and Saint Augustine.

Sappho perhaps reflected Plato's metaphysics, but turned it into a synthesis of ethics and aesthetics: "What is beautiful is good, and who is good will soon be beautiful." Yet many Greeks were skeptical about beauty. Theophrastus, who succeeded Aristotle at the Peripatetic school, described beauty as "a mute deception"; and Theocritus said it was "an evil in an ivory setting" (Laertius, 1972: 463). Euripides, often a critic of his society, spoke strongly against beauty in *Orestes* (408 B.C.), when Electra blames the beautiful Helen for all the deaths in the Trojan War (lines 126-7):

> Oh, what a vileness human beauty is,
> Corroding, corrupting everything it touches.

Vain, Dung and God: Christianity and Beauty

Beauty has been equally controversial in Judaeo-Christian thought. The Bible warns against beauty; according to *Proverbs* (31:30) "beauty is vain."[4] Isaiah (28:1) said that "beauty is a fading flower," and Jeremiah inveighed against beauty (4:30), and the ascetics ignored the conventional beauty and dress norms, from Samson to John the Baptist. This philosophy is entirely compatible with the early Greek ascetic tradition expressed in Plato's Orphism.

On the other hand, the Biblical story of creation asserts the goodness of creation: "And God saw everything that he had made, and behold, it was very good" (Gen. 1:31). Furthermore in the Song of Solomon, the bride and the king praise each other's beauty and goodness in earthy and physical rather than metaphysical terms.

Christ did not impinge directly on this discussion of face and beauty, but he did further the debate between, for want of better words, the hedonists and the ascetics, on the body. On the one hand the body is important and good. Thus Christ taught his disciples to look after the physical as well as the spiritual needs of others. On the other hand Christ himself led an ascetic life of poverty, chastity and obedience, with fasting, prayers, watches and solitude and even death. Saint Paul likewise taught a balance. On the one hand the body is good and holy: "Know ye not that your bodies are the members of Christ?...Know ye not that your body is the temple of the Holy Ghost?" (I Cor. 6:15, 19). On the other hand the body is also an enemy: "I bruise my own body and make it know its master" (I Cor. 9:27; cf. Synnott, 1988a).

Saint Paul's asceticism was probably no more typical of the Roman Empire than Plato's had been in Greece or the prophets' had been in Ancient Israel. Ovid (1957, 1968), whose numerous affairs were celebrated in somewhat libidinous poetry, and whose advice on hygiene, make-up and beauty was the first of its kind, was probably far more typical of the era. The Stoic philosophers, however, did also practice asceticism. In his essay "On adornment," Epictetus advised a young man "with his hair elaborately arranged," "If you would be beautiful, make this the object of your effort, human virtue...For you are not flesh, nor hair, but a rational will: if you get this beautiful then you will be beautiful" (1968: 142, 145).

The Christian love of beauty is evident in Christian creations: the Gothic cathedrals, the stained glass, the Gregorian chant, illuminated manuscripts, the religious statuary and art—all created "to the greater glory of God" and reflecting the beauty and goodness of God and inspiring towards the worship of God. Yet always there is tension and movement, a balance, and a fine line between love of beauty for its own sake and for the love of God.

In his development of Plato's ascetics and metaphysics, Plotinus retained Plato's idea of the ladder of beauty (I:6; 1956: 56-64); and Beauty, together with the One and the Good are the names of the Absolute: the One is "beauty above beauty" (VI:7, 32). He also maintained Plato's dualism, polarizing Matter and Soul, evil and good, ugly and beautiful: "A Soul becomes ugly...by sinking itself into the alien, by a fall, a descent into the body, into Matter" (I:6, 5; 1956: 60). He seems to have experienced this dualism personally, for Porphyry, his friend and biographer, records that he "seemed ashamed of being in the body," and refused to sit for his portrait (1956: 1). Indeed, he dismissed beauties of the body as "copies, vestiges, shadows" of Beauty, and not to be pursued. What should be pursued, he said, is beauty of the soul (V.8; 1956: 433):

We ourselves possess beauty when we are true to our own being; our ugliness is in going over to another order; our self-knowledge, that is to say, is our beauty; in self-ignorance we are ugly.

And he advised his readers: "Let each become godlike and each beautiful who cares to see God and Beauty" (I: 6; 1956: 64). This equation of God and Beauty is reiterated by Saint Augustine in his famous prayer. But for Augustine matter is not evil and ugly, nor is physical beauty a shadow; matter is good, and beauty reflects God, for God is Beauty, and Beauty is God (*Confessions*, Bk. 10, 27; 1961: 231-2):

I have learnt to love you late, Beauty at once so ancient and so new! I have learnt to love you late! You were within me, and I was in the world outside myself. I searched for you outside myself and, disfigured as I was, I fell upon the lovely things of your creation...The beautiful things of this world kept me from you and yet, if they had not been in you, they would have had no being at all.

Saint Augustine was fascinated by beauty and, following Plato, used his love of beauty in its many aspects to help him love the beauty of God (cf. *Confessions*, Bk. 10, 6; 1961:211-2). As with Plato, the beautiful is the good, but the temporal is not the spiritual, and the two should not be confused (*Confessions*, Bk. 11, 4; 1961: 256-7):

It was you, then, O Lord, who made [earth and the heavens], you who are beautiful, for they too are beautiful; you who are good, for they too are good; you who ARE, for they too are. But they are not beautiful and good as you are beautiful and good.

Saint Jerome (345-420), a contemporary of Saint Augustine's, was less pre-occupied by beauty but observed the face; indeed his is a classic statement of facism, echoing Cicero: "The face is the mirror of the mind, and eyes without speaking confess the secrets of the heart" (Letter 54; 1975: 251).

Boethius (c475-525), who was immensely popular throughout medieval Europe and whose ideas permeate the thought of Chaucer and Dante, continued the mainstream of thinking about beauty from Plato to Augustine. Indeed God is described as the "height of beauty" (1969: 97). Yet Philosophy, in the person of a lady, warns Boethius against (physical) beauty (1969: 92):

The sleek looks of beauty are fleeting and transitory, more ephemeral than the blossom in spring. If, as Aristotle said, we...could see right through things, even the body of an Alcibiades, so fair on the surface, would look thoroughly ugly once we had seen the bowels inside. Your own nature doesn't make you beautiful. It is due to the weak eyesight of the people who see you.

This ascetic orientation in Christian thought emphasized the difference between Creator and Creation, and was expressed in practical terms in the asceticism of the Desert Fathers in the early church, and in the monastic movements of the eleventh to the thirteenth centuries. Concomitant with the new asceticism was a new militarism in the Crusades; and Saint Bernard of Clairvaux, who inspired the Second Crusade, echoed Plotinus when he said that "Interior beauty is more comely than external ornament, more even than the pomp of kings." Indeed he declared bluntly that (physical) beauty is "dung" (Eco, 1986: 9,7):

We who have turned aside from society, relinquishing for Christ's sake all the precious and beautiful things in the world, its wondrous light and colour, its sweet sounds and odours, the pleasures of taste and touch, for us all bodily delights are nothing but dung...

Physical beauties are "dung" for Saint Bernard, as they are "copies, vestiges, shadows" for Plotinus, and "fleeting and ephemeral" for Boethius. Yet for Saint Augustine all things are beautiful for they are created by God who is Beauty and are in his image. Physical beauty has therefore been a matter of some controversy in Christian thought, depending on whether the body is evaluated positively or negatively.

Yet elsewhere the same Saint Bernard argues that spiritual beauty shines in the body which in turn, as an image (mirror?) of the mind, becomes beautiful (Eco, 1986: 10):

When the brightness of beauty has replenished to overflowing the recesses of the heart, it is necessary that it should emerge into the open, just like the light hidden under a bushel: a light shining in the dark is not trying to conceal itself. The body is an image of the mind, which, like an effulgent light scattering forth its rays, is diffused through its members and senses.

Gilbert of Hoyt expressed a similar view: "have regard also for the bodily countenance whose grace can be seen in its abundant beauty; for the exterior face can refresh the spirit of those who look upon it, and nourish us with the grace of the interior to which it witnesses" (Eco, 1986: 10). The body, in this view, may be inferior to the immortal soul, but the body and the face reflect light and grace and beauty. They *mirror* the soul.

Saint Thomas Aquinas, however, did not believe that "inner" and "outer" were connected, that physical beauty mirrored spiritual beauty. Indeed he distinguished clearly between them: "Beauty of body consists in shapely limbs and features having a certain proper glow of colour. So also beauty of spirit consists in conversations and actions that are well-formed and suffused with intelligence" (*Summa Theologiae* 2-2: 145, 2; Vol. 35, 1981: 75). Furthermore we share the former with the "lower orders" of being, and the latter with angelic and infinite being (Hart, 1959: 394).

Aquinas defined beauty as "that which pleases," and insisted that "the beautiful and the good are identical in reality; it is only the mind that makes a distinction between them" (*S.T.* 1-1: 27,1; Vol. 19, 1981: 77; cf. *S.T.* 1: 5,4,1). Furthermore "beauty goes with (conveniat) every virtue" (*S.T.* 2-2: 141, 2; Vol. 43, 1981: 11). Indeed beauty is one of the transcendentals, the attributes of being, which are unity, truth and goodness. Beauty is also one of the attributes of God, for God as Existence is Infinite Goodness and Infinite Beauty. Aquinas therefore not only reflects Plato's ancient philosophy of beauty, but also Augustine's prayer to Beauty (Hart, 1959: 351, 386-93). Beauty is therefore of supreme value in Thomistic metaphysics; and he revived the Platonist equation of Beauty as Truth and Goodness.

Despite Aquinas' clear and clean separation of physical and spiritual, many others were not so inclined to admit the distinction, as we have seen. It was but a short step for the medievals to identify physical beauty with moral beauty, i.e., truth and goodness; and conversely to identify physical ugliness with moral ugliness, i.e., evil. Just as beauty had metaphysical significance, so had the face, for Aquinas, both from its location and from its intelligence functions. Aquinas observed (*S.T.* 1: 91,3,3; Vol. 13, 1981: 29):

other animals have their faces close to the ground, as if to look for food and provender; while man has his face on top, in order that his senses, and especially the sense of sight...may be free to become aware of sense objects in every direction, on the earth and in the heavens, so that from them all he may gather intelligible truth.

The face is close to God both literally and figuratively. These two additional dimensions to the face therefore reinforce the symbolic power of facial beauty. During and after the Renaissance the spiritual dimensions of Christian thought were to some degree secularized; but before considering this, it is necessary to review the thinking about the face as the mirror, not of the soul, but of personality and character.

The Face as Mirror: Aristotle and Physiognomics

Aristotle did not develop Plato's theory of beauty as goodness, indeed he distinguished between them, for goodness "implied conduct as its subject, while the beautiful is found also in motionless things"; but he did define beauty: "The chief forms of beauty are order and symmetry and definiteness," or proportion in other translations (*Metaphysics* 1078; 1984: 1705). The idea of beauty as proportion inspired not only the Greek sculptors, notably Praxiteles, but also Leonardo da Vinci, Durer, Vitruvius, and Corbusier. Francis Bacon, however, perhaps finding this definition a trifle mathematical, insisted that: "There is no excellent beauty that hath not some strangeness in the proportion" (1985: 189).

Faces, rather than beauty, were what fascinated Aristotle; and his treatise *Physiognomics* established physiognomy as a science, although it was probably written by one of his followers at the Peripatetic school after his death. Aristotle argued that the face is a "particularly suitable" part of the body to indicate "mental character" (1984: 1250). One example will suffice (1984: 1246):

The face, when fleshy, indicates laziness, as in cattle: if gaunt, assiduity, and if bony, cowardice, on the analogy of asses and deer. A small face marks a small soul, as in the cat and the ape; a large face means lethargy, as in asses and cattle. So the face must be neither large nor little: an intermediate size is therefore best.

Where Aristotle had emphasized the structure of the face, Cicero emphasized its expressiveness: "everything is in the face, and the face in turn is totally dominated by the eyes...the face is the mirror of the soul...for this is the only part of the body capable of displaying as many expressions as there are emotions" (Vol. 2, 1960: 176). This second dimension of facism reinforced Aristotelian physiognomics; and Aristotle's teachings dominated European thought until Lavater's texts in the eighteenth and nineteenth centuries. The Renaissance, however, saw the addition of two complementary themes: astrology and the Neo-Platonist doctrine of correspondences. The rise of astrology from the fourteenth century resulted in a new contribution to physiognomics as astrologers described faces according to the seven planetary types, and detailed the influence of the 12 constellations by the markings on the face. Not only was a new cosmic principle added to the "science" of physiognomy, but physiognomy also became predictive rather than "merely" descriptive (de Givry, 1973; Thomas, 1974).

Furthermore, despite the continued prominence of the face and face-reading, other parts of the body were increasingly considered significant as symbols of the self and as indicators of the past, present and future of the subject. Cheiromancy, or palm-reading, became increasingly popular; and indeed as systematic "fortune-telling" it is now far more popular than physiognomics. Metaposcopy, or the readings of the lines and markings of the forehead enjoyed a brief vogue in the seventeenth century (de Givry, 1973).

The "doctrine of correspondences" emphasized the correspondence between matter and spirit, microcosm and macrocosm, Man and the Universe. As Macrobius expressed it: "The world is man writ large and man is the world writ small." It was believed that Man, the microcosm, mirrored the universe, the macrocosm; and that the face, the hand, the forehead in turn mirrored the Man. All corresponded. All is one. All is cosmic (Tillyard, 1963).

This synthetic *mentalite´* tended to blur the scholastic distinction between matter and spirit, corporeal and spiritual beauty, and thus to reinforce the art or science of physiognomy, and also facism and the beauty mystique. Both the face and beauty were now of cosmic significance. Plato and Aristotle were synthesized; and Plato's interest in beauty and Aristotle's fascination with the face were integrated in the orientation towards facial beauty. The body is therefore not only physical and moral, but also cosmic. This is clear, for instance, in *Cymbeline* (Act IV, Sc. ii), when Imogen recognizes the body of Cloten:

> I know the shape of's leg: this is his hand;
> His foot Mercurial; his Martial thigh;
> The brawns of Hercules: but his Jovial face—

Physiognomy, palmistry and metaposcopy flourished in the sixteenth and seventeenth centuries. The decline of astrology and the rejection of the doctrine of correspondences in the late seventeenth century, with the rise of science, rationalism and mechanism did not destroy physiognomy, however, but merely transformed it from a predictive, cosmic mode back to the traditional Aristotelian descriptive mode. Indeed physiognomy as a "science" remained very popular throughout the eighteenth and nineteenth centuries. Johann Lavater's classic work *On Physiognomy* which ran through 18 editions in many languages from its first publication in 1775 to 1885, was dedicated to the proposition: "If you would know men's hearts look in their faces." Lavater also formulated "A Hundred Rules of Physiognomy."

The effectiveness of Lavater's physiognomics is indicated by the reluctance of the Captain of the H.M.S. Beagle to allow Darwin on the expedition to South America. According to Darwin's account, the Captain "was an ardent disciple of Lavater...and he doubted whether anyone with my nose could possess sufficient energy and determination for the voyage" (1950:36). Lavater's influence is also evident in the corpus of nineteenth century European literature (Tytler, 1982). Later specialized works were published on noses (Warwick, 1848), ears (Cherry, 1900), and resemblances between men and animals (Redfield, 1852)—ideas that had lasted 2,000 years.

Interest in physiognomics declined again in the second half of the nineteenth century, perhaps in part because of the vigorous attack against it by Hegel in *The Philosophy of the Mind* (1807/1967: 342-8), but also due to the rise of phrenology—dismissed by Hegel also: "Bumps and hollows, there is room for selection!" (1967: 361). The rise and fall of phrenology was relatively rapid, but the "science" persists in the occult world with the re-printing of old classics (Fowler, 1969; Wells, 1971) and new work by a self-styled witch (Leek, 1970).

Physiognomics enjoyed a brief renaissance in business circles in the early 1900s, under the leadership of one Dr. Holmes Whittier Merton (Brandt, 1980: 95-6); and re-appeared as "characterology" in later decades (e.g., McCormick, 1920). Indeed physiognomics is still popular in some circles, and trade books are numerous (Whiteside, 1981; Baker and Bellack, 1981), including works on Chinese physiognomics (Mar, 1975; Young, 1984). Studies on body language and face language promise to reveal the truths about moods and feelings, as well as character (Fast, 1971; Hall, 1973; Nierenberg and Calero, 1973; Davis, 1973). And extravagant and unsubstantiated claims may be made: "The face reveals facts not only about a person's mood, but also about his character, health, personality, sex life, popularity, ability to make money, social status and life expectancy" (Knapp, 1980: 179). Perhaps the most presumptuous physiognomist of the century, however, is Kahlil Gibran: "Show me your mother's face; I will tell you who you are" (1962: n.p.).

Aristotle and the science that he founded, are therefore alive and well in our culture. Yet, while the themes of beauty and the face can be distinguished conceptually in their origins in Plato and Aristotle respectively, in fact they blend and merge with each other in the Renaissance and indeed in contemporary thought. Here we examine the convergence between the face and beauty as symbol of the self.

Facism and the Beauty Mystique

During the Renaissance both physical beauty and the face were of cosmic significance; beauty, because in Augustinian philosophy, it led to God and, by reversal, reflected God; and in Thomistic philosophy Beauty is one of the attributes of God. The face, because individual characters were inscribed there, and future fortunes could be read there by trained "diviners." Also, the face was, and is, the prime focus of beauty.

All these themes permeate the *Divine Comedy* of Dante (1265-1321). The contrasts between beauty/ugliness, good/evil, love/hate, joy/horror, light/darkness, God/Satan, permeate the work; indeed it cannot be understood without a prior understanding of these synthetic equations. The ugliness, horror and evil of the three-headed Satan, weeping from his six eyes, devouring sinners, with "runnels of tears and slaver" dripping from his triple chin is in sharp contrast with the former Lucifer, Light-bearer, "once as fair as now he's foul" (Vol. 1, Canto 34). Yet Dante cannot describe the beauty of Beatrice, transformed after their vision of the angelic circles (Vol. 3, Canto 30); it is the same when Saint Bernard bids Dante to gaze at the Virgin Mary, Mother of God (Vol. 3, Canto 32):

'Now to that face which most resembles Christ
Lift up thy gaze; its radiance alone
Can grant to thee the power to look on Christ.'

I looked and on that countenance there shone
Such bliss...

That nothing I had looked on heretofore
Had held me breathless in such wonderment,
Or unto God so close a likeness bore.

For Dante, beauty is a reflection of the glory of God (1955: 67); and the face is the expression not only of the individual, but also of God. Even the structure of the face, the medievals believed, is witness to God. Dante remarked "he who reads OMO in man's countenance": (Vol. 2, Canto 22, 1.32)—which refers to the words "[H]OMO DEI" = "man [is] of God" inscribed on the face. The figure below shows the eyes, representing two O's, the lines of the eyebrows and nose forming the M; and the ears, nostrils and mouthing forming the D, E and I (1955: 248, 251).

Perhaps the finest exposition of the medieval idea of beauty, which closely followed Plato's was offered by the courtier, Baldesar Castiglione (1478-1529; 1984: 330-2; emphasis added.):

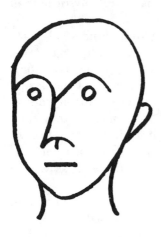

"[H]OMO DEI"

beauty is a sacred thing...[it] springs from God and is like a circle, the centre of which is goodness. And so just as one cannot have a circle without a centre, so one cannot have beauty without goodness. In consequence, only rarely does an evil soul dwell in a beautiful body, and so *outward beauty is a true sign of inner goodness*. This loveliness, indeed, is impressed upon the body in varying degrees as a token by which the soul can be recognized for what it is, just as with trees the beauty of the blossom testifies to the goodness of the fruit.

Therefore for the most part *the ugly are also evil, and the beautiful good*. And it can be said that beauty is the pleasant, gay, charming and desirable face of the good, and that ugliness is the dark, disagreeable, unpleasant and sorry face of evil...it can be said that in some manner the *good and the beautiful are identical*, especially in the human body. And the proximate cause of physical beauty is, in my opinion the beauty of the soul.

This belief that physical beauty is caused by spiritual beauty is characteristic of the Renaissance; but Castiglione went on to suggest that the lover of physical beauty may grow to love intellectual and spiritual beauty, may go from love of particular beauties to the love of universal beauty and ultimately God (1984: 340-1). Castiglione not only reflects Plato, Augustine and Aquinas but also justifies secular and sensual delight in beauty: a superb synthesis of "biology" and theology, the profane and the sacred, sex and God. If physical beauty is but "a ray of the supernatural" divine beauty, it is right that beauty should be worshipped: it is indeed "a sacred thing." And clearly a beautiful person is nearer to God than an ugly one, not only because of beauty but also because of virtue.

Castiglione's was the most fully developed theory of the time; Francis Bacon agreed in *De Augmentiis Scientiarum*, but was more concise: "Virtue is nothing but inward beauty; beauty nothing but outward virtue" (1864: Vol. 9, 156). Conversely, in his essay on deformity, he states: "Deformed persons are commonly even with nature, for as nature hath done ill by them, so do they by nature; being for the most part (as the Scripture saith) *void of natural affection*; and so they have their revenge of nature" (1985: 191-2; Bacon's emphasis). The Lord Chancellor, and the most distinguished essayist of the early seventeenth century not only believed that beauty was a sign of virtue, but also that deformed (ugly) people are "void of natural affections," do ill by nature, "have their revenge of nature," and have chips on their shoulders, even if they sometimes prove excellent persons. The analysis is less mystical than Castiglione's but the conclusions are very similar.

Bacon's contemporary in France, the essayist Montaigne (1553-1592), was most interested in faces, but undecided on the value of physiognomics. He advised that: "The face is a weak guarantee; yet it deserves some consideration" (1965: 811). He was also a strong adherent of the beauty mystique, and a great admirer of beauty. He found it "incongruous" that Socrates, with the "beauty of his soul" was so ugly, as they said; for "there is nothing more likely than the conformity and relation of the body to the spirit." He added: "I cannot say how much I consider beauty a powerful and advantageous quality...I consider it as within two fingers' breadth of goodness" (1965: 809-10).

The equation of beauty and goodness, the conformity of body and soul, the value of the face—the central themes are sketched very clearly. Miranda also subscribed to the beauty mystique. In *The Tempest* (1.ii) she identified physical and moral beauty on first seeing Ferdinand:

> I might call him
> A thing divine, for nothing natural
> I ever saw so noble...
> There's nothing ill can dwell in such a
>   temple.

For Miranda, the man is good-looking *therefore* "a thing divine" and *therefore* good. Caliban, on the other hand, is both evil and ugly—a monster both literally and figuratively; Prospero calls him "A devil, a born devil...and...with age his body uglier grows" (IV.ii). The conflict between good and evil is also a conflict between beautiful and ugly.

Miranda was not alone in her beliefs. Thomas Walkington (1607) was equally moved: "When I doe gaze with a longing looke on the comelinesse of the feature without, I am more than halfe persuaded of the admirable decencie within" (in Camden, 1941: 401). And Thomas Browne in *Religio Medici* (1642) asserted clearly that: "there are mystically in our faces certain characters which carry in them the motto of our Soules wherein he that cannot read A.B.C. may read our natures" (1964: 57).

Milton (1608-74) also subscribed to the beauty mystique. Adam and Eve are beautiful in paradise before the Fall (*Paradise Lost*, Bk. 4: 288ff):

> Two of far nobler shape, erect and tall,
> God-like erect, with native honour clad
> In naked majesty, seemed lords of all,
> And worthy seemed; for in their looks divine
> The image of their glorious Maker shone,
> Truth, wisdom, sanctitude severe and pure—

Even Satan, newly expelled from heaven, is at first still glorious and majestic (Bk. 1: 59ff; Bk. 2: 302ff); but as his evil intent develops he appears "squat like a toad" (Bk.4: 800); and finally then "mixed with bestial slime," a serpent (Bk. 9: 165). Finally, after the Fall, he and all the devils are punished by God and transformed permanently into "a crowd of ugly serpents!" (Bk. 10: 538-9). Where Dante had written, till words failed, of the increasing beauty of goodness and love in his ascent to heaven, Milton stressed the increasing ugliness of sin. But the equations of the beauty mystique were identical for both.

The Romantic poets of the late eighteenth and early nineteenth centuries were captivated by beauty, natural beauty in particular, but human beauty also, and even the idea of beauty. Wordsworth wrote about a little eight year old girl in "We Are Seven," and captures the essence of the beauty mystique: "Her eyes were fair, and very fair;/ Her beauty made me glad." William Blake in his satirical "Proverbs of Hell" includes a classic facist proverb: "He whose face gives no light, shall never become a star." Another proverb states that: "Exuberance is Beauty." Coleridge, like many others, was impressed by the beauty of Lord Byron: "so beautiful a countenance, I scarcely ever saw...his eyes the open portals of the sun—things of light and for light" (Abrams *et al*, 1968: 1457). Certainly Coleridge did not consider the notorious rake virtuous, even if beautiful; yet he equated beauty with sun and light, both familiar analogues of God. Byron himself wrote a famous poem that begins: "She walks in beauty, like the night/ Of cloudless climes and starry skies"; and concludes in the now familiar strains of beauty mystique, equating beauty and goodness: "The smiles that win, the tints that glow,/ But tell of days in goodness spent,/ A mind at peace with all below./ A heart whose love is innocent." Shelley composed "A Hymn to Intellectual Beauty," in which he states: "I vowed that I would dedicate my powers/ To thee and thine—have I not kept the vow?" (Socrates had made a similar promise to Love, as we have seen.) Yet it was John Keats, dead at 26, who summarized the Romantics' views in "Endymion":

A thing of beauty is a joy forever:
Its loveliness increases; it will never
Pass into nothingness;

And he concluded his "Ode on a Grecian Urn" with the much-quoted lines:

Beauty is truth, truth beauty—that is all
Ye know on earth, and all ye need to know.

The consensus within European cultural history has been impressive. Beauty is objective, related to goodness and to God, and moral and physical beauty are related; it is located primarily in the face which also reflects character and perhaps the future. And beauty as physically attractive not only reflects Divine beauty, and inner moral beauty, but also inspires physical desire, i.e. is sexy. Nonetheless there were some who objected, and observed the relativity of beauty. Montaigne who, as we have seen, was both a moderate facist and an adherent of the beauty mystique, was also the first to offer an early anthropology of beauty (1965: 355-6):

We imagine its forms to suit our fancy...The Indies paint it black and dusky, with large swollen lips and a wide flat nose. And they load the cartilage between the nostrils with big gold rings, to make it hang down to the mouth.... In Peru, the biggest ears are the fairest, and they stretch them artificially as much as they can.... Elsewhere there are nations that blacken their teeth with great care, and scorn to see white ones; elsewhere they stain them red.

Voltaire, likewise, was more impressed by the relativity than the objectivity of beauty; for him, beauty is in the culture of the beholder, not in the philosophy of Plato (1941: 53).

Ask a toad what beauty is, the *to kalon*? He will answer you that it is his toad wife with two great round eyes issuing from his little head, a wide, flat mouth, a yellow belly, a brown back.

The philosophical implications of such subjectivism were drawn by David Hume (1711-1776). In his essay "Of the Standard of Taste," he remarks (1965: 6):

Beauty is no quality in things themselves: it exists merely in the mind which contemplates them; and each mind perceives a different beauty. One person may even perceive deformity, where another is sensible of beauty...To seek the real beauty, or real deformity, is as fruitless an inquiry, as to pretend to ascertain the real sweet or real bitter.

In sum, beauty is in the eye of the beholder (but the "eye" is culturally determined, as Montaigne and Voltaire had shown). Hume therefore summarily rejected the aesthetic theories of Plato, Aristotle, Augustine, Aquinas and Bacon. These conflicts between rationalism and empiricism, objectivism and subjectivism, were heightened, if not resolved by Hume. Tastes might vary, but they are not equal; nor are sentiments about an object equally sound. Nonetheless, he insisted in "The Sceptic": "Beauty is not a quality of the circle...It is only the effect, which that figure produces upon a mind, whose particular fabric or structure renders it susceptible of such sentiments" (1965: 125). Beauty is socially constructed, is Hume's point; and it has taken over 200 years for the anthropological insights of Voltaire, and before him of Montaigne, and the philosophical insights of Hume, to be utilized in sociology (Berger and Luckman, 1967).

Yet Hume was also a traditionalist, and in his most famous work, *A Treatise of Human Nature* (1738: 2,1,8) he restated Aquinas' definition of beauty (that which pleases), adding a corollary on ugliness or deformity (1985: 350):

beauty is such an order and construction of parts, as...is fitted to give a pleasure and satisfaction to the soul. This is the distinguishing character of beauty, and forms all the difference betwixt it and deformity, whose natural tendency is to produce uneasiness. Pleasure and pain, therefore, are not only necessary attendants of beauty and deformity, but constitute their very essence.

The addition of pleasure and pain to the ancient Platonist-equation contributed another dimension to the beauty-ugliness mystique. Kant rejected Hume's empiricism and relativism. In his complicated *Critique of Judgement* he returned to a Platonist-type idealism: "the beautiful is the symbol of the morally good" (1951: 198). More lyrical was Schiller in his essay "On the Sublime" and in his letters on aesthetics (1782). In one letter he writes: "Beauty alone makes the whole world happy, and each and every being forgets its limitations while under its spell" (1967: 217; letter 27).

Hegel was equally captivated by beauty. In his *Aesthetics* (1835) Hegel states that "everything beautiful is truly beautiful as sharing in this higher sphere [of the spirit] and generated by it" (1975:2). And in his *Lectures on the Philosophy of Religion* (1827), he says: "the beautiful is essentially the spiritual that expresses itself sensibly...in such a way that the sensible does not have being on its own account, but only has complete significance within the spiritual and through the spiritual, and is the *sign* of the spiritual" (1987: 585, cf. 477). In Hegel's view the human sensory form is determined by the spirit, the exterior by the interior, thus we create ourselves physically as well as spiritually (1975: 433-4):5

The external human form is alone capable of revealing the spiritual in a sensuous way. The human expression in face, eyes, posture, and air is material...but within this corporeality itself the human exterior is not only living and natural, as the animal is, but is the bodily presence which in itself mirrors the spirit. Through the eyes we look into a man's soul, just as his spiritual character is expressed by his whole demeanour in general.

Hegel adds that "a face altogether regular in form and beautiful may nevertheless be cold and expressionless" (1975: 173); but he insists that the body, especially the face, manifests the soul: "the face has a...centre in which the soulful and spiritual relation to things is manifested" (1975: 729). Again, a man's "glance is what is most full of his soul, the concentration of his inmost personality and feeling" (1975: 732). These ideas about the face go straight back to Plato and, as we shall see, are still "true" today.

Schopenhauer (1788-1860) agreed with Hegel about the spirituality of the face but, unlike Hegel, was a convinced physiognomist. He wrote: "That the outer man is a picture of the inner, and the face an expression and revelation of the whole character, is a presumption likely enough in itself, and therefore a safe one to go by." His facism is clearer in the emphatic statement that "the face of a man is the exact expression of what he is, and if he deceives us, that is our fault, not his" (n.d.: 250, 254). Hence he recommended physiognomics: it is the study of truth.

The reality of beauty not only fascinated poets and philosophers but also naturalists. In *The Descent of Man* (1871), Darwin discussed the variations in, and functions of, animal beauty and the differences in cultural definitions of beauty; he concluded that: "It is certainly not true that there is in the mind of man any universal standard of beauty with respect to the human body" (1981: Vol. II, 353). Nonetheless, in his view, beauty was immensely significant in the evolutionary scheme of things, contributing to sexual selection; this would, "after the lapse of many generations modify to a certain extent the character of the tribe" in line with the aesthetic values of the tribe (Darwin, 1981: Vol. II, 369). Beauty, therefore, contributes to sexual selection and to the descent of Man.

Beauty has been the light which has illuminated Plato's idealism, as the face inspired Aristotelian physiognomics; by the modern age, both the beauty mystique and facism were grounded in Platonist metaphysics, Aristotelian physiognomics and Thomistic theology. They had been reinforced by the cosmic holism of ancient astrology and the doctrine of correspondences; furthermore Dante and Castiglione had added secular dimensions to the spiritual during the Renaissance. Montaigne and Voltaire had philosophized about the relativity of beauty, and Hume had discussed the subjectivity of beauty. Schiller, Hegel and Schopenhauer had praised the face as a symbol or mirror of the self. The romantics, notably Keats, equated beauty with Truth—a coinciding of virtues which reflected Plato; and Darwin accorded a biological role to beauty in his theory of evolution. The significance of beauty and the face even seemed to be legitimized by the Bible, notably by the verse: "A man may be known by his look, and one that hath understanding by his countenance, when thou meetest him" (Ecclus, 20:19; cf. also 25:17; 26:9; 37:17).

The significance of beauty and the pre-eminence of the face are therefore secure in Western culture, with roots deep and strong in both the Judaeo-Christian and the Graeco-Roman traditions.

The Face and Contemporary Culture

In the twentieth century, the twin beliefs that the face (and the body) mirror the soul, and that beauty and goodness are one, and are reflected in the face, still persist as they did in the past. In a well-known passage Wittgenstein stated that "the human body is the best picture of the human soul" (1968: 178). One cannot help observing that Wittgenstein himself did not have a notoriously beautiful body. Also, the implications for the physically handicapped are clear.

George Simmel was fascinated by the face and declared bluntly in his essay "The Aesthetic Significance of the Face" that "in the features of the face the soul finds it clearest expression"; and again: "the face strikes us as the symbol, not only of the spirit, but also of an unmistakable personality" (1901; 1965: 276, 278).[6] The face tells the truth.

Emerson, the American philosopher and poet, often wrote about beauty. In one essay, "Beauty," he says, echoing Bacon, that "Beauty is the mark God sets upon virtue"; and adds, in Platonist mode that "Beauty, in its largest and profoundest sense, is one expression for the universe. God is the all-fair. Truth, and goodness, and beauty are but different faces of the same all" (1968: Vol. 1, 19, 24). In another essay, "Michael Angelo," he asserts his belief that "Beauty is the virtue of the body, as virtue is the beauty of the soul." Indeed: "a beautiful person is sent into the world as an image of the divine beauty, not to provoke but to purify the sensual into an intellectual and divine love." Furthermore, "perfect beauty and perfect goodness are one" (1968: Vol. 12, 240, 217). Continuing on this theme he asserts that "Beauty is its own excuse for being" (1968: Vol. 9, 38); and is "welcome as the sun wherever it pleases to shine, which pleases everybody with it and with themselves, seems sufficient to itself...Her existence makes the world rich" (1968: Vol. 2, 178). These are classic statements of the beauty mystique.

However, by the turn of the century the new social sciences were impacting on traditional philosophies. Thorstein Veblen offered the first sociological theory of beauty, suggesting that "the utility of articles valued for their beauty depends closely upon the expensiveness of the article" (1953: 94); beginning with spoons, he then discussed the aesthetic value of parks and lawns, cats and dogs, and finally dress, men and particularly women. Of the ideal of feminine beauty, he observed (1953: 107):

The ideal requires delicate and diminutive hands and feet and slender waist. These features...go to show that the person so affected is incapable of useful effort and must therefore be supported in her idleness by her owner. She is useless and expensive, and she is consequently valuable as evidence of pecuniary strength.

Thus the beautiful woman is a status symbol; she not only does not work, but cannot work; long hair, corsets, high heels, long dresses, and so on, are intended to indicate this: they too are status symbols; and the decoration of the woman with jewelry, making her an expensive ornament, reinforces this process, as does the attention to fashion and "the alleged beauty or 'loveliness' of the styles in vogue at any given time" (1953: 121, 125-6). Feminists in the second half of this century developed some of these ideas further, as we shall see.

Freud argued somewhat differently: "There is to my mind no doubt that the concept of 'beautiful' has its roots in sexual excitation and that its original meaning was 'sexually stimulating' " (1977: 69n2). Indeed Freud seemed mildly perplexed by beauty: "Beauty has no obvious use: nor is there any clear cultural necessity for it. Yet civilization could not do without it," apparently because the enjoyment of beauty can compensate for the threat of suffering. He suggests that: "The love of beauty seems a perfect example of an impulse inhibited in its aim" (1985: 270-1). Yet Freud's theory of beauty originating in "sexual excitation" neatly complements Darwin's theory of sexual selection, quite apart from any compensation roles it may play.

Rollo May is reminiscent of Socrates and Shelley in the title of his autobiography, *My Quest for Beauty* (1985). This reflects Kahlil Gibran (1883-1931): "We live only to discover beauty" (1968:27). Edward O. Wilson, the founder of sociobiology and surely closer to Darwin than to Freud, also eulogizes beauty, the beauty of science.[7] He quotes Hermann Weyl, the perfecter of quantum and relativity theory: "My work always tried to unite the true with the beautiful; but when I had to choose one or the other, I usually chose the beautiful" (1984:6). There is an echo of Keats here; but for Keats beauty and truth could not clash. Wilson himself suggested that "Mathematics and beauty are devices by which human beings get through life with the limited intellectual capacity inherited by the species" (1984: 61). Indeed he suggested that beauty may lie "in the genes of the beholder" (1984: 109), i.e. much that we perceive as beautiful, is determined by some sort of genetic memory of mankind's earliest and optimal environments in the savannah, on hills and by water. Here, of course, Wilson referred to natural rather than to facial beauty; but the idea is intriguing.

Twentieth century scientists have therefore introduced new equations of beauty: beauty as status symbol (Veblen), as sexual excitation (Freud), as aesthetic goal (May), and as genetically determined and as mathematical (Wilson).

These added dimensions to beauty and to the face coincided with increased attention to both from beauticians and cosmeticians. The German physician Anna Fischer-Duckelmann, in her long (970 page) work on feminine hygiene in 1901 included a number of beauty hints and stated that "Beauty is power," especially for women. The book was very successful, sold half a million copies in seven years, and was translated into 10 languages (Kern, 1977: 162-3). The doctor perhaps expressed what was already known of Helen of Troy and Cleopatra, but had not been said; yet it was not until the 1970s that sociologists and social psychologists began investigating in detail this power of beauty.

In *The Complete Beauty Book* (1906), the American Elizabeth Anstruther defined beauty simply as "health, dress and winsomeness, all of which are cultivable." Indeed she downplayed physical beauty: "Perfection of features would be nice, of course, but so would a good many other kinds of perfection which are not possible in this workaday world." On the one hand, "a clean skin,...bright eyes, white teeth, a good figure, beautifully kept hair, attractive hands, and a graceful carriage, everyone may have who wills them." Also health, wholesomeness and "bubbling good spirits." Beauty, in this view, is not a matter of classical good looks, but of health, dress and charm or good manners. But Anstruther warned that "the history of the world's beauties has always been tragic" (1912: 1-4)—a somewhat negative view of physical beauty.

By the 1950s, beauty was being re-defined again. Health, dress and charm were being treated separately, not as components of physical beauty. *The Family Circle's Complete Book of Beauty and Charm* (Milo and Marshall, 1951) explicitly separated beauty and charm in their title, but did not separate them in the text. In their view, "To achieve lasting beauty...you will have to develop the feeling of beauty." The authors described a number of "routines" in detail, including the following: enjoy being alive; be sensitive to beauty; enjoy new experiences; have nice things; think beauty—think of yourself as a beautiful person; and others (1951: 2-4). They insisted that beauty comes from within: "it is within yourselves that you find the source of your beauty." The authors advised that "beauty is as beauty does"—an essentially moral definition of beauty which follows Epictetus and Plotinus; and they asserted that "the inward wellsprings of beauty are in your attitudes towards yourself." The emphasis on high self-esteem and beautiful (= ethical) behavior and positive attitudes is subtly different from Anstruther's insistence on charm and manners, for Anstruther did not recognize a distinction between inner and outer. Milo and Marshall were also more positive about beauty, and insisted that: "The great beauties of history have also been great wits and charming women—they did not rely on their looks alone for their reputation" (1951: 374-83). History, like beauty, is constantly being revised.

Ten years later another beauty expert stated clearly that "Beauty is a duty. Love of self, as reflected in the care of your person and the enhancement of your looks, is an expression of a healthy personality" (Hauser, 1961: 4). The notion that beauty is a duty, particularly for women has been asserted since the Victorian era, and both physical and spiritual beauty were discussed (Steele, 1985: 102-5). Hauser too discussed beauty as a moral phenomenon: "Body and mind nourish each other, and both of them nourish beauty...happiness is literally translated into physical beauty." His *bon mots* included "Laugh and be beautiful, I say"; "Love is the best of all cosmetics"; "Most beautifying of all is the knowledge of being loved, that someone finds you beautiful and desirable"; "Lift the spirit and you lift the face" (1961: 18-25, 153). For Milo and Marshall (1951), philosophy was crucial. Hauser paid lip-service to this theme, emphasizing happiness rather than self-esteem, but it was peripheral to his work, most of which was concerned with nutrition, skin care and cosmetology. In this century, therefore, beauty was being re-defined from an *effect* of attitudes, beliefs and philosophy, variously defined as charm, self-esteem, happiness, education, and virtue, to a purely physical phenomenon of bones and muscle, diet and make-up.

In the eighties, the redefinition of beauty continues. The Avon Book of Beauty is titled *Looking Good Feeling Beautiful*; the book offers beauty advice and tips on exercise, relaxation and diet, and promises "You'll not only look good, but feel beautiful...every day of your life" (Avon, 1981: 157). In this view, the physical *determines* the emotional in a total capsize of the causal directions asserted by Milo and Marshall (1951) and Hauser (1961). Similarly the *Vogue Complete Beauty* emphasizes the circularity of this issue, but comes down firmly on the side of the physical as well as paramount: "Feel beautiful and you will look beautiful. But how do you go about feeling beautiful? The answer is a circular one. You must start by looking good" (Hutton, 1982:11). These are complete redefinitions of beauty within 30 years: from beauty as primarily psychological to primarily physical, from inner to outer, from mind to body, from attitudes to techniques.

Beauty and Ugliness

"Beauty is only skin deep"; "appearances are deceptive"; "all that glitters is not gold"; "handsome is as handsome does"; and "never judge a book by its cover": folk wisdom and popular culture warn insistently against taking beauty "at face value."[8] Nonetheless, pressures to look good seem to have intensified, particularly for men (Cash *et al*, 1986: 30). Furthermore the beauty "hype" continues, fuelled by poets and philosophers, major corporations and beauticians.

Indeed our everyday language indicates the prevalence of the beauty mystique. We might say that someone "looks good," "looks divine," or is "divinely beautiful": phrases which neatly equate beauty, goodness, and God. Conversely, the phrases "as ugly as sin" or "looks like hell" equally neatly equate ugliness, evil and the devil. To be attractive is, by definition, to attract. To be lovely is to be lovable and, by implication, to be loved. Conversely, to be unlovely is to be unlovable and unloved; and to be ugly is to be repulsive and to repel. Beauty and ugliness are evaluated linguistically therefore, not only as physical opposites but as moral opposites.

Ugliness and physical deformities, particularly facial deformities, are stigmatized (Goffman, 1963; Kampling, 1981). Ugliness causes pain, said Hume, but in the observer, quite apart from the "victim." Cleft lips or palates, lop ears (microtia), drooping eyelids (ptosis), cranio-facial deformities of various sorts, birth-marks, as well as burns and scarring may traumatize the individuals concerned and those with whom they interact. Such conditions, whether congenital or accidental, or simply matters of taste, may be changed by cosmetic surgery; but the psychic and social significance of ugliness is immense (Stallings, 1980; Kaczorowski, 1988). Prejudice and discrimination against the ugly are virtually a cultural norm.

Indeed discrimination against the ugly has been institutionalized in the so-called "ugly laws" in some American cities, whereby those of "unsightly" appearance in public places were liable to arrest (Note, 1987: 2035).

There is a second dimension to ugliness. Just as physical beauty is believed to symbolize inner moral or spiritual beauty or goodness, so too physical ugliness is believed to symbolize an inner ugliness or evil (as with Homer's Therstis). The equation is reversible: the ugly are evil, but the evil are also ugly. Thus those who are perceived as evil, i.e. enemies of one sort or another: military, ethnic, racial, political, etc., are "uglified"—portrayed as ugly. This second process consolidates and reinforces the original stigmatization of the ugly: propaganda includes "uglification."

In Germany, for instance, Hitler presented the Jews as both physically ugly and morally ugly in *Mein Kampf* (1924); the Aryans, on the other hand, were physically and morally beautiful, and biologically and spiritually superior. Riefenstahl's film, "The Will to Power," showed the Nazis as beautiful, blonde, noble and strong. Similarly, in Ireland and England during the Fenian crisis, cartoonists from each side showed the other as ugly: as apes, Yahoos, Frankensteins, vampires, and generally unpleasant (Curtis, 1971). Again, in the United States, from the earliest days of contact, Blacks were stigmatized by Whites. The linguistic opposition of white and black connoted life and death, "purity and filthiness, virginity and sin, virtue and baseness, *beauty and ugliness, beneficence and evil, God and the devil*" (Jordan, 1969: 7; Emphasis added). Centuries later Black nationalists responded with "Black is beautiful!"—by implication, white, its opposite is ugly; and Malcolm X added that the white man is the devil and the enemy (1966: 212-3, 251, 266). The issues remained polarized, but the moral poles were reversed; now Blacks were beautiful and good; and whites were evil and ugly.

Finally, Cesare Lombroso, the Italian criminologist, concluded that "born" criminals were not only atavistic throwbacks and moral imbeciles but also that a physical "criminal type" existed, distinguished in their bodies by prehensile feet, left-handedness and hernias, and in their faces by "outstanding ears, abundant hair, a sparse beard, enormous frontal sinuses," prognathism, broad cheekbones, a low and retreating forehead, oblique eyes, a small skull and in women, a masculine face (1911/1968: xviii, 369-72). It was therefore often possible to distinguish born criminals from the rest of the population: they were extremely ugly. The face is the clue to the criminal self.

Lombrosian ideas still persist. In *The Secret Adversary*, first published in 1922 and still in print, Agatha Christie describes villains as looking villainous; one was "A villainous looking man with close-cropped hair"; a second had "a weak, unpleasant face...his shoulders cringed a little as he talked, and his eyes, small and crafty, shifted unceasingly"; and a third was still more obvious: "He was obviously of the very dregs of the society. The low, beetling brows, and the criminal jaw, the bestiality of the whole countenance..." (1987:51, 48, 53). He was, in sum, Neanderthal. This is perhaps less description than invective; but the processes by which the evil, however defined, are portrayed as ugly, and the good are shown as good-looking, both express and reinforce facist beliefs and the beauty mystique. Appearance symbolizes "reality."

The beauty mystique is rooted not only in physiognomy and philosophy, linguistics, ethnic relations, war and criminology, but also in our literary heritage. Our fairy stories imbue children with the mystique. In Grimm's story, "Cinderella," it is the remarkably beautiful and amazingly good Cinderella who wins the heart of the prince. In "Beauty and the Beast," Beauty, who is both good and intelligent enough to see through ugliness, breaks the spell over the beast, who promptly turns into a handsome prince. The moral of the stories is not only that virtue triumphs, but so does beauty. Hans Andersen's story, "The Ugly Duckling," tells how the poor duckling was loathed and persecuted by his brothers and sisters, and everyone else. Even his mother wished he had never been born. His problems are only resolved when he becomes a beautiful swan. All three of these stories exemplify the beauty mystique, and socialize children into the cosmic value and practical utility of beauty; and "Sleeping Beauty" and "Snow White" transmit the same morals.

Adult literature emphasizes the same themes. In Mary Shelley's *Frankenstein* (1817), the monster was so monstrous that even his creator rejected him and fled; yet was he intrinsically "benevolent and good," in accord with Rousseau's view of humanity. Society however rejected him for his ugliness—even young children, the monster learned, were prejudiced, and abhorred deformity. He explained: "Once I falsely hoped to meet with beings who, pardoning my outward form would love me for the excellent qualities which I was capable of unfolding." But he found no Beauty for his Beast. Spurned by all, shot at, hated, lonely and miserable, "I declared everlasting war against the species." He kills, again and again, but is filled with remorse. He, and his victims, were destroyed by the beauty mystique: the hatred and fear of ugliness.

Truth is often as strange as fiction, as the case of John Merrick, the so-called Elephant Man, exemplifies. He was so ugly, so deformed, that people paid to see him; and when travelling he had to wear a bag over his face. Dr. Treves, his very experienced doctor, admitted that on the basis of his looks and his inability to articulate "I supposed that Merrick was imbecile and had been from birth." But he found out that he was wrong. The man was "highly intelligent...possessed an acute sensibility and—worse than all—a romantic imagination" (Montagu, 1979: 17-18).

In *The Strange Case of Dr. Jekyll and Mr. Hyde* (1886), the good doctor not only becomes the evil Mr. Hyde, but he also becomes ugly—his face is transformed and his body is deformed (Stevenson, 1984:84):

Even as good shone upon the countenance of the one, evil was written broadly and plainly on the face of the other. Evil besides...had left on that body an imprint of deformity and decay.

And in Oscar Wilde's story, *The Picture of Dorian Gray* (1891), the enigma was how Gray could be so evil, so debauched, and yet still be so good-looking; only the picture could resolve the contradiction. The same idea that the face is the mirror of the person is conveyed in George Orwell's well-known dictum that "At 50 everyone has the face he deserves" (1971: 579).

The same point was made in an American Catholic high school text in the early sixties (Elwell, 1961: 556):

The faces of the pure, even those who otherwise lack natural beauty, are usually clear-eyed, noble, strong, open, innocent, appealing. But the faces of the impure, whether beautiful or homely, in proportion to their depravity often become hard-eyed, coarse, weal, callous, naughty, brazen, sensuous, repellent. Yes, impurity leaves its ugly marks.

A recent children's book, however, asserts the primacy of moral over physical beauty (Dahl, 1982: 9):

If a person has ugly thoughts, it begins to show on the face. And when that person has ugly thoughts every day, every week, every year, the face gets uglier and uglier until it gets so ugly you can hardly bear to look at it. A person who has good thoughts cannot ever be ugly. You can have a wonky nose and a crooked mouth and a double chin and stick-out teeth, but if you have good thoughts they will shine out of your face like sunbeams and you will always look lovely.

The nastier people become, the uglier they look; this view repeats Milton's description of Satan; conversely the morally good person "will always look lovely." Essentially the same point is made by the theologian Charles Davis (1976: 38):

The bodily beauty of men and women, the beauty that shines forth physically, is not purely physical. Everyone will admit this in regard to the human face. Facial beauty insofar as it comes from perfect physical proportions, firm flesh, and finely textured skin, can of itself be dead and unattractive. Indeed, such features may be the basis of an ugly countenance, expressing a selfish or hateful personality. But a face can have a quite extraordinary beauty in the mobile expressiveness with which it presents a rich, lovable personality, despite features in themselves physically ugly. The same is true of the body as a whole. Its living beauty is never exclusively physical.

Facism and the beauty mystique are not only literary, they are primarily visual. They may be discussed in theological works and children's stories, literary essays and philosophical treatises; but they are most apparent in films and television programs, advertising and comics (Longmore, 1985; Synnott, 1983; Bogden *et al*, 1982); and in fine art, religious and secular, the beloved is beautiful. This mystique, however, has costs as well as benefits. Discrimination and prejudice against the ugly persist. Not everyone agrees that virtue shines through physical ugliness. One 32 year old man states (Cash *et al*, 1986: 32):

I was an ugly child, I was an ugly teenager, and now I'm an ugly adult. I get angry when I hear some-one say that looks don't matter. It isn't true. Most people won't give me a chance because of how I look.

Tolstoy's brisk dismissal of Plato, Aquinas, and Castiglione is apposite in this matter: "It is amazing how complete is the delusion that beauty is goodness" (1978: 538).

Physiognomics also still persists as one aspect of facism. The classic example is Professor Moriarty's comment on meeting Sherlock Holmes for the first time: "You have less frontal development than I should have expected" (Doyle, 1950: 241). More recent and more popular examples can be found in Ian Fleming's James Bond novels; Bond's face is described in *From Russia with Love*: "General G. held the photograph out at arm's length. Decision, authority, ruthlessness—these qualities he could see" (Fleming 1957/1977: 44-5). Where he could see them is not obvious. The Bond stories, however, are excellent examples of the beauty mystique, with the good guys good-looking and the bad guys ugly (Synnott, 1988b).

Conan Doyle, Agatha Christie and Ian Fleming are typical of a massive literary genre from the late eighteenth century to the present employing the techniques of physiognomics (Tytler, 1982). Facism and the beauty mystique are even more popular in the conventional portrayal of right and wrong; recent examples in this century include such authors as Leslie Charteris, John Buchan, Sapper, Dennis Wheatley, Alistair Maclean and others. Journalists often employ these techniques (Booker, 1969: 283). So do artists: Hogarth and Rowlandson were particularly adept at this—the evil are ugly; on the other hand Renaissance artists portrayed Christ and Our Lady as beautiful, and the devils as ugly.

Perhaps the most lyrical writer on beauty today is the poet and philosopher Kahlil Gibran. In his bestseller *The Prophet* (1923) he writes (1985: 82-3).

> beauty is. . .an ecstasy
> . . .a heart enflamed and a soul enchanted.
> . . .an image you see though you close your eyes and a
> song you hear though you shut your ears.
> . . .a garden for ever in bloom and a flock of angels ever in flight.
> People of Orphalese, beauty is life when life unveils her holy face.
> But you are life and you are the veil.
> Beauty is eternity gazing at itself in a mirror.
> But you are eternity and you are the mirror.

Poets and artists, philosophers and theologians, politicians and criminologists, novelists and dramatists, naturalists and scientists, psychologists and cosmeticians. . .people in all walks of life have adored beauty, even where they have perceived it and defined it differently. The symbolic value of the face and beauty can therefore hardly be overstated. Nonetheless, despite this unanimity, the face may *misrepresent* the self, and the body *disguise* the soul.

The Face as Mask

Your face, my thane, is as a book where men
May read strange matters. To beguile the time
Look like the time; bear welcome in your eye,
Your hand, your tongue; look like the innocent flower,
But be the serpent under't.

(*Macbeth*, Act 1, Sc.vi, 64 ff)

More succinctly, Lady Macbeth reiterates the doctrine of face as mask in an early statement advocating what we now call impression management: "False face must hide what the false heart doth know" (*Macbeth*, Act 1, Sc.vii, 81). The face, therefore, may also be false, a disguise, a mask, a distorting mirror, a pretense: "one may smile, and smile, and be a villain" mused Hamlet (*Hamlet*, Act 1, Sc.v).

The situations in *Macbeth* and *Hamlet* were perhaps extreme; yet popular culture and daily life are full of similar advice to wear a mask: "Cheer up! Don't look so miserable!" "Keep a stiff upper lip!" And, as the song says, "Smile, even though you're crying inside." All these exhortations, and many others, testify to the social necessities of wearing a mask in public, and therefore of seeming to be what one is not, or of seeming to feel, to a greater or lesser degree, what one does not feel. We are expected to present ourselves, and thus our faces, in culturally approved ways. Park has emphasized (in Goffman, 1959: 19):

It is probably no mere historical accident that the word person, in its first meaning, is a mask. It is rather a recognition of the fact that everyone is always and everywhere, more or less consciously, playing a role...It is in these roles that we know each other; it is in these roles that we know ourselves.

Goffman developed these themes in this exposition of dramaturgical theory, but the crucial point for our purposes is the role of the face as part of the "personal front" in the performance. In "face to face" interaction the face is, self-evidently, of critical significance, as it is in acting; but Goffman's homely example from the Shetland Isles places the role of acting firmly in the context of real life (1959: 8):

When a neighbor dropped in to have a cup of tea, he would ordinarily wear at least a hint of an expectant smile as he passed through the door into the cottage. Since lack of physical obstructions outside the cottage and lack of light within it usually made it possible to observe the visitor unobserved as he approached the house, islanders sometimes took pleasure in watching the visitor drop whatever expression he was manifesting and replace it with a sociable one just before reaching the door. However, some visitors in appreciating that this examination was occurring, would blindly adopt a social face a long distance from the house, thus ensuring the projection of a constant image.

The social face is the public face, and requires the rapid changing of masks or expressions. Only under conditions of extreme emotion or alone or among friends does the mask "slip" and the private face, the "real" person appear. Thus the face will often be shielded, either with gestures or by veils or handkerchiefs. Privacy, the private face, is preserved. Facial expressions therefore are generally carefully monitored to preserve the desired mask; but to maintain this mask, make-up is sometimes useful.

The Face as Art: Make-up and Surgery

Most women, and some men, wear make-up, at least sometimes. And in this connection two phrases require examination; people sometimes say "I must put on my face," or "I'm not dressed yet," meaning that they must make up their faces. Thus the face must be dressed, just like the body; and the face must be "put on," just like clothes. Both expressions imply a distinction between the physiological face and the social face. The social face is the face "we put on"; it is part of getting dressed. This is the public face, the decorated face, the created face: make-up is art. It is also the *particular* face we select from a range of possible options, depending on our self-definition, the person we wish to project, our artistic skill and our interests in impression-management: make-up is mask.

Make-up therefore serves two principal functions: self-expression and self-creation. The two functions are in part contradictory since the first assumes that there is *one* self to express: the "real me"; while the second function following Robert Park, assumes that we are as *many* selves as we have roles to play. If "All the world's a stage," as Goffman (1959) has suggested, then make-up is merely stage make-up, supporting us in our various roles through life. It is socially desirable, necessary or useful precisely because we are actors. Putting on, or changing, make-up not only changes our faces but also ourselves. Make-up is role-support.

One may wear make-up for many reasons: to look younger than one is, or to look older, to hide pimples, etc. Indeed the late Way Bandy (1981), an American make-up artist, has presented 15 cosmetic designs for women and men. These include the glamorous face, the great American face (a dynamic self-assured look, crisp, blond, blue-eyed), and the natural face (paradoxically, made up for that unmade-up look). Males may select from the traditional, modern, new and debonair faces. In this view, the face is a canvas upon which the desired image is painted, and the desired self therefore presented. As Bandy put it: "Do not look for your face in this book. Look for the face or faces you would *like to be*, and I will guide you toward your dreams" (1981: 6). Not only is the choice of faces interesting, but so also is the choice of words: not "faces you would like to have" but "faces you would like to *be*," i.e. faces are created; make-up is identity.

In sum, looking different is *being* different; and in our culture it is fashionably necessary for women to look and be different, to vary from time to time and place to place. A recent article in *Mademoiselle*, a fashion leader for teenagers and young women, is entitled "Why do I always look the same?" and states "Suddenly it hits you—you're sick and tired of seeing yourself in the mirror looking exactly the same, every day" (February, 1985: 140) and offers make-up and hair-style hints to solve the problem.

To some degree, no doubt, this advice can apply to men; but traditionally most men do not wear make-up, nor do they change their hairstyles for week-ends or evenings, nor do most wear much in the way of fashion accessories, and if they do wear rings or gold chains they tend to wear the same ones all the time. Indeed for men, looking the *same*, the same as other men and the same as before, is as important as looking *different* is for women: different from others and different

from before. Kanter, who studied a major American corporation, states·
"Managers at Indsco had to look the part. They were not exactly cut
out of the same mold like paper dolls, but the similarities in appearance
were striking" (1978: 47). Even appearance, especially hair, is political
(Synnott, 1987). The opposite sexes present themselves differently; and
the different ideals of beauty or handsomeness are expressed in, and
reinforced by, different aesthetics and the use of make-up.

Most women wear make-up to look "good," i.e. beautiful, but also
to "feel" good, it is said. "I wear the entire spectrum of make-up every
day of my life, not only because it makes me look my best, but when
I look my best I feel my best." Hayes-Steinert adds that "Make-up is
good for your skin. Make no mistake about that!" (1980: 18, 30). But
alleged health benefits are not the principal reason. Another make-up
artist insists that make-up should be "a vivid, vibrant expression of the
woman inside" (Rex, 1986: 1). The rules of make-up are now extremely
detailed and require "artistry." The face is not only custom-designed
to hide problems, highlight certain features, express moods or selves,
etc.; but it is also scientifically colour-coordinated with complexions,
tans, eyes, clothes-colours, and so on (cf. Hayes-Steinert, 1980; Clark,
1981). Diplomas are awarded in cosmetology. Make-up is an art, but
also a science.

The more the face is made up, however, and the more effective the
artistic statement, the greater the *disparity* between the physiological
and the social faces...to the delight of satirists. The Roman poet and
epigrammatist Martial satirized the make-up imperative almost 2,000
years ago: "You lie stored away in a hundred caskets and your face does
not sleep with you" (in Carcopino, 1940: 168-9). Shakespeare has Hamlet
complain to Ophelia: "God has given you one face, and you make yourself
another" (Act 3, Sc.i). And poets like Matthew Prior (1664-1721), Jonathan
Swift ("A beautiful young nymph going to bed"), and Pope ("The Rape
of the Lock") delightedly satirized the entire beautification process. More
recently the Beatles continued the satire in "Eleanor Rigby": "wearing
a face that she keeps in a jar by the door."

Make-up is temporary, but cosmetic surgery is more permanent.
About 591,000 aesthetic plastic surgery operations were performed in
the United States in 1986, and 1,260,000 reconstructive procedures; this
is a 24% increase over 1984, making plastic surgery one of the fastest
growing specialities in medicine in the United States. The vast majority
(87%) of aesthetic procedures were performed on women, presumably
reflecting the greater role of beauty in the female life-cycle. For men
the most common operations were rhinoplasties/noses (21,000) and
blepharoplasties/eyes (15,000), followed by rhytidectomies/face-lifts
(7,000) and otoplasties/ears (7,000). The face is therefore overwhelmingly
the area of concern. This is not entirely true for women. The most common

operations for women were, in order, breast augmentation (94,000), blepharoplasties (85,000), rhinoplasties (82,000), suction assisted lipectomies on the thighs, abdomens and buttocks (73,230), and rhytidectomies (67,000). Women therefore have nine times more operations than men, and are concerned not only about the face but also about the breasts and the torso. The data indicates in quantitative terms just how much more important beauty of face *and* figure are for women (American Society of Plastic and Reconstructive Surgeons, News Release, 1987).

The Face as Battlefield

Make-up and beautification are extremely controversial. The face is now a battlefield between contending groups asserting different values and interests. The four principal arguments against the use of make-up and/or against the value of beauty are, in chronological order, the ascetic argument, the health argument, the feminist argument, and the animal rights argument. Other arguments may also be advanced, but the proponents of the above points of view are organized, and the conflicts are virtually institutionalized.

The ascetic argument is deeply rooted in Judaeo-Christian culture, as we have seen. Jeremiah (4:30) condemned make-up and beautification long ago:

And you, O desolate one, what do you mean that you dress in scarlet, that you deck yourself with ornaments of gold, that you enlarge your eyes with paint? In vain you beautify yourself.

Saint Clement of Alexandria (c150-c215) forbade women to dye their hair, to pierce their ears, "nor are the women to smear the faces with the ensnaring devices of wily cunning." He pointed out that "love of display is not for a lady but a courtesan," and that "cosmetics and dyes indicate that the soul is deeply diseased." He advised men that "the man, who would be beautiful, must adorn that which is the most beautiful thing in man, his mind." He argued that "it is monstrous for those who are made 'in the image and likeness of God' to dishonour the archetype by assuming a foreign ornament" (1956: 273-87). Saint Jerome (345-420) was even more blunt (Letter 54, 1975: 241; cf Letter 38, 1975: 163):

What have rouge and white lead to do on a Christian woman's face?...They are fires to influence you men, stimulants to lustful desire, plain evidence of an unchaste mind.

Saint John Chrysostom (347-407), Archbishop of Constantinople, warned that "the beauty of woman is the greatest snare" (1956: 442); a snare for men. (Feminists later advised that it was a snare for women, too.) Thomas a Kempis (1380-1417), the Augustinian monk and mystic, also warned against the beauty mystique: "Do not be vain about your beauty or strength of body, which a little sickness can mar and disfigure" (Bk. 1, Ch. 7; 1952: 34). But the Avon *Beauty Guide* pamphlet disagrees: "Make-up is fun. Make-up looks like you, only better" (Griffin, 1979: 16). Beauty is ideological.

Make-up is fun, says Avon; but Jeremiah says it is in vain. The difference epitomizes not only different attitudes towards the face and the body, but also different philosophies of life: fun or the service of God; and the two alternatives are seen, at least by Jeremiah, as mutually exclusive. This negative attitude persisted in Christendom; but cosmetics did not come into general use in England until the reign of Queen Elizabeth (1558-1603). The Puritans later re-iterated the traditional perspective that make-up was sinful. One Puritan divine, Phillip Stubbes, stated emphatically in 1583 that "whosoever do colour their faces or their hair with any unnatural colour, they begin to prognosticate of what colour they shall be in hell" (Stubbes, 1973: n.p.). This was a somewhat tactless remark since his Queen's hair was both red and dyed; but he was quoting Saint Ciprian.

Health rather than morality has become a major issue since the eighteenth century. Ceruse or white lead was a commonly used type of make-up; but the celebrated beauty Maria Gunning, Lady Coventry, died in 1760: the first "victim of cosmetics," she has been called; and the actress-courtesan Kitty Fisher died in 1767. Both died of lead poisoning. By 1784 the Ladies Magazine stated that "a little rouge is pardonable but white paint is now looked on as disgraceful and dangerous" (Angeloglou, 1970: 85). Since then there have been many victims of cosmetics and, more remotely, of the beauty mystique. The dangers include skin cancers from sun-tanning, blindness from mascara, cancers from hair dyes, death from silicone injections, burns on various parts of the body from hairsprays, colognes and deodorants, numerous infections and irritations from bubble baths, poisonings, usually of children, from many products, hormone changes from many products, and the possibilities of genetic mutations, not to mention the dangers from cosmetic surgery. The list is long (Nader, 1986; American Society of Plastic and Reconstructive Surgeons, 1987; Goldwyn, 1984). Beauty is dangerous and painful.

The feminist attack on the cult of female beauty and its servant, make-up, began, effectively, with the publication of Simone de Beauvoir's *The Second Sex* in 1949 describing and analyzing the subordinate position of women. In her view, women's interests in beautification are *political* and a contributing factor in the oppression of women. Make-up is a symbol of this oppression. And the face became, once again, a battleground. de Beauvoir insisted that "Woman's narcissism impoverishes her instead of enriching her; by dint of doing nothing but contemplate herself, she annihilates herself" (1953: 707). Beauty is no substitute for hard work; and she observes that "Make-up can substitute for creating a work of art" (1953: 529, 534). Beauty, in sum, is political.

The feminist movement gathered strength in the sixties. And there were demonstrations against the Miss America beauty contests in 1968 and 1969. Offending articles of make-up and beautification were thrown into the Freedom Trash Can as symbols of servitude. There had been objections to the beauty contests before, usually by male clerics on moral grounds, but these were the first protests by women on political grounds (Deford, 1971). The five thousand child beauty contents held in the United States each year, however, continue to socialize children, male and female, into the beauty mystique (Baker, 1984: 91).

The feminist critique of the beauty mystique continued into the seventies and eighties, emphasizing that beautification was unnecessary, time-consuming, expensive, unhealthy, ecologically disastrous, degrading, inauthentic and ultimately futile and contributing to self-hatred (Greer, 1971; Kinzer, 1977; Lakoff and Scherr, 1984; Brownmiller, 1984). In her book *The Beauty Trap*, Baker insists that "freeing ourselves from the beauty trap is something that every woman must accomplish if she is ever to be content with herself" (1984: 8).

The fourth and most recent attack on make-up and cosmetics, but not on the beauty mystique as such, has come from the animal rights lobbies. According to one source, between one and two billion animals die in drug tests (veterinary, medical or dental), but many die in cosmetics research. In Britain, of 3.5 million experiments conducted in 1984, 17,512 experiments were conducted on living animals in cosmetic research. This is down from 24,421 experiments in 1981 (*Compassion*, 1985-6: 6). Without the space to go into detail, suffice it to say that members of the Animal Liberation Movement object to the use of all (or some) animals in research, and specifically to the waste of animals, the cruelty to animals, and the conditions of research; and they point out the relative inutility of much research, given that results are often not transferable from one species to another (Singer, 1977: 47-51; Ryder, 1985). The movement has had some success in persuading many cosmetics corporations to modify their research methods. One advertisement featured a white rabbit with sticking plaster over its eye, and the question: "How many rabbits does Revlon blind for beauty's sake?" (Spira, 1985). In this view, beauty is not just a "trap" for humans.

The moral, political, ecological, and health attacks on beauty, beauty aids and cosmetics have been powerful. Some people refuse to wear make-up for religious reasons (e.g. nuns, Doukhobours, Mennonites, Hassidic Jews), some for feminist reasons, some to protest cruelty to animals, and some because they are allergic to the products. Yet most women wear make-up sometimes, and an increasing number of men. Despite these criticisms of the social and personal costs of the beauty mystique and beauty aids, it seems that the public sees the benefits as outweighing the costs. The face therefore remains a battlefield, literally, from the first human victim, Maria Gunning, through the physical and psychological casualties of those obsessed with beauty, to the thousands of animal victims of research every year.

Conclusion

Social discourse on beauty is ancient, but sociological discourse on beauty has been relatively little and relatively late, as we have seen. Interest is increasing, however, and this paper attempts to place the discourse on beauty in both historical and philosophical perspectives, and also within the context of contemporary popular culture.

Sociologists have for decades investigated the social significance of physical attributes, notably gender, age and colour; yet each of these three areas has been divorced from their common denominator: a sociology of the body. Furthermore, aesthetic relations are perhaps as socially significant as class relations, gender relations or race relations, despite, or perhaps because of, their *non-institutionalized* status. Aesthetic relations are so taken-for-granted as to be invisible. Yet "facism" and "beautyism" may be as problematic as other "isms" and ideologies in the stigmatization of minorities. Aesthetic relations have been relatively neglected in the discipline, I would suggest, despite their commanding role in popular culture and indeed in personal and social relations.

Beauty and the face are, as we know both by experience and from scientific research, extremely powerful symbols of the self (as are age, gender, and colour). The beauty mystique vested largely in the face derives much of this power from its multi-dimensionality or, to change the metaphor, from the many levels and types of meanings which accrue to beauty in our culture. Yet each age seems to construct the meaning and value of beauty differently, and indeed although people echo each other, each individual seems to perceive beauty somewhat differently. Beauty is many things to many people. On the one hand, beauty is perceived positively, but variously as goodness (Plato), and a symbol of goodness (Castiglione and others), as fun (Avon) and as a duty (Hauser), as good for the health and psyche (Hayes-Steinert and others), as truth (Keats) and as power (Fischer-Duckelmann); as a status symbol (Veblen) and as sexual excitation (Freud); as determined culturally (Montaigne, Voltaire, Darwin), subjectively (Hume) and genetically (Wilson); as objective (Plato, Aquinas) and subjective (Hume) as physical (Avon, *Vogue*), psychological (Milo and Marshall, Hauser) and metaphysical (Plato and Aquinas, again); as a gift from God (Aristotle), earned (Castiglione and others) and learned (Avon, Bandy, Hutton); and as life and eternity (Gibran). These all may be considered positive, by their proponents; but they are not necessarily mutually exclusive—indeed they may be complementary.

Furthermore facism and the beauty mystique are institutionalized in such novelists as Shelley, Wilde, Christie, Stevenson and Fleming; they are expressed in fairy stories and children's stories, as we have seen; and in films and television programs, advertising and comics. Hence their power.

Yet beauty and particularly beautification are also extremely controversial. Beauty is said by ascetics to be "vain" (Proverbs), "a fading flower" (Isaiah), "a mute deception" (Theophrastus), "evil" (Theocritus), a "snare" (Chrysostom), and "dung" (Saint Bernard). Feminists have frequently argued that beauty and beautification have many negative consequences for women; health workers have warned that they have many negative consequences for the health of men and women; and animal liberationists observe that cosmetics research in particular (quite apart from the fur and the food industries) are destructive of animal life and welfare. All four critiques of the beauty mystique, or aspects of the beauty mystique, persist at the present time, although often in different populations and with different impacts on popular culture.

The discourse on beauty has continued for centuries and will no doubt continue. Indeed, as we have seen, this last century has seen new ideas about beauty developed by biologists (Wilson), philosophers (Gibran), psychoanalysts (Freud), cosmetic corporations and fashion magazines (Avon, Vogue), and beauty advisors (Bandy, Milo and Marshall, and others), as well as sociologists (Veblen, Goffman). Nonetheless one can see, I think, some of the poles around which the discourse has centered, and sometimes the shifts in *mentalité* from one pole to another. The principal topics of discourse seem to be as follows:

sacred	:	profane
absolutism	:	relativism
objectivity	:	subjectivity
holism	:	particularism
exteriority	:	interiority
positive	:	negative

Put in such dichotomous terms, these topics are reminiscent of Parsons' pattern variables or the ancient Pythagorean oppositions; but I suspect that reality is rarely so polarized. Indeed the debates have often occurred on the middle ground, over matters of degree or synthesis rather that over differences of kind. Furthermore these issues are not necessarily mutually exclusive, indeed many are intrinsically linked and interdependent, as we have seen. The themes weave in and out of each other, and each thinker seems to create a new, unique and distinct pattern from the different colours and textures available; occasionally new colours and textures surprise the tradition.

Beauty may be either sacred or profane, or both, under different aspects. For Plato, as we have seen, physical beauty may lead one up the "ladder of beauty" to God, but is is inferior to spiritual beauty; but where Plato had emphasized the beauty-negative and body-negative Orphic tradition, Saint Augustine emphasized the body-positive tradition of Genesis, and the ladder linking beauty to God. Aristotle ignored the metaphysical Platonist tradition: beauty is in proportionality and is mathematical—physical, secular and material. Aquinas separated physical and metaphysical beauty (in contrast to both Plato, who united them, and Aristotle who denied the latter), but Beauty remained an attribute of God. The secularization of beauty, "the unhinging of Beauty from God," in David Howes' phrase, began with the Renaissance and was accelerated by mechanism and the Industrial Revolution. Beauty, formerly transcendent, has become an immanent value: physical and technical. The metaphysical links between individual physical beauty and Absolute moral Beauty on the ladder of beauty have now been severed. Utilitarian considerations are paramount. For Hayes-Steinert, beauty and make-up are psychologically useful: "When I look my best I feel my best" (1980: 18); similarly Bandy (1981) and others offer a catalogue of faces from which to choose, with instructions on how to create these faces and *be* new people—beauty is technique. Punk beauty is ugliness, intended to shock and horrify. In Veblen's view beauty is useful as a status symbol. These examples indicate both the persistence of the beauty mystique, and its changed and various forms; beauty is physical but no longer metaphysical; it is art, not God.

Today the face is often seen as part of the presentation of the self and impression-management (Goffman, 1959). Experts on "dressing for success," "style," and "power looks" describe not only the dress but also the appropriate faces and "looks" for various environments and purposes with respect to beards, make-up, and hair-styles. In this dramaturgical view, beauty has no metaphysical meaning, as it had for the Greeks; no spiritual analogues as it had, and has, for Christians; and the face has no cosmic significance, as it had in astrological thought. It is purely secular and instrumental, and is assessed by utilitarian practical criteria.

Discourse on the body has also shifted from objective to subjective definitions, and from absolute to relative definitions. To the Ancients and the early Christians absolute Beauty existed, and God was absolute Beauty. All things beautiful participated in God and reflected God. The original equation was formulated by Plato but persisted through Augustine to Aquinas, Dante and Castiglione, and even to Emerson and Gibran. But Montaigne and Voltaire described a beauty that is culturally determined, having no objective existence; and Hume in particular insisted that beauty is not only culturally relative but also individually subjective. Beauty, in these views, is in the eye and the culture of the beholder, not in God. Indeed, for many observers, God does not exist.

In the earlier paradigm it was logical and necessary to attempt to develop a theory of beauty; thus Plato, Aristotle, Bacon, Hegel and others developed theories of beauty. With the rise of relativism, however, the multiplicity of beauties began to replace Absolute Beauty as topics of enquiry. One universal theory of beauty for all mankind no longer seemed possible. Darwin, as we have seen, noted that the difference in values and tastes were still of prime significance for evolution; but in his *Aesthetics*, Hegel was more concerned with music, painting and sculpture, than with human beauty; and, more recently, the debates have focussed on comparing the theories of beauty (Cassitt, 1962; Eco, 1986) or showing the changing fashions in beauty (Brophy, 1963; Clark, 1980) rather than in seeking, in Hume's phrase, "to ascertain the real sweet or real bitter."

Thus for Keats beauty is the supreme moral value, not God or moral goodness—which indicates secularism; but what Keats found beautiful, a Grecian urn, for instance (purely physical with no intrinsic moral value), others might consider ugly, as Hume noted—which indicates relativism and subjectivism.

A third theme in the discourse on beauty has been the holism-particularism paradigm. Medieval thought was essentially holistic: all was one, and in many ways. Greek metaphysics, Christian theology, and Arabian astrology emphasized respectively the ladder of beauty (Plato) and monism (Aristotle), the goodness of creation (Genesis 1), and the unity of all Christians in the Church and the Mystical Body of Christ (John 15; I Corinthians 6:15-20; 12: 12-31), and the doctrines of correspondences and the microcosm and the macrocosm. This multi-dimensional holism began to break down with the rise of mechanism, science and, generally, reductionism. Specialization increased; and beauty too has become specialized—not only as an art form, as we have seen, but also in the itemization of body parts: the blue eyes of Paul Newman, the violet eyes of Elizabeth Taylor, the cleft chin of General Haig, the lips of Clara Bow, the eyebrows of Marlene Dietrich or Mariel Hemingway, the muscles of Arnold Schwarzenegger or Sylvester Stallone, the breasts of Lana Turner or Dolly Parton, the slimness of Twiggy, Elvis's pelvis, and so on. This particularism is evident perhaps most clearly in the practice of cosmetic surgery, and in the social construction of the body as a machine composed of various parts rather than as a temple of the Holy Spirit (Synnott, 1988a).[9] It is particularly evident in this quotation from the Avon Beauty Guide (so different from Castiglione) (Griffin, 1979: 55):

Beauty is the sum of many parts. Skin care, makeup, hair care...They're important. But there's more...fragrance...jewelry...and attitude. The way you feel good about yourself...They're all part of being beautiful. Your own, personal kind of beautiful. Like a private puzzle you piece together bit by bit. And turn into one glorious whole that's unique in all the world. YOU.

This brief extract implies not only particularism (the puzzle of the parts), but also individualism (the unique beauty), and secularism (the physical aspects). The emphasis on attitude is interesting, for it is exceptional in beauty guides of this decade, although very common in beauty books of the first half of this century; it is a lingering relic of the relation between interior and exterior described by Plato, Castiglione and even by Saint Jerome.

The interior-exterior debate has two dimensions, or two questions which are implicit; is beauty a matter more of the soul or the body? The inner beauty—outer beauty problem. And is beauty exterior to the individual or interior? For Plato beauty was outside the body: one climbed the ladder to absolute beauty; but also it was physical, at least to begin with, as exemplified by Alcibiades, whose virtue was questionable; but the ideal situation was the harmony of the beauty of body and soul. Augustine, however, takes the reverse of Plato's position: God comes *down* the ladder; "you were within me," says Augustine. He echoes Christ's teaching here: "I am in my Father, and ye in me, and I in you" (John 14:20). Saint Paul developed this doctrine further, as we have seen. Thus God and Beauty are immanent. The emphasis has shifted from Plato's God in the seventh heaven, "out beyond the shining of the farthest star" to interiority—an inner beauty which is visible (or is not, opinions varied) in the exterior, especially in the face. Miranda spoke to this unity of inner and outer: "There's nothing ill can dwell in such a temple"; but Montaigne regretted the incongruity in the case of Socrates. The general consensus however insists on unity: moral beauty "shines through" say Saint Bernard and Dahl; but the exceptions include Mary Shelley and Tolstoy.

Purely physical beauty, however, is often dismissed as "evil," "deception" or "vileness" by worldly-wise Greek skeptics, as "vain" or "a fading flower" by the prophets, as "dung," a "snare" and "fleeting" by Christian ascetics and as a "trap" by some feminists. Some described the physical body not so much as the exterior of the *soul*, and reflecting the moral beauty or ugliness of the soul, but as the exterior of the *body*; i.e. the "innards" are considered. Thus Boethius: "even the body of an Alcibiades, so fair on the surface, would look thoroughly ugly once we had seen the bowels inside." This clarifies Saint Bernard's reference to physical beauty as "dung." The debate has continued into the twentieth century, with some authors emphasizing the priority of the physical interior: the body (nutrition, exercise), some the psychological interior:

the mind (education), and some the metaphysical interior: the soul (virtue). Others emphasize beauty as exterior (Avon, *Vogue*, and others), insisting that the outer effects the inner: "if you look good, you feel good." Finally this shift of focus results in Goffman describing the face as a *mask* adopted for various roles in the play of life; there is no longer any room for the spiritual in his sociology.

Aristotle said that beauty was a gift of God; Castiglione said it was earned by virtue, as did Bacon, Emerson, and many others; but the moderns, Avon, Hayes-Steinert, Bandy and others, more cosmetically-oriented, say that beauty is learned, like other skills. Either way, beauty is still highly valued (with some exceptions, as we have seen), but for entirely different reasons.

Sociologists and social psychologists have emphasized the significance of beauty as a status symbol, as enhancing self-esteem through the looking-glass effect, as contributing to social mobility, greater popularity in school and higher grades, and lesser sentences in court, as eliciting more helping-behavior from others, and other such socially useful advantages; and they have observed the *halo* effect of beauty and attractiveness, and the *horns* effect of plainness and ugliness, and noted the exceptions to these effects (Berscheid *et al*, 1973; Cash and Janda, 1984; Berscheid and Walster, 1972; Berscheid and Walster, 1974). The halo and horns effects are difficult to understand, however, without a prior understanding of the immense significance of beauty in the history of Western thought and action, and in all the spheres of our lives from art to zoology including, as we have seen, philosophy and theology, poetry and literature, television and films, religion and science, comics and cosmetology, advertising and animal rights, politics, law, feminism and economics, psychology and sociology and sexology, among both men and women, from birth till death.

Despite the social power of beauty and the face, or perhaps because of it, they are controversial. Some say beauty is goodness, others say it is evil, some believe beauty is truth, others argue it is deception; Avon says it is fun, but Proverbs says it is in vain. Some insist it is sacred, others that it is only skin-deep; some believe moral beauty is more important than physical, while others care only about the physical. Some think that beauty is vitally important as power, or as a symbol of inner beauty or as a status symbol; others warn "Never judge a book by its cover." Is beauty in the eye of the beholder? or is it objective? Does beauty lead up the "heavenly ladder" to God, or up the wooden stairs to the bedroom? The debates continue around these and other themes, and have inspired or legitimated hedonism and asceticism, idealism and materialism, relativism and absolutism: and the debates will no doubt continue in the future.

Euripides, Solomon and Ovid spoke of love, beauty and sex in similar terms to those of Shakespeare, Freud, Darwin and modern beauty magazines, equating beauty with sexual desire; so, in a sense, nothing is new. Facism and the beauty mystique remain secular. Equally, perhaps the most famous line in the musical "Les Miserables" was: "To love another person is to see the face of God." This equation of love, the face and divinity, however, was precisely identified by Plato in *The Symposium* over 2,000 years ago. Facism and the beauty mystique therefore remain sacred and again, in a sense, nothing is new.

Yet the same themes are re-worked and re-interpreted in each age; indeed with the rise of Black nationalism and "Black is Beautiful," and feminism with the rejection of "the beauty trap," and the appearance of Hippies, Skins and Punks, together with constantly changing fashions, beauty is now being re-defined several times in each generation, and a new "face" appears every few years; so, in a sense, everything is always new.

Notes

Special thanks to Sharon Byer, David Howes, Janucz Kaczorowski, Joseph Smucker, and Nicholas Synnott. Also the Social Sciences and Humanities Research Council of Canada for their grant Number 410.88.0301.

[1]There were apparently beauty contests on the island of Lesbos; but in Sparta the women were not allowed to use cosmetics, jewelry or perfumes, nor could they wear coloured clothing (Pomeroy, 1975: 83, 55; Lefkowitz and Fant, 1977: 52).

[2]Beauty is therefore not only an integral part of Plato's metaphysics, but it is also integrated with his psychology and his theory of the "three types of men," pursuers of wisdom, honour or sensory gratification discussed in *Phaedrus*. These are the men of gold, silver and bronze in the famous "noble lie" (*Republic* 3: 414-5), who in turn have three different types of soul, rational, spirited or appetitive located respectively in the head, chest and belly; only the first of these, pursuing wisdom and beauty, is immortal (*Timaeus* 69-70, 89-90). Plato's metaphysics, politics, psychology and anatomy therefore reinforce each other.

[3]Aristotle also defined the beautiful, or the noble in the Bollingen edition, as "that which is desirable for its own sake and also worthy of praise; or that which is both good and also pleasant because good" (*Rhetoric*, 1366a: 33; cf. also *Poetics* 1448b: 4).

[4]Christina Rossetti wrote a poem called "Beauty is vain." Anticipating contemporary feminists she asks "Shall a woman exalt her face/Because it gives delight?" She concludes, gloomily, "Whether she flaunt her beauty/Or hide it away in a veil/...Time will win the race he runs with/And hide her away in a shroud."

[5]If this idea seems a little fanciful to those of us accustomed to the idea of genetic inheritance, it is as well to remember not only our own aesthetic and physiological patterns, including dieting, obesity, tanning, body-shaping courses, plastic surgery, weight-lifting, and so on, but also Sartre's development of this idea in a moral dimension.

[6]In *The Mikado*, Katisha protested this admiration of facial beauty: "You hold that I am not beautiful because my face is plain. But you know nothing. You are unenlightened. Learn, then, that it is not in the face alone that beauty is to be sought... I have a left

shoulder-blade that is a miracle of loveliness. People come miles to see it. My right elbow has a fascination few can resist."

[7]Note that, according to Plato, this is higher up the ladder of beauty than the beauty of objects.

[8]Popular wisdom may be changing, and now warns against ugliness. Two sayings express this, my students have informed me: "Beauty is skin deep, but ugliness goes right to the bone." And: "I know I'm fat; but you're ugly, and I can always go on a diet."

[9]Intermediate between the cosmic holism of the past and the physical particularism of the present stands the psychological holism of Elizabeth Barrett Browning. In one of her *Sonnets from the Portuguese* (185) she wrote: "Do not say/'I love her for her smile— her look—her way/of speaking gently'...For these things in themselves, Beloved may/ be changed, or change for thee... But love me for love's sake."

Works Cited

Adams, M.H. et al. *The Norton Anthology of English Literature*. New York: Norton, 1968.

a Kempis, Thomas. *The Imitation of Christ*. Penguin Books, 1952.

American Society of Plastic and Reconstructive Surgeons, News Releases, 1987.

Angeloglou, Maggie. *A History of Make-up*. London: Macmillan, 1970.

Anstruther, Elizabeth. *The Complete Beauty Book*. New York: Appleton, 1912 [1906].

Aristotle. *The Complete Works of Aristotle*. Edited by Jonathan Barnes. Princeton University Press, Bollingen Series, 1984.

Aquinas, Saint Thomas. *Summa Theologiae*. Blackfriars, 1981.

Augustine, Saint. *Confessions*. Penguin Books, 1961.

Avon. *Looking Good, Feeling Beautiful. The Avon Book of Beauty*. New York: Simon and Schuster, 1981.

Bacon, Francis. *The Works of Francis Bacon*, Vol. 9. Edited by James Spedding et al. Boston: Taggard and Thompson, 1864.

———. *The Essays*. Penguin Books, 1985.

Baker, Jane Osborne. "The Rehabilitation Act of 1973: Protection for Victims of Weight Discrimination?" *U.C.L.A. Law Review* Vol. 29, 1982: 947-71.

Baker, Nancy C. *The Beauty Trap*. London: Piatkus, 1984.

Baker, Samm Sinclair and Leopold Bellack, M.D. *Reading Faces*. New York: Holt, Rinehart and Winston, 1981.

Bandy, Way. *Styling Your Face*. New York: Random House, 1981.

Banner, Lois W. *American Beauty*. New York: Alfred A. Knopf, 1983.

Berger, Peter L. and Thomas Luckmann. *The Social Construction of Reality*. New York: Anchor Books, 1967.

Berscheid, Ellen and Elaine Walster. "Beauty and the best," *Psychology Today*, March 1972: 42-46, 74.

Berscheid, Ellen, Elaine Walster, and George Bohrnstedt. "The Happy American Body," *Psychology Today*, July 1973: 119-31.

Berscheid, Ellen and Elaine Hatfield Walster. "Physical Attractiveness" in L. Berkowitz (ed.), *Advances in Experimental Social Psychology*, Vol. 7. New York: Academic Press, 1974.

———. *Interpersonal Attraction*. Addison-Wesley, 1979.

Berscheid, Ellen and Steve Gangestad. "The Social Psychological Implications of Facial Physical Attractiveness," *Clinics in Plastic Surgery*, Vol. 9, No. 3, July 1982: 289-96.

Berthelot, J.M. et al. "Les Sociologies et le Corps," *Current Sociology*, Vol. 33, No. 2, Summer 1985.

Boethius. *The Consolation of Philosophy*. Translated by V.E. Watts. Penguin Books, 1969.

Booker, Christopher. *The Neophiliacs*. London: Collins, 1969.

Boone, Sylvia Ardyn. *Radiance from the Waters: Ideals of Feminine Beauty in Mende Art*. Yale, 1986.

Bourdieu, Pierre. *Distinction*. Harvard University Press, 1984.

Brain, Robert. *The Decorated Body*. New York: Harper and Row, 1979.

Brandt, Anthony. "Face-Reading: The Persistence of Physiognomy." *Psychology Today*, Vol. 14, No. 7, December 1980: 90-96.

Brophy, John. *The Face in Western Art*. London: Harrap, 1963.

Browne, Thomas. *Religio Medici*. Oxford: The Clarendon Press, 1964.

Brownmiller, Susan. *Femininity*. New York: Linden Press/Simon and Schuster, 1984.

Bullough, Vern L. *The Subordinate Sex: A History of Attitudes Towards Women*. Penguin Books, 1974.

Burwell, Barbara Peterson and Polly Peterson Bowles. *Becoming a Beauty Queen*. Prentice Hall, 1987.

Camden, Carroll. "The mind's construction in the face," *Philological Quarterly*, XX, 1941: 400-12.

Carpocino, Jerome. *Daily Life in Ancient Rome*. New Haven: Yale University Press, 1940.

Carritt, E.F. *The Theory of Beauty*. London: Methuen, 1962.

Cash, Thomas F. and Louis H. Janda. "The eye of the beholder," *Psychology Today*, December 1984: 46-52.

Cash, Thomas F., Barbara A. Winstead, and Lois H. Janda. "The Great American Shape-Up," *Psychology Today*, April 1986: 30-37.

Castiglione, Baldesar. *The Book of the Courtier*. Penguin Books, 1984.

Charteris, Leslie. *The Brighter Buccaneer*. London: Hodder and Stoughton, 1962 [1933].

Cherry, Samuel and Anna. *Otyognomy, or the External Ear as an Index to Character*. New York: The Neely Co., 1900.

Christie, Agatha. *The Secret Adversary*. London: Triad-Grafton, 1987.

Cicero. *De Oratore*. 2 Vols. London: Heinemann, 1960.

Clark, Felicity. *Vogue Guide to Make-Up*. Penguin Books, 1981.

Clark, Kenneth. *Feminine Beauty*. New York: Rizzoli, 1980.

Clement of Alexandria. "The Instructor" in Rev. Alexander Roberts and James Donaldson (eds.), *The Ante-Nicene Fathers*, Vol. 2. Grand Rapids, Michigan: Eerdmans, 1956.

"Compassion." *Journal of Beauty Without Cruelty*. Winter 1985-Spring 1986.

Curtis, Lewis Perry. *Apes and Angels: The Irishman in Victorian Literature*. Newton Abbott: David and Charles, 1971.

Dahl, Roald. *The Twits*. New York: Bantam Skylark, 1982.

Dante. *The Divine Comedy*. Translated by Dorothy Sayers and Barbara Reynolds, 3 Vols. Penguin Books, 1955.

D'Arcy, M.C., s.j. *Thomas Aquinas*. London: Ernest Benn, 1930.

Darwin, Charles. *The Descent of Man*. Princeton University Press, 1981 [1871].

———— *The Expression of the Emotions in Man and Animals*. New York: Philosophical Library, 1955 [1872].

———— *Autobiography*. Edited by Sir Frances Darwin. New York: Henry Schuman, 1950.

Davis, Charles. *Body as Spirit*. New York: Seabury, 1976.

Davis, Flora. *Inside Intuition*. New York: Signet Books, 1975.

de Beauvoir, Simone. *The Second Sex*. New York: Knopf, 1953.

Deford, Frank. *There She Is: The Life and Times of Miss America*. New York: The Viking Press, 1971.

de Givry, Emile Grillot. *Illustrated Anthology of Sorcery, Magic and Alchemy*. New York: Causeway Books, 1973.

Dion, K., E. Berscheid, and E. Walster. "What is Beautiful is Good," *Journal of Personality and Social Psychology*. Vol. 24, 1972: 285-90.

Douglas, Mary. *Natural Symbols*. Penguin Books, 1973.

Doyle, Sir Arthur Conan. *The Memoirs of Sherlock Holmes*. Penguin Books, 1950.

Ebin, Victoria. *The Body Decorated*. London: Thames and Hudson, 1979.

Eco, Umberto. *Art and Beauty in the Middle Ages*. New Haven: Yale University Press, 1986.

Elwell, Clarence Edward. *Our Quest for Happiness*. Chicago: Mentzer, Bush, 1961.

Emerson, Ralph Waldo. *The Complete Works*. Vols. 1, 2, 9, 12. New York: Ams Press, 1968.

Epictetus. *The Discourses*. Translated by P.E. Matheson. New York: The Heritage Press, 1968.

Fast, Julius. *Body Language*. New York: Pocket Books, 1971.

Fisher, Angela. *Africa Adorned*. New York: Harry N. Abrams, 1984.

Fleming, Ian. *From Russia With Love*. London: Triad-Panther, 1977 [1957].

Fowler, Orson Squire and Lorenzo Niles Fowler. *Phrenology*. New York: Chelsea House, 1969 [1835].

Freedman, Rita. *Beauty Bound*. Lexington, Mass.: D.C. Heath, 1986.

Freud, Sigmund. "Three Essays on the Theory of Sexuality" (1905) in *On Sexuality*. The Pelican Freud Library, Vol. 7, Penguin Books, 1977.

_____ "Civilization and its Discontents," in *Civilization, Society and Religion*. The Pelican Freud Library, Vol. 12, Penguin Books, 1985.

Gibran, Kahlil. *The Prophet*. New York: Alfred Knopf, 1985 [1923].

_____ *Spiritual Sayings*. New York: Citadel Press, 1962.

_____ *Secrets of the Heart*. Kansas City, Missouri: Hallmark, 1968.

Goffman, Erving. *The Presentation of Self in Everyday Life*. New York: Doubleday Anchor, 1959.

_____ *Stigma*. Englewood Cliffs, N.J.: Prentice-Hall, 1963.

Goldwyn, Robert M. *The Unfavourable Result in Plastic Surgery*. Two Vols. Boston: Little, Brown and Company, 1984.

Greer, Germaine. *The Female Eunuch*. London: Paladin Books, 1971.

Griffin, Sunny. *Avon Beauty Guide*. Avon Products, 1979.

Hall, Edward T. *The Silent Language*. New York: Doubleday/Anchor.

Hart, Charles A. *Thomistic Metaphysics*. Prentice-Hall, 1959.

Hauser, Gayelord. *Mirror, Mirror on the Wall*. New York: Farrar, Strauss and Cadahy, 1961.

Hayes-Steinert, Jan. *Your Face After Thirty*. New York: Berkeley Books, 1980.

Hegel, G.W.F. *The Phenomenology of Mind*. New York: Harper Torchbooks, 1967 [1807].

_____ *Aesthetics*. Oxford: Clarendon Press, 1975.

_____ *Lectures on the Philosophy of Religion*. Vol. 2. *Determinate Religion*. Edited by Peter C. Hodgson. University of California Press, 1987.

Hitler, Adolph. *Mein Kampf*. London: Hurst and Blackett, 1942 [1924].

Homer. *The Odyssey*. Penguin Books, 1981.

_____ *The Iliad*. Penguin Books, 1983.

162   Digging into Popular Culture

Hume, David. *Of the Standard of Taste and Other Essays.* New York: Bobbs-Merrill, 1965.

———. *A Treatise of Human Nature.* Penguin Classics, 1985.

Hutton, Deborah. *Vogue Complete Beauty.* London: Octopus Books, 1982.

Jerome, Saint. *Select Letters.* Translated by F.A. Wright. Harvard University Press, 1975.

Jordon, Winthrop D. *White Over Black.* Penguin Books, 1969.

Kaczorowski, Janucz. *The Good, the Average and the Ugly: Socio-economic Dimensions of Physical Attractiveness.* M.A. Thesis, Department of Sociology, McGill University, Montreal, 1988.

Kampling, Jo. *Images of Ourselves: Women With Disabilities.* London: Routledge and Kegan Paul, 1981.

Kant, Immanuel. *Critique of Judgement.* Translated by J.H. Bernard. New York: Collier-Macmillan, 1951.

Kanter, Rosabeth Moss. *Men and Women of the Corporation.* New York: Basic Books, 1978.

Kern, Stephen. *Anatomy and Destiny: A Cultural History of the Human Body.* New York: Bobbs-Merrill, 1975.

Keyes, Ralph. *The Height of Your Life.* Boston: Little, Brown, 1980.

Kinzer, Nora Scott. *Put Down and Ripped Off: The American Woman and The Beauty Cult.* New York: Crowell, 1977.

Kirk, Malcolm. *Man as Art.* New York: Viking Press, 1981.

Knapp, Mark L. *Essentials of Nonverbal Communication.* New York: Holt, Rinehart and Winston, 1980.

Laertius, Diogenes. *Lives of Eminent Philosophers.* Translated by R.D. Hicks. The Loeb Classical Library. London: Heinemann, 1972.

Lakoff, Robin Tolmach and Raquel L. Scherr. *Face Value: The Politics of Beauty.* London: Routledge and Kegan Paul, 1984.

Lavater, Johann. *Essays on Physiognomy.* London: Vernor and Hood, 1806.

Leek, Sybil. *Phrenology.* London: Collier-Macmillan, 1970.

Lefkowitz, Mary R. and Maureen B. Fant. *Women in Greece and Rome.* Toronto: Samuel-Stevens, 1977.

Liggett, John. *The Human Face.* London: Constable, 1974.

Lombroso, Cesare. *Crime: Its Causes and Remedies.* Montclair, New Jersey: Patterson Smith, 1968 [1911].

Longmore, Paul K. "Screening Stereotypes: Images of Disabled People," *Social Policy,* vol. 16, No. 1, Summer 1985: 31-37.

Mademoiselle. February 1985: 140-5.

Mar, Timothy. *Face Reading.* New York: Signet Books, 1975.

Maruyama, Geoffrey and Norman Miller. "Physical Attractiveness and Personality" in Brendan A. Maher and Winifred B. Maher (eds.), *Progress in Experimental Personality Research,* Vol. 10. New York: Academic Press, 1981.

Mauss, Marcel. "Techniques of the Body," *Economy and Society.* Vol. 2, 1973: 70-88.

May, Rollo. *My Quest for Beauty.* San Francisco: Saybrook, 1985.

McCormick, L. Hamilton. *Characterology: An Exact Science.* Chicago: Rand McNally, 1920.

Mead, Margaret. *Male and Female.* New York: Morrow Quill, 1977 [1949].

Miller, Paul Steven. "Coming up short: Employment discrimination against little people," *Harvard Civil Rights-Civil Liberties Law Review.* Vol. 22, 1987: 231-71.

Millman, Marcia. *Such a Pretty Face.* New York: Berkeley Books, 1981.

Milo, Mary and Jean King Marshall. *Family Circle's Complete Book of Beauty and Charm.* Garden City, New York: Garden City Books, 1951.

Montagu, Ashley. *The Elephant Man*. New York: E.P. Dutton, 1979.

Montaigne. *The Complete Essays of Montaigne*. Translated by Donald M. Frame. Stanford University Press, 1965.

Morris, Desmond. *Manwatching*. New York: Abrams, 1977.

Murphy, Robert F. *The Body Silent*. New York: Henry Holt, 1987.

Nader, Ralph. *Being Beautiful*. Washington: Center for the Study of Responsive Law, 1986.

New York Times, 11.9.84., 25.11.84.

Nierenberg, Gerald I., and Henry H. Calero. *How to Read a Person Like a Book*. New York: Pocket Book, 1973.

Note. "Facial discrimination: Extending handicap law to employment discrimination on the basis of physical appearance," *Harvard Law Review*. Vol. 100, 1987:2035-52.

Orwell, George. *The Collected Essays, Journalism and Letters of George Orwell*. Edited by Sonia Orwell and Ian Angus. Vol. IV. Penguin Books, 1970.

Ovid. *The Art of Love*. Bloomington: Indiana University Press, 1957.

——— *Amores*. Translated by Guy Lee. London: John Murray, 1968.

Patzer, Gordon L. *Looking Good: The Physical Attractiveness Phenomenon*. New York: Plenum, 1985.

Plato. *The Collected Dialogues*. Edited by Edith Hamilton and Huntington Cairns. Princeton University Press, Bollingen Series, 1963.

Plotinus. *The Enneads*. Translated by MacKenna and Page. London: Faber and Faber, 1956.

Polhemus, Ted (ed.). *Social Aspects of the Human Body*. Penguin Books, 1978.

Pomeroy, Sarah B. *Goddesses, Whores, Wives and Slaves: Women in Classical Antiquity*. New York: Schocken Books, 1975.

Raines, Marshall L. "Status and Structure of the Cosmetics Industry," in M.S. Balsam and Edward Sagarin (eds.), *Cosmetics Science and Technology*. Vol. 3. New York: John Wiley, 1974.

Redfield, James. *Comparative Physiognomy or Resemblances Between Men and Animals*. New York, 1852.

Rex. *Making-Up*. New York: Clarkson N. Potter, 1986.

Russell, Alan (ed.). *The Guinness Book of Records, 1987*. London: Guinness books, 1986.

Ryder, Richard D. "Speciesism in the Laboratory," in Peter Singer (ed.), *In Defence of Animals*. Oxford: Blackwell, 1985.

Sacks, Oliver. *The Man Who Mistook his Wife for a Hat*. New York: Harper and Row, 1987.

Schiller, Friedrich. *On the Aesthetic Education of Man*. Oxford: Clarendon Press, 1967.

Schopenhauer, Arthur. *Essays*. Translated by T. Bailey Saunders. New York: A.L. Burt, (n.d.).

Shelley, Mary. *Frankenstein*. New York: Bantam Books, 1981.

Simmel, George. *Essays on Sociology, Philosophy and Aesthetics*. Edited by Kurt H. Wolff. New York: Harper Torchbooks, 1965.

Singer, Peter. *Animal Liberation*. New York: Avon-Discus, 1977.

Spira, Henry. "Fighting to Win," in Peter Singer (ed.), *In Defence of Animals*. Oxford: Blackwell, 1985.

Stallings, James O. *A New You*. New York: Signet Books, 1980.

Standard and Poor. *Industry Surveys*. January 1988. New York.

Steele, Valerie. *Fashion and Eroticism*. New York: Oxford University Press, 1985.

Stubbes, Phillip. *The Anatomy of Abuses*. New York: Garland, 1973 [1583].

Stevenson, Robert Louis. *The Strange Case of Dr. Jekyll and Mr. Hyde, and Other Stories.* Penguin Books, 1984.

Synnott, Anthony. "The Presentation of Gender in Advertising: The New York Times," *International Journal of Visual Sociology.* Vol. 1, No. 1, 1983: 47-64.

—— "Shame and Glory: A Sociology of Hair," *British Journal of Sociology.* Vol. 38, No. 3, September 1987: 381-413.

—— "Physical, Mystical and Spiritual: The Body in Christian Thought," *Santé,* Culture, Health. Vol. 5, No. 3, 1988a: 267-89.

—— "Ian Fleming and James Bond: Facism and the Beauty Mystique." Unpublished paper. Department of Sociology, Concordia University, 1988b.

Thevoz, Michel. *The Painted Body.* New York: Rizzoli, 1981.

Thomas, Keith. *Religion and the Decline of Magic.* New York: Charles Scribner, 1974.

Tillyard, E.M.W. *The Elizabethan World Picture.* Penguin Books, 1963.

Tolstoy, Leo. "The Kreutzer Sonata" in John Bayley (ed.), *The Portable Tolstoy.* New York: Viking Press, 1978.

Turner, Bryan S. *The Body and Society.* Oxford: Blackwell, 1984.

Tytler, Graeme. *Physiognomy in the European Novel.* Princeton: Princeton University Press, 1982.

Veblen, Thorstein. *The Theory of the Leisure Class.* New York: The New American Library, 1953 [1899].

Virel, Andre. *Decorated Man.* New York: Harry N. Abrams, 1980.

Voltaire. *Philosophical Dictionary.* New York: Carlton House, 1941.

Warwick, Eden. *Nasology: Or Hints Towards a Classification of Noses.* (Pseudonym for George Jabet). London, 1848.

Wells, Samuel R. *How to Read Character.* Tokyo: Tuttle, 1971 [1871].

Whiteside, Robert L. *Face Language.* New York: Simon and Schuster Pocket Book, 1975.

Wilson, Edward O. *Biophilia.* Harvard Univeristy Press, 1984.

Wittgenstein, Ludwig. *Philosophical Investigations.* New York: Macmillan, 1968.

X, Malcolm. *Autobiography.* New York: Grove Press, 1966.

Young, Lailan. *Secrets of the Face.* London: Hodder and Stoughton, 1984.

The Landscape of Modernity:
Rationality and the Detective

James D. Smead

This study approaches the study of several aspects of culture in a new and exciting way. It discusses the fusion of character and the physical environment into a cultural landscape. The author argues that seeing is a cultural activity and that aesthetic assertions necessitate objectification and are always constrained by the cultural context in which they arise. The result is a new cultural and literary geography that draws a new three- or four- dimensional map that scholars might well use as a guide.

The detective novel is an important form of American cultural production. Vivid descriptions of the physical landscape are fused with intricate descriptions of character and action. What emerges is a landscape of the body, of the self, of modern culture. I have chosen to explore this landscape of modernity through John D. MacDonald's novel *A Tan and Sandy Silence*. I am interested in MacDonald's description of the detective's body and mind as a landscape and how this parallels his description of the physical landscape. The parallel MacDonald makes between a healthy body and a healthy interaction of individuals with their environment is based largely on the assumption that the individual can be independent from political, economic institutions in society. MacDonald's often stated respect for both the body and the landscape is ultimately contradicted by his objectification of tourists, women, and landscape. This process of objectification can be clearly identified when MacDonald fuses tourists and women with the landscape, allowing him to discuss them in primarily aesthetic terms.

The story of *A Tan and Sandy Silence* begins when Travis McGee becomes aware that a woman he knows, Mary Broll, has been mysteriously absent for three months. Her husband, Harry, is upset because he needs her to sign some papers which concern a condominium development in Florida. McGee follows Mary's tracks to Grenada, where he finds that another woman is posing as Mary, and the other woman is actually her husband's lover, Lisa. McGee poses as a wealthy developer so he can get close to Lisa and he learns that Mary was murdered by Lisa's cousin, Paul. Lots of money and sex get involved all through here but are basically unimportant to the development of the story. The cousin, Paul, hits McGee on the head and ties his hands and feet. After Paul kills Lisa in a dehumanizing manner and while he prepares to kill McGee, McGee makes his escape. He stumbles down the beach and jumps, still bound hand and foot, into a strong current that draws him away from the land and Paul. McGee floats out to sea and is saved by a boat full of naked women, who nurse him back to health. Back in Florida, the cousin, Paul, extorts money from the husband, Harry, and then kills him. Paul is himself killed in a final confrontation with McGee when he accidentally buries himself, instead of McGee, in a big gob of hot asphalt.

I start the analysis with MacDonald's notion of the body. MacDonald defines the body as either healthy or unhealthy; this attitude is applied equally to all of his characters. Good health is obtained through sustained interaction with natural elements: the land, the sea, and the air. If the environment is diseased, the body will be negatively affected. The individual can have a similar effect on the land. Both the characters and the landscape carry the marks of disease and violation; scars are the traces left by the process of recovery. What society has often believed to be progress interrupts what would otherwise be the healthy interaction between body and landscape.

McGee exemplifies the natural man who has been violated by social progress: he is a "knuckly, scabrous, lazy, knobbly old ruin," according to a lover in *A Tan and Sandy Silence* (MacDonald 23). As she traces the marks on his body, finding the leavings of lived stories: "the gullied scar in [his] thigh," "the symmetrical dimple of the entrance wound of a bullet," "the white welt of scar tissue nearly hidden by the scruffy, sun faded hair" (MacDonald 21). McGee's scars provide a cultural contrast to the brown skin, bleached hair, and long strong muscles which are the natural result of years working and sailing around Florida and the Caribbean.

McGee can exercise control over his life if he can balance physical conditioning with the excitement of adventure. McGee sees the exhilaration of balancing between pleasure and pain, or death as the feeling of being alive. "I know what counts is the feeling I have when I make my own luck," he admits after surviving the outrageous events in this novel.

The way I feel then is totally alive [...] I have an addiction. I'm hooked on the smell, taste, and feel of the nearness of death and on the way I feel when I make my move to keep it from happening. (MacDonald 149)

The edge between control and excess provides, for McGee, the reason for living. The nearness of death which gives his life meaning, leaves its mark on the body when he misjudges. His instinct is "a precision tool"; if it fails, he is as "vulnerable as if sight or hearing had begun to fail" (MacDonald 25). Scars result from inattention and neglect; yet, as a record of mistakes, those scars simultaneously document the ability to assume and maintain control. McGee uses his body as does a cat. Every movement, every activity is exercise for his body. Health is obtained through interaction with the elemental, animal aspects of land and people. When the walk along the edge of consuming excitement leads McGee to sensual excess, he regains control through intense physical exertion. McGee's loss of balance leads to his physical harm, his cure is time and sleep.

The scars of missed opportunities and mistaken judgment that identify the destruction done to the external landscape have been caused by both well meant ignorance and savage disregard of the environment. The destruction is created "[i]n spite of all good intentions," McGee observes in the early morning half-light. A night of sexual excess has set him to pondering the way in which his "dirty two-legged species is turning the lovely southeast coast into a sewer" (MacDonald 24). Individuals are seen as causes of the pollution observed in the water and air; these problems are explained as violations of aesthetic taste as well as a disruption in the natural balance between nature and culture. McGee makes an aesthetic judgment when he describes the physical landscape as corrupted with cultural refuse created for the tourists escaping the frozen northern rust belt for the scrubbed and plasticised new south. Standing alongside "a shiny row of vending machines under a roof made of plastic thatch, incredibly green" or following "small, plastic orange arrows" down a "black velvet vehicle strip," McGee's disgust with the visual violation of his landscape is apparent (MacDonald 133).

McGee's final confrontation with Paul and his horrible ending in the hot glob of asphalt takes place just past a

huge billboard telling of the fantastic city of the future that would rise upon the eleven square acres of sandy waste, [...] where clean industry would employ clean smiling people, where nothing would rust, rot, or decay.(MacDonald 138)

The juxtaposition of the future city that exists only in an advertisement with the crazed individual who dies by his own hand establishes a parallel that allows MacDonald to displace society's responsibility for violating the landscape. The green plastic thatch roofs and sanitized cities of mass culture that individuals have created for the tourist are, for MacDonald, the decay gradually corrupting the landscape. Tourists, for McGee, are so pervasively a part of the cultural landscape they are "invisible, except to the man trying to sell them something" (MacDonald 127).

McGee's conflation of tourists into the surrounding landscape is possible because he no longer views them as people; they are visual elements within a framed landscape. Interchangeable members of an anonymous group, McGee objectifies them by the commonly shared characteristics and possessions he finds aesthetically objectionable. This same process of arbitrary categorization allows McGee to define women as "miles of bunnies along the tan Atlantic sand." The women soaking up sun on the beach comprise an undifferentiated landscape of "five and a half tons of vibrant and youthful and sun-toned flesh." These "children" are, for McGee, "an exquisite reservoir called Girl, aware of being admired and saying " 'drink me!' " (MacDonald 28). Placing responsibility for their violation on the "children" themselves allows him to construct a landscape with them as little more than visual elements. A woman can be constructed as an accomplice in this process because, according to John Berger, "her own sense of being in herself is supplanted by a sense of being appreciated as herself by another" (Berger 46). Berger further expands on the dualism of a woman's cultural role when he states:

Women watch themselves being looked at. This determines not only most relations between men and women but also the relation of women to themselves.... Thus she turns herself into an object-and most particularly an object of vision: a sight. (Berger 47)

In McGee's world, healthy women are expected to participate in this process of objectification. They should keep their bodies as fit as their body-type will allow; as in nature, imperfections in appearance are expected, although those same imperfections are often reason enough for McGee's rejection. The marks from successful plastic surgery, covered expertly with "careful and elegant grooming " (MacDonald 16), are ultimately less offensive than "a small double chin," a scar on an "upper lip near the nostril," or a "narrow tan roll of fat across [a] trim belly" (MacDonald 96). The culturally produced image of a woman is given priority over the notion that a woman is part of nature. The scars existing on McGee's body are traces of the battle between good (natural) and evil (cultural). The acceptable scars on a woman's body are traces of the battle between the natural aging process (evil) and the cultural desire to alter that process (good).

An open and honest interaction between MacDonald's characters is privileged, as is an honest interaction with the environment and, ironically, the acceptance of imperfection as natural. Although sexuality is defined as a natural physical need, and healthy women are those who express an appropriate interest—usually in McGee himself—he ultimately retains romanticized ideas of a correct relationship between men and women. Not only does McGee define "stray pubic hairs" peaking around the fabric of a revealing bikini bottom as the stuff of "jockstrap sex, unadorned" (MacDonald 96), but the dominance he exercises in sexual relationships contradicts his parallel between the body and the landscape, and the privileged position he gives to shared physical expression.

The visual aesthetic of a "natural" landscape of women is juxtaposed to

> The great white wall of high-rise condominiums which conceal the sea and partition the sky. They are compartmented boxes stacked high in sterile sameness. The balconied ghetto. Soundproof, by the sea. (MacDonald 28)

As in the earlier discussion of women as an objectified feature of the landscape, McGee is congratulating himself on his appreciation of natural beauty. McGee also, as before, engages in an equivalent act of uncaring violation.

In contrast with the extensive commercial decay of the Florida landscape, Grenada is relatively pure. "The air is full of spice and perfume"; the island itself is "fabulously erotic" (MacDonald 49). The "beach is velvet under a brilliance of stars" (MacDonald 49). Although the public land may contain the remains of "what had been the Grenada Expo...warping plywood shedding thin scabs of bright holiday paint" (MacDonald 101), McGee finds the beauty of the land relatively undisturbed only on private property (MacDonald 102). The differentiation between public and private is of particular importance to MacDonald; responsibility for stewardship of the land is here awarded to the individual. Ownership of the land is best left to individuals, and particularly those who privilege its beauty over commercial exploitation.

While sightseeing in moments stolen from the rigors of protecting "his" beaches and women, McGee evidences a profound appreciation of surrounding beauty. From a lighthouse McGee finds

> a view so breathtakingly, impossibly fabulous that it became meaningless. It was like being inserted into a living postcard.... The only way a person could accommodate himself to a place like that would be to live there until he ceased to see it and then slowly and at his own pace rediscover it for himself. (MacDonald 103)

McGee's aesthetic response to this landscape is principally an objectified construction of pictorial elements, and can be nicely illuminated by turning to John Jakle's discussion of sightseeing, in *The Visual Elements of Landscape*. The response to this visual landscape is in fact conditioned by the same touristic activity McGee regularly deplores (Jakle 35). Although aware that sightseeing is an activity engaged in by tourists, McGee mistakenly identifies the clothing and cameras as signifying the activity of tourism. He desires to eventually experience the landscape through living with it as a native. Essentially, McGee desires to replace the vicarious aesthetic construction of "seeing," with what Jakle would call the participatory experience of the native (Jakle 152).

McGee rejects the style of tourism because he equates the style with an estrangement from the land, from the physical self, and from an honesty with self. This estrangement is likely to be manifest by a lost balance between the natural and culturated self and results in a violation of both landscape and self. McGee is able to maintain this balance in some areas of his life. A good example of this balance can be seen in his understanding of the sea. Living on his houseboat, he rarely loses contact with the feel and appearance of the water. McGee reads the water carefully; every change in its movement, color, and surface signifies changes to which he may need to respond. His intuition has been honed to provide rational responses to changes in the water. McGee's style of life is a tracing of the edge between complete commitment and excess, and often allows little space to carefully choose the most appropriate response to a situation placing his life in danger.

An example from the narrative is here appropriate. Sensitivity to the dynamics and subtle changes in the sea makes possible McGee's escape from the individual holding him prisoner. McGee reads water as he sits dazed on the beach, and uses a tidal flow to carry him to sea—still bound hand and foot. The possibility of death by drowning is described by McGee without fear, as he floats along in a current that draws him swiftly out to sea. The rational, calm acceptance of his hopeless situation helps keep him alive.

Along with the beauty of the land, sea, and individuals also goes the danger, according to McGee, of a "world [that] is strange, becoming more strange, a world spawning" people who are barely human (MacDonald 144). The society that creates the damaged personality is for MacDonald a society of individuals. Assuming the self-assigned roll of protector, McGee has defined himself as opposed to both ruthless condominium developers with no understanding of the land and aberrant individuals who are "unable to concede [the] humanity of people" (MacDonald 132). Society can corrupt an individual, but only a private individual can correct the destructive actions of society. McGee is rewarded by his thrills in an experience of "the smell, taste and feel of the nearness of death" (MacDonald 149). As McGee protects the land and makes it safe for "lithe maidens" to innocently play games in the surf (MacDonald 74), the violence he draws to himself is violence which would otherwise be inflicted on the landscape or innocent women.

Each scar on McGee's body is a sign of the violence that would otherwise deface "his" smooth sandy beaches or the smooth skin of "his" young girls. Ultimately, MacDonald sees the strong (white male) individual as a tamer of modernity and a protector of the land and the innocent. The "freedom" allowed in American society is necessary for the natural beauty and goodness to continue as society progresses. MacDonald believes this natural goodness is threatened by aberrant individuals on a case by case basis. Individuals do bad things and occasionally distort the natural ebb and flow of events. This cycle of violence continues if it is not set right, as MacDonald urges in *A Tan and Sandy Silence*, and is not inherent in political, economic, and social institutions. Systems are bad only because individuals pervert the natural progression of events.

Readers can obtain vicarious thrills at McGee's escapades, and enter into self-congratulatory disgust as they recognize the exploitation of the land. Yet a more troubling and perhaps more destructive objectification of landscape and women can be understood by readers as they engage the world through the eyes of MacDonald's detective character, Travis McGee.

Works Cited

Berger, John. *Ways of Seeing*. 1972. New York: Penguin, 1977.

Fiske, John, et al. *Myths of Oz: Reading Australian Popular Culture*. Winchester, MA: Unwin Hyman, 1987.

Jakle, John A. *The Visual Elements of Landscape*. Amherst: Univ. of MA Press, 1987.

MacDonald, John. "A Tan and Sandy Silence" in *Five Complete Travis McGee Novels*. New York: Avenel Books 1971; rpt. 1985, pp. 1-153.

Media-Based Therapy:
The Healing Power of Popular Culture

Joseph J. Moran

In our society, saturated as it is with personal and emotional problems and solutions, we need to get at a fuller understanding of ways to solve those problems. Since popular culture may cause many of the problems, perhaps it, or some elements of it, can suggest or generate solutions. Moran suggests that it "can be used to enhance psychotherapy as practiced by mental health professionals." This paper, then, suggests ways popular culture students may bring new understanding and insight to themselves and to a large field in our society.

"Barney, haven't you seen enough Rock Hudson movies to know how to sweet talk a girl?" This line, taken from the *Andy Griffith Show*, hardly needs examination. Barney is overwhelmed by the prospect of going on a date. And, Andy has done as much in the one sentence to explain how to acquire the social graces and the self-confidence to go out with a young woman as would be possible in hours of earnest one-to-one conversation with a counselor. In addition, Andy's words strongly suggest that popular culture has significant potential for helping people who might have any one of a host of behavioral and/or emotional problems. This paper explores the ways in which popular culture as it appears in mass media can be used to enhance psychotherapy as practiced by mental health professionals.

The use of media in the pursuit of psychotherapeutic goals has a long history. Morris-Vann noted that the Greeks were known to place the inscription *Medicine for the Soul* on their libraries, and that the Romans held the belief that reading transcripts of orations could improve mental health.[1] For the last three hundred years newspaper advice columns have been striving to help troubled people solve life's problems.[2] Recently, a survey has found that popularized self-help books are being prescribed widely by practicing psychologists as part of ongoing treatment, and that the psychologists are generally positive regarding their efficacy.[3] In the 1980s, the term, media counseling, was adopted to refer to counseling conducted as part of radio broadcasts so that the therapy for the individual serves as entertainment and education for the many in the audience.[4]

The professional fields of art therapy, music therapy, and bibliotherapy have been developed to capitalize upon the possibilities for using media in therapeutic settings. These three therapies have generally been conducted as components of comprehensive therapy programs. For example, music therapy might be held twice a week for a group of inpatient substance-abuse clients or art therapy might be conducted individually for autistic children who attend a special school.[5] Bibliotherapy—therapy that involves the reading of literature—might be conducted for a group of students who had been involved previously in individual therapy at their university counseling center.[6] These three fields have much in common.[7,8,9] Although they are not based upon a theory of either therapy or human development, they share the assumption that media can help a client express important thoughts and feelings that are not readily experienced and expressed in the absence of the media. Once expressed the feelings can be used by the therapist according to the principles of psychotherapy. These therapies are also based upon the belief that producing and responding to art gives an individual a sense of mastery that in itself contributes to mental health.

All of these therapies have been effective, but the application of each has been limited. Art and music therapy can not be practiced by most therapists because most therapists lack the required knowledge and artistic skills. Bibliotherapy has developed around literature that is described by bibliotherapists as universal, beautiful, and profound.[10] As a result of this elitist orientation to literature, bibliotherapy has not been used readily with unsophisticated and/or resistant clients. In sum, media can serve important therapeutic functions, but techniques are needed to open the use of media to a wider range of therapists and clients.

The term media based therapy is coined to denote the use of expressly popular culture materials in the psychotherapeutic process. This paper will document uses of popular culture in the therapeutic interventions and explain some of the apparent advantages of using interventions based on popular culture materials. Particular emphasis will be placed on ways of making traditional psychotherapy effective with clients who typically have been difficult to treat. Examples are offered for both group and individual therapy in each of the steps in psychotherapy: screening interview, diagnostic interview, therapeutic intervention, and termination.[11,12]

The screening interview may offer fewer opportunities for using media than any of the other steps in the relationship. The point of the screening is to determine whether a potential client can benefit from treatment, and, if so, whether the appropriate treatment is available from the screening therapist or from some other source. Normally, the interview is largely informational in that the client, or in the case of child, the parents of the client, describe the problem(s) they are seeking help for. Duration, frequency, intensity, and related problems are of primary concern. The therapist and the potential client are both helped by an open relationship. The therapist's ability to establish rapport quickly is of considerable importance. There is one situation in a screening interview where use of popular culture materials is strikingly effective. This is the case of the interview with a child, which is usually conducted immediately after the therapist has met with the parents. Children are brought to psychotherapists for all sorts of reasons, they are told all sorts of things about what is going to happen, and they imagine all sorts of happenings. They usually trail the therapist, looking up and scanning the office for clues about how to behave and what to say. While there are many good and bad ways to begin with such children, it is usually relatively easy to establish rapport by asking them to name their favorite television programs. For example, "Todd, your mother said you are 7 years old and go to second grade. (Child nods yes to both statements.) I think she said sometimes you like school and sometimes you don't. (Child smiles.) Now I want to ask you some questions, and I am going to write down your answers. Do you watch television? (Child says yes.) What are your three favorite television programs?" With marked regularity, the client opens up and remains open even after the therapist has shifted to more threatening and central concerns. The point is that the child has been convinced that the therapist is interested in him, in what is important to him, and will meet him on his own turf. It is apparently not necessary for the psychotherapist to be familiar with every cartoon series, only that he or she be willing to ask and listen as the child describes his favorites.

The diagnostic interview is usually held the second time a therapist and client meet. Diagnosis is a process with two purposes. One is to classify the client according to symptoms, and the second is to detail the unique constellation of the individual's thoughts, feelings and behaviors. The classification is a technical matter. It is important for research purposes and making medical insurance claims. The second step, understanding the interrelationships among the client's thoughts, feelings, and behaviors, is the basis for planning treatment. As part of the second step, Gardner uses a technique that involves what might be called incidental media based therapy.[13] He asks adolescent and adult clients to list the people they would most like to be. Often the answer is an entertainer, sports figure, or TV character. Familiarity with the individuals listed not only establishes rapport but enables the therapist to follow effectively with questions whose answers give information about such matters as emotional needs, personal goals, work ethic, and felt inferiorities. By using this indirect approach, the therapist avoids being prematurely intrusive and obtains information that many clients would not be capable of providing even if they had been asked directly.

In a similar way, by listening to a child describe a favorite television program, a therapist can learn a lot about the child's world view. Consider a six year old, first born, middle class girl who is brought to a therapist because she cries about not wanting to got to school even though she gets only good grades from her teacher. Asking a six year old why she cries is unlikely to be productive. Listening to her first choose and then describe television programs that emphasizes that characters are rewarded for doing well and punished for doing badly suggests a hypothesis. Perhaps she is praised for her good work, but rather than concluding she is fortunate to be competent, she has concluded that something terrible will happen to her (her parents will be disappointed) if she fails to live up to her usual standards. She cries because she wants to escape from the situation where a failure is possible. This is a diagnostic hypothesis that can be readily checked. An advantage of deriving the hypothesis in this way is that it can be explained to the parents as based on observation of their child and not pulled out of a hat or based on experience with other children. Consequently, they are likely to cooperate with interventions intended to test the hypothesis.

Before concentrating on specific therapeutic interventions, it is helpful to consider the distinction Weiner made between strategies and tactics in psychotherapy.[14] Strategy refers to the objectives a therapist is pursuing at a particular point in time. Tactics refer to the specific methods the therapist employs in pursuing the objectives. Popular culture materials seem to provide the raw material for a number of successful tactics. In part, the potential of tactics based on popular culture materials comes from the opportunities for matching the materials with the characteristics and/or experiences of the clients. For example, Moreno has shown that group therapy for black males can be facilitated by using blues songs to introduce emotional themes into the sessions.[15] The blues are particularly good at evoking emotional reactions and their connection to the suffering of Black Americans seemed to add to their effectiveness among his clients. This example also suggests an important restriction that applies to the use of media with clients. Since stereotyping and other authoritarian processes lead to negative reactions, materials should be chosen jointly by therapists and clients. The therapist would not say, "You're from Appalachia so we'll listen to some Blue Grass." Rather, the therapist might end a group session saying, "Next time I'd like to use some music to get us started talking. We can use any kind of music. I was thinking about three types. Tell me which you prefer, and please bring in recordings that start you thinking."

Turning to some general therapeutic considerations, many people come to therapy with considerable reluctance. There are too many sources of such reluctance to be catalogued here. But, it can be noted that using popular materials probably helps to overcome the reluctance of some clients. There are people who arrive at the therapist's office under some type of duress. Perhaps a wife has threatened to leave unless the client "gets help." Such a client is likely to resent the power and prestige implicitly attributed to the therapist by the client's wife. If the therapist appears to be elitist, the problem is likely to intensify. On the other hand, using popular materials mitigates the perception of a gulf between the therapist and client. Similarly, therapy sometimes becomes effective after it becomes fun, and using popular culture materials can replace such anxieties as fear about being a disappointing client with the fun of responding to entertaining as well as meaningful material.[16]

Although there are reports of clients who regularly attended sessions without conversing with the therapist and made dramatic progress, typically the client must be engaged in discussion of the problems that occasioned the therapy. Some people encounter a stumbling block at the outset of therapy because they lack the experience and sophistication to step outside themselves and talk about themselves from the standpoint of an observer. For such people it is easier to talk about others and the problems of others. A therapist might very will build on the ability to talk about others by having them first analyze fictional characters. The therapist would be able to learn more about the individual's conception of the interpersonal world at the same time that the client builds skills that will support self-analysis later in therapy. It would seem that a substantial portion of these clients also lack the sophistication to respond to literature that could be described as universal, beautiful and profound. For such clients popular culture materials such as TV sitcoms will reduce the need for grappling with literature and help them get on with learning to analyze human motives and relationships on familiar territory.

A related point is that popular culture materials often deal with mundane problems. In other words, problems that are closer to the actual problems of clients than are the problems of literary characters such as Oedipus and Ozymandias. Consider the schizoid person or the overdefended person who denies experiencing feelings except on rare occasions. By virtue of presenting very simple feelings such as being afraid to ask for a date, or being embarrassed about not having a date, TV programs offer clients practice at discussing the type of feeling they actually confront without threatening the clients personally—perhaps to the point where they resist or leave therapy.

One of the well established findings regarding therapeutic interventions is that people learn to modify their behaviors especially well from observing models.[17] In addition, people imitate more readily models who are similar to them in age, race, sex, social class, etc. These principles can be effectively applied through the use of popular materials. Consider the case of a learning disabled 14 year old girl from a rural background who has been overprotected by her parents. She is brought to the clinic because she has complained that she has no friends and wishes she had never been born. Should it happen that among other things she is deficient in the social skills required for peer acceptance, the therapist would need to devise some way for her to acquire those skills. One possibility would be to select for regular viewing a television program or programs with a female character who is about the same age as the client to serve as a model or social skills. The model would likely be effective because she conveys a tremendous amount of information about non-verbal communication such as tone of voice, mannerisms, and dress. Finally, the model is distinct from the client so that she becomes a subject for discussion. Perhaps she has been sanitized for television, perhaps she is too cheery. It is likely that the client would like to be similar to the model but also different from her in some ways so the client and the therapist could plan how to be like and unlike the model. The use of the televised model provides the client not only with a basis for learning social skills, but also with a safe topic for practicing conversation skills with the therapist, and later to launch discussions about personal emotional issues and questions about identity.

There is a negative sense in which popular culture can be used in psychotherapy. The overwhelming majority of people who come for therapy regularly consume popular culture and are influenced by it. Therefore, they arrive for counseling with impressions that are fostered by popular culture, of which they are only dimly aware, and which are potentially self-defeating. For example, many television programs describe an interpersonal or family problem and reach a resolution of the problem within a half hour period. They create the impression that solutions to significant problems can come easily. A parent might have gotten the sense that one good talk with an adolescent child will clear up even serious problems if just the right words are uttered. Such a parent would need to be educated so he or she does not leave therapy prematurely feeling as though the therapist is incompetent or their problem is exceptional and hopeless. All sorts of misconceptions are possible. Rather than list them here, suffice it to say that therapists do well to ask, "How is your situation different from what we see in books, movies, and television?"

A final point regarding the general uses of popular culture materials has to do with building self-esteem. When popular culture is involved in the therapeutic process, in some ways the client is put on equal footing with therapist. By definition, popular culture does not belong to any select group, nor is it the specialty of the therapist. The client's reactions to popular materials are just as valid as the therapist's reaction. Similarly, the client can suggest what he, she, or they might view or read for next time. This type of equity not only bolsters self-esteem, it prevents flight from therapy.

It is appropriate to consider uses of popular culture materials in specific types of therapy and with specific types of clients. Applications of popular television to marital counseling have been described by Patricia Hersch.[18] She noted that watching programs such as *Thirtysomething* is particularly good at opening discussions of topics that a given couple might consider taboo such as the problems children have when parents divorce. Similarly, since *Thirtysomething* often focuses on the ambivalent feelings of the characters the show is helpful in educating clients to appreciate their own and their spouse's ambivalent feelings. An entirely different approach is the use of romance novels. They are immensely popular among women presumably because of their emphasis on the romantic as opposed to the erotic aspects of love.[19] If a husband were to think his wife was unusual or unreasonable in desiring more romance in their relationship, he might adjust his attitude after reading one or two of them and processing his response to the novels in the presence of his wife and their therapist. Similarly, if a man had missed all those Rock Hudson movies, he could read the same novels to learn how to be romantic. A woman who has not read such a novel might do so to experience a validation of her feelings.

Play therapy is often the treatment of choice for work with children. it typically involves props or toys of some sort. Often, a therapist will want to choose the materials the child will play with because there is a need to deal with particular issues. For example, if a child is living in a chaotic family setting, it might be desirable to invite the child to play with dolls that seem to constitute a family. On the other hand, it can be revealing to invite a child to bring in his or her own toys. In these days of television advertising, a child's toys are his or her own popular culture collection. The toys provide insight into the child's life outside the therapy session. They also give information about the child's maturity level, interest in competition or cooperation, as well as an indication of what felt inadequacies the child is trying to compensate for. For example, a ten year old boy of who brings in a large fully armed military figure is likely to be having trouble establishing a sense of himself as adequately masculine. In this sense, each time the child brings in a toy he or she is presenting the therapist with an opportunity for ongoing diagnosis or evaluation of progress which is independent of observations and descriptions of the child by the parents. The toys are also instant sources of conversation between the therapist and the child regardless of how shy or resistant the child normally is and more importantly provide the means of focusing on the themes that are central concerns for the child.

One of the increasingly common and serious problems for a therapist who is working with dysfunctional families is finding ways to bring parents and children together in ways that allow them to learn improved types of interaction. Some parents resent the time they are asked to spend with their children. Others try elaborate activities such as trips to the ocean or to amusement parks. Unfortunately, the problems with logistics and/or unfulfilled expectations often turn these trips into disasters. An effective procedure is to have selected members or the entire family watch television together. When a father who usually interacts with his son by correcting him at Little League practice, sits on the couch with his arm around the boy while watching a Sunday evening children's movie, the impact on both can be dramatic. In addition, shows can be selected with the particular family in mind. Reruns of shows like *Leave it to Beaver* might be helpful for some relatively unsophisticated and fractionalized families because everyone could have a model of cooperative behavior within a family. Of course, that show might be all wrong for a dual earner, urban household with three teen-age girls. *The Cosby Show* would likely be very good for helping parents learn psychologically based discipline techniques to replace techniques based on physical power.

Psychotherapy with adolescents involves many problems that cannot be detailed within this paper. Establishing rapport, maintaining confidentiality, and encouraging independence without fostering rebellion are examples of these problems. Although adolescents present many challenges to the therapist, they also present opportunities through their attachment to popular culture materials. In large part adolescents seem to acquire and express their identity by the way they consume popular culture materials. Indeed, for many people the word teen-ager is linked closely with popular culture. They think of rock music and brash clothing, especially message carrying T-Shirts. The overall dress, and T-shirts in particular, can always be considered diagnostically for information about the adolescent's identity and sense of alienation or belongingness in his or her community. However, troubled adolescents usually do not like to discuss their dress. On the other hand, contemporary music can be used in a number of ways with adolescents. Rock is often used by adolescents as a form of rebellion against parents and as a means of withdrawing from parents. "I'm just listening to some music in my own room. How can you complain about that." It also serves to give the adolescent a sense of connection with the peer group and, therefore, is a source of emotional support. Resistant adolescents can often be engaged by a therapist who invites them to bring to a session or two some of their music simply for listening. The goal of this tactic is to demonstrate to the adolescents that their generation, their preferences, and they as individuals are considered worthwhile by the therapist. It may be that the therapist would arrange to have the music serve as background for discussions with the expectation that the music will help elicit suppressed emotional material just as it is thought to do in traditional music therapy.

Adolescents are inclined to resist the influence of adults by casting them as old fashioned and therefore lacking in credibility. Attempts to engage them through the use of media can easily fail if the materials are in any way dated. However, popular culture materials can have the advantage of being current in style so they are not so readily dismissed by adolescents. In fact, several writers have described the beneficial effects of using popular music in adolescent therapy groups.[20],[21],[22] On the other hand, adolescents sometimes resist having their materials such as rock music made meaningful so the use of popular culture materials can easily backfire with adolescents. With adolescents as much as with any group, care should be taken to involve them in selecting media materials for inclusion in therapy.

There is a well known technique for conducting therapy with children which is based upon mutual story telling.[23] This technique can be approximated with adolescents by inviting the adolescent to relate the plot to a movie. The therapist can reciprocate by summarizing a movie that illustrates a point the therapist wants to make. This technique is based upon the assumption that in telling the story or summarizing the movie the therapist is able to impart material such as a sense of competence or a sense of belongingness directly into a client's unconscious and without giving the client's psychological defenses the usual opportunity to mitigate the impact of the material. The appearance of VCR's has made this a particularly viable technique with the large group of adolescents who live in small towns or rural areas and are now enthusiastically watching movies in great numbers.

In ending this section on tactics involving popular culture materials, it is advisable to consider the negative influences of popular culture materials. As noted, televised models are extremely powerful influences on behavior. It must be that some people are acquiring their problematic behaviors from these models. Children are probably particularly susceptible to this difficulty. Therefore, a therapist might want to know what television their child clients watch to determine if some of the programs the child watches should be eliminated from his schedule. For example, a hyperactive or aggressive child might be better off not watching fast paced, violent cartoons.

It is easy to overlook the termination stage of psychotherapy. After all, it normally occurs because an effective therapeutic process has lead to satisfactory progress. However, for many clients it is a stressful time. They feel good about their progress, but they are apprehensive about maintaining their gains and sad about losing the relationship with the therapist. The therapist can reduce these problems by using media in a fashion similar to what has been called reading therapy.[24] The therapist might give suggestions about books, movies, drama, TV, etc. that the client could enjoy and use to practice whatever has been learned in therapy.[25] Such suggestions constitute a meaningful, and professional "gift" to the client which moderates the sense of being abandoned. They probably also help the client maintain gains by extending the learning period to the point where the new behaviors and patterns become second nature.

It is clear from interest shown in published literature that psychotherapists are increasing their use of popular materials in therapeutic tactics. This paper is part of the beginning of the documentation of their use. In looking back at the documented and suggested uses of popular culture materials, it seems that a major purpose for using popular materials is to facilitate therapy with relatively unsophisticated and/or relatively resistant clients. At this point it should be mentioned that within psychotherapy circles there has been a lament that traditional practice has been successful with only a restricted class of clients. The acronym YAVIS was developed to describe individuals who are good candidates for psychotherapy.[26] It stands for young, attractive, verbal, intelligent, and single. It is very close in meaning to the popular term YUPPIE. At this point popular culture materials offer great promise for treating more effectively the great mass of people who are outside the exclusive YAVIS-YUPPIE category. Evaluating the success of popular materials in fulfilling this promise seems to be an appropriate task for the immediate future.

At present, there are solid reasons for thinking that popular culture materials have important uses in psychotherapy. But as yet the case for their use is far more a rational argument than an empirical one. And empirical evaluation of media based therapy is likely to be a complicated business. It probably will have to involve at least two sources of information—the behaviors of practicing psychotherapists and the results of experimental studies. If psychotherapists report an increase in its use over time, and if researchers publish more articles describing the successful use of explicitly popular culture materials to achieve specific goals with specific types of clients, the argument for the use of popular culture materials will be established.

Notes

[1]Morris-Vann, Artie M. *Once Upon a Time...* (Southfield, Michigan: Aid-U Publishing Company, 1979).

[2]Moran, Joseph J. "Newspaper psychology: Advice and Therapy," *Journal of Popular Culture.* 22 (1989): 119-127.

[3]Starker, Steven. *Oracle at the Supermarket.* (New Brunswick: Transaction Publishers, 1989).

[4]Paterson, John G., and Blashko, Carl A. "Media counseling: A new frontier for health professionals," *National Journal for the Advancement of Counseling.* 8 (1985): 25-30.

[5]Murphy, Marcia. "Music therapy: A self-help group experience for substance abuse patients," *Music Therapy.* 3 (1984): 52-62.

[6]Mazza, Nicholas, and Price, Barbara D. "When time counts: Poetry and music in short-term group treatment," *Social Work with Groups.* 8, 2, (1985): 53-66.

[7]Feder, Elaine, and Feder, Bernard. *The Expressive Arts Therapies.* (Englewood Cliffs, New Jersey: Prentice Hall, 1981).

[8]Hynes, Arleen McCarty and Hynes-Berry, Mary. *Bibliotherapy—The Interactive Process: A Handbook.* (Boulder: Westview Press, 1986).

[9]Wadeson, Harriet. *The Dynamics of Act Psychotherapy.* (New York: John Wiley and Sons, 1987).

[10]Hynes and Hynes-Berry, op. cit.

[11]Gardner, Richard A. *Psychotherapy with Adolescents.* (Cresskill, New Jersey: Creative Therapeutics, 1989).

[12]Weiner, Irving B. *Principles of Psychotherapy.* (New York: John Wiley and Sons, 1975).

[13]Gardner, op. cit.

[14]Weiner, op. cit.

[15]Moreno, Joseph J. "The therapeutic role of the blues singer and considerations for the clinical applications of the blues form," *Arts in Psychotherapy.* 14 (1987): 333-340.

[16]Rozensky, Ronald H., and Pasternak, Joseph, F. "Obi-wan Kenobi, 'The Force' and the art of the biofeedback: A Headache treatment for overachieving boys," *Clinical Biofeedback and Health: An International Journal.* 8 (1985): 9-13.

[17]Kagan, Jerome, and Segal, Julius. *Psychology an Introduction.* (New York: Harcourt Brace Jovanovich, 1988).

[18]Hersch, Patricia. "Thirtysomethingtherapy," *Psychology Today.* 22, 10, (1988): 62-63.

[19]Radway, Janice A. *Reading the Romance: Women, Patriarchy, and Popular Literature.* (Chapel Hill, North Carolina: University of North Carolina Press, 1984).

[20]Mazza and Price, op. cit.

[21]Wells, Nancy, F., and Stevens, Ted. "Music as a stimulus for creative fantasy in group psychotherapy with young adolescents," *Arts in Psychotherapy.* 11 (1984): 71-76.

[22]Frances, Allen, and Schiff, Matthew. "Popular music as a catalyst in the induction of therapy groups for teenagers," *International Journal of Group Psychotherapy* 26 (1976): 393-398.

[23]Gardner, Richard A. *Therapeutic Communication with Children: The Mutual Story Telling Technique.* (New York: Science House, 1971).

[24]Hynes and Hynes-Berry, op. cit.

[25]Weiner, Sanford R., and Lu, Francis G. "Personal transformation through an encounter with death: Cinematic and psychotherapy case studies," *Journal of Transpersonal Psychology.* 19 (1987): 133-149.

[26]Hariman, Jusuf. *Does Psychotherapy Really Help People?* (Springfield, Illinois: Charles E. Thomas Publishers, 1984).

Contributors

Pat Browne, is editor and business manager of the Bowling Green State University Popular Press, Bowling Green, Ohio.

Ray B. Browne, is Chair of the Department of Popular Culture, Bowling Green State University, Bowling Green, Ohio.

K.S. Coates is Professor of History at University of Victoria, Victoria, B.C., Canada.

John Forrest is with the Anthropology Department, State University of New York, Purchase, New York.

Elizabeth A. Lawrence, is a Professor of Environmental Studies, Tufts University, School of Veterinary Medicine.

Barbara J. Little, teaches Anthropology at the University of Maryland, College Park, Maryland.

Joseph J. Moran, is a licensed psychologist and Associate Professor of Educational Foundations at Buffalo State College, Buffalo, New York..

W.R. Morrison, is Director of the Centre for Northern Studies, Lakehead University, Thunder Bay, Ontario.

Ade Peace, is on the Faculty of Arts, University of Adelaide, G.P.O. Adelaide, South Australia.

Paul A. Shackel is Research Archaeologist, Division of Archaeology, Harpers Ferry National Historical Park, Harpers Ferry, West Virginia and Research Associate, Department of Sociology and Anthropology, George Mason University, Fairfax, Virginia.

Malcolm K. Shuman, is an assistant professor with the Louisiana Geological Survey at Louisiana State University, Baton Rouge, Louisiana.

James D. Smead, is with the Communication Department, Indiana-Purdue University, Ft. Wayne, Indiana.

Anthony Synnott is with the Sociology Department, Concordia University, Montreal, Quebec.